MW01146039

AGAINST ABSOLUTE GOODNESS

OXFORD MORAL THEORY

Series Editor
David Copp, University of California, Davis

AGAINST ABSOLUTE
GOODNESS

Richard Kraut

OXFORD
UNIVERSITY PRESS

OXFORD
UNIVERSITY PRESS

Oxford University Press, Inc., publishes works that further
Oxford University's objective of excellence
in research, scholarship, and education.

Oxford   New York
Auckland   Cape Town   Dar es Salaam   Hong Kong   Karachi
Kuala Lumpur   Madrid   Melbourne   Mexico City   Nairobi
New Delhi   Shanghai   Taipei   Toronto

With offices in
Argentina   Austria   Brazil   Chile   Czech Republic   France   Greece
Guatemala   Hungary   Italy   Japan   Poland   Portugal   Singapore
South Korea   Switzerland   Thailand   Turkey   Ukraine   Vietnam

Copyright © 2011 Oxford University Press

Published by Oxford University Press, Inc.
198 Madison Avenue, New York, New York 10016

www.oup.com

Oxford is a registered trademark of Oxford University Press

All rights reserved. No part of this publication may be reproduced,
stored in a retrieval system, or transmitted, in any form or by any means,
electronic, mechanical, photocopying, recording, or otherwise,
without the prior permission of Oxford University Press.

Library of Congress Cataloging-in-Publication Data
Kraut, Richard, 1944–
Against absolute goodness / Richard Kraut.
p. cm.
Includes bibliographical reference (p.).
ISBN 978-0-19-984446-3 (alk. paper)
1. Good and evil.   2. Moore, G. E. (George Edward), 1873–1958.   I. Title.
BJ1401.K72 2011
170—dc22   2011007438

To
T. M. Scanlon
and
Judith Jarvis Thomson

CONTENTS

CONTENTS

CONTENTS

ACKNOWLEDGMENTS

This book began as a paper, "What Is Intrinsic Goodness?" that I hastily put together to fill in for a speaker who had withdrawn from a local conference. My aim was to contrast two ways of thinking about intrinsic value. One of them I called (following G. E. Moore) "absolute" goodness. The other is relativized to an individual: it is what is noninstrumentally good *for* someone. The distinction received some attention in my book *What Is Good and Why*, but I realized, soon after it appeared, that I needed to say far more about the notion of goodness that Moore championed. I would like to thank Martha Nussbaum for her comments on the paper I read, and I am also grateful to the criticism I received from Agnes Callard and Rosalind Hursthouse, who served as referees for *Classical Philology*, where my revised conference paper appeared.

I was able to give more serious attention to these issues when I received a Starr Fellowship from Lady Margaret Hall, Oxford, for the 2008–2009 academic year. I am deeply grateful to the faculty of LMH and particularly to my host, Christopher Shields, for their hospitality. To the Weinberg College of Arts and Sciences of

Northwestern University, I am indebted for the leave of absence that allowed me to accept this fellowship. During my year in Britain, audiences in Oxford, King's College, London, Reading, and St. Andrews showed me how much more thought I needed to give this subject before I could hope to make my ideas convincing. Subsequently, audiences at the University of Miami, the University of Minnesota, the University of Wisconsin, the University of Chicago, and Northwestern University were equally helpful.

Earlier versions of this book benefited from the criticism of Robert Audi, Jerry Dworkin, Anne Eaton, Sam Fleischacker, Jon Garthoff, Andy Koppelman, Tony Laden, David Reeve, and Marco Zingano. More recently, the entire manuscript was carefully examined and criticized by David Copp, David Enoch, Guy Fletcher, Daniel Groll, Mark LeBar, Jeff McMahan, Russ Shafer-Landau, and Julie Tannenbaum. I am particularly indebted to David Copp and Jeff McMahan for the extensiveness of their critiques. Despite all the help I received, I am painfully aware that the final product is not all that it should be. The responsibility for that rests with me alone.

This book is dedicated to two formidable philosophers with whom I was associated at different points in my career. I am grateful to the kindness of both. T. M. Scanlon and I were together for a brief period at Princeton, he as a new faculty member, I as a bewildered graduate student. With Judith Jarvis Thomson, I served on the Board of Officers of the American Philosophical Association. As the reader will see, each has left a mark on my thinking. Their contributions to value theory planted the seeds of my skepticism about absolute goodness.

AGAINST ABSOLUTE GOODNESS

Chapter 1

Moore and the Idea of Goodness

Are there things we should value because they are, quite simply, good? *— important*

Like many perplexing philosophical questions, this one is deceptive in its simplicity. It is tempting, at first, to reply: yes, of course. Friendship, after all, is a good thing. So, too, are natural beauty, tasty and nourishing food, playful activity, participation in sports, intellectual adventure, good theater and poetry, and much else besides. It is obvious that we should value them, and when we ask *why* we should do so, it seems appropriate (though not particularly surprising or profound) to reply: "because they are valuable," that is, "because they are good things."

But the trickiness of our question becomes apparent when we notice that it is one thing to say that something is good *for* someone and another to say, quite simply, that it is good (period) or valuable (period). Consider friendship and beauty, to take the first two examples. We are confident that we should value them. But it is difficult to be equally confident that the reason we should value them is that they are, quite simply, good things. Perhaps, instead, the reason they should be enjoyed, appreciated, treasured (or valued in other ways) is that they are good *for* us. Or perhaps both of these are reasons for valuing friendship and beauty: both because they are, quite simply, good, and because they are good for us. Another possibility is that beauty is valuable because it is good (period), whereas friendship is valuable because it is good *for* those who are friends. After all, it is not evident that beauty or its appreciation is *beneficial*; by contrast,

3

it seems undeniable that a friend is not merely to be appreciated, but to be helped as well. In any case, valuing something because it is good (period) is not to be confused with valuing it because it is good *for* us.

Consider two of the other examples I used: good theater and poetry. Should they be valued because excellent plays and poems are good *for* us? Whatever we think of that idea, it should be distinguished from a different one: we might say a good play or poem should be appreciated because it (or because appreciating it) is a good or valuable thing (period).[1] Another way to express that idea would be to say that the world is made a better place when good literary works are understood and enjoyed—regardless of whether appreciating such works is good *for* people.[2] On the other hand, we might be suspicious of both these ideas. We might think that good plays and poems are to be valued neither because doing so is good for us, nor because they are quite simply good, but only because they are good plays and poems. A good peach, we might point out, is just that: a good peach; valuing it by biting into it and enjoying its taste is not a good thing and does not make the world a better place by adding to the value it contains. So, too, we might insist, a good play is merely that: a good play; neither it nor its appreciation is quite simply a good thing and does not make the world a better place.

---

1. This, or something close to it, is suggested by Joseph Raz in *The Practice of Value* (Oxford: Clarendon, 2003). Speaking of literary, musical, and cinematic works and so on, he says: "If it is a good instance of its genre, then it is a good work absolutely, not only of its kind" (p. 45). Similarly, good apples and good lectures have, by virtue of being good of their kind, a further feature: they are valuable (pp. 40–41). I return to this idea in appendix C.

2. As Christine M. Korsgaard notes, "We ... sometimes judge particular things to be good absolutely, meaning that here and now the world is a better place because of this thing." See "Two Distinctions in Goodness," *Philosophical Review* 92 (1983), p. 169. Reprinted in *Creating the Kingdom of Ends* (Cambridge: Cambridge University Press, 1996), pp. 249–274.

To repeat: the question I pursue in this study is whether there are things we should value because they are, quite simply, good. But I hope I have conveyed more fully what this question involves. I am not asking whether there are things we should value because they are good *for* someone or because they are good things of a kind (good plays, good poems, good friends). Rather, for no reason other than their being good—or, as I have been saying, good *period*. Latin and French phrases can be used to the same effect: we can ask whether we should value certain things because they are good *simpliciter, tout court, sans phrase*. We can also ask this same question by using synonyms of "good"—such words, for example, as "excellent" or "valuable". So: are there things we should value because they are, quite simply, valuable and excellent? If there are, we could call them "impersonally good." That would emphasize the point that their being good (period) is different from their being good *for some person*.

G. E. Moore uses the words "absolute" and "absolutely" to designate what is good *simpliciter*, and I, too, will use them frequently to remind readers that he is one important influence on this study.[3] "The only possible reason that can justify any action," he says in *Principia Ethica*, "is that by it the greatest possible amount of what is good absolutely should be realised."[4] Notice how many different assertions and assumptions are contained within that statement: First, it presupposes that there is such a property as absolute goodness. Second, it assumes that when an action has this property, that is a reason to undertake it. Third, it asserts that this is the only possible reason to perform any action. Fourth, it takes it for granted that goodness has magnitude—that some actions bring about more

---

3. Moore's usage is still current, as notes 1 and 2 show.
4. Revised ed. (Cambridge: Cambridge University Press, 1993). Original ed. 1903, section 60, p. 153.

of it than others. Fifth, it claims that we ought always to produce the greatest possible amount of good.

In this study, I will pay no attention to Moore's fifth thesis—that we ought always to maximize what is absolutely good—because I want to focus entirely on two of his presuppositions: that there is such a thing as absolute goodness, and that when something has this property, this gives us a reason to value and pursue it. Moore, in other words, gives an unequivocally affirmative answer to the question I am raising: "Are there things we should value because they are, quite simply, good?" He goes beyond saying yes to that question; he adds that goodness is the *only* property that can justify what we do and that we must bring about as much goodness as we can. But we would be missing something important in his philosophy if we debated only those further assertions and accepted what they presuppose: that there is such a thing as absolute goodness and that we should value what is good precisely because it is good.

One of Moore's chief aims, furthermore, is to call attention to the difference between two ways in which the question "What is good?" can be understood. First, it can be treated as a request for a specification of which things have that property. "Pleasure is good" and "pleasure alone is good" are possible answers to that question. Second, it can be treated as a request for a definition of goodness— not the sort of definition that can be found in an ordinary dictionary, but the kind that goes deeper by shedding light on the nature of goodness. Moore regarded it as a matter of the greatest philosophical importance that this second question cannot be answered. He argued that some of the most influential moral philosophers— both those who advocated what he called "naturalistic ethics" and those who propounded what he called "metaphysical ethics"— were utterly misguided because of their failure to recognize the indefinability of goodness.

That tenet of Moore's philosophy—the indefinability of good—will be set aside here, for the same reason that I am leaving aside his thesis that good is to be maximized. Both doctrines presuppose the existence of absolute goodness. He combines both with the assumption that whatever is good (period) should be valued simply because it is good (period). As the title of this book suggests, I believe Moore was wrong about that. I am "against absolute goodness" not because I think we should shun it and seek absolute badness instead, but because I doubt that the property of absolute goodness, as Moore understands it, has a useful role to play in moral philosophy or in everyday practical thinking. We should take seriously the possibility that absolute goodness is not a reason-giving property. There are, of course, many good things: books we should read because they are good novels, cameras with which we should take photographs because they are good cameras, friends we should love because they are good friends. Furthermore, that something is good *for* you, or *for* someone else, is, of course, often an excellent reason for you to value it. But are there things you should value because they are, quite simply, good? I doubt it. That is because I doubt that goodness can ever be, all by itself, a reason for valuing something.

Suppose a reader of this book agrees with me, after studying my arguments, that goodness is not itself a reason to value anything. Such a reader might ask: "But even so, is there no such property as being, quite simply, good? Granted, Moore misunderstood the role such goodness should play in our thinking. Yet does not absolute goodness exist? Have you shown that there is no such thing as being good (period)? Or that nothing could have this feature?"

The answer that will emerge is that when calling something good (*simpliciter*) is merely a way of saying that there is reason to value it, and is not construed as a reference to the very property (namely, goodness) on the basis of which it is to be valued, then talk about goodness (period) does have a useful role to play in practical reasoning. Friendship, sports, adventure: these are good things, in that there is some reason to value them (a different reason in each case). But it does not follow that there is some single thing that they have in common, namely, their sharing in the property of goodness. Sentences in which we call something a good thing are meaningful, but not all meaningful sentences ascribe properties. "Here is the book," for example, does not ascribe a property called "hereness" to the book, for there is no such property.[5] Similarly, if I am right, there is no such property as mere goodness—"absolute" goodness, as Moore calls it. Or to put my point more cautiously, we have no reason to suppose otherwise. Once we abandon the idea that absolute goodness is a reason-giving property, we have no reason to hold that nonetheless some things have the property of being, quite simply, good. Positing such a property would do no evaluative work for us. It would be empty, practically speaking, to say that there is such a property but that nothing has it, or has had it, or ever will.

Admittedly, it is tempting (for some, it is even irresistible) to think of goodness as an evaluative property that belongs to certain things, just as beauty—which surely is an evaluative property—belongs to exemplary paintings, scenic vistas, certain human faces and bodies, and so on. What all these beautiful things have in common may be difficult or impossible to say, but nonetheless it seems plausible that beauty is a feature that some things have and that we must learn to recognize and appreciate it in its many guises,

5. I borrow the analogy between "here" and "good" from Dean Pettit, "The Semantics of 'Good'" (unpublished). These terms, he argues, are not meaningful by virtue of their association with a property. That claim is entirely in line with my own thinking. Perhaps his analogy could be put this way: To say "that is good" is to locate the object in question above something else (contextually indicated) in evaluative space, just as "here is the book" locates the book in the vicinity of the speaker.

even if we cannot define it. Furthermore, if an object is beautiful, that feature of it gives us reason to value it, by seeking it out and contemplating it with due appreciation. To call something beautiful is not merely to say that it ought to be appreciated, but to say which of its properties grounds such appreciation. If I am right, however, goodness is not like beauty in these ways. The goodness (period) of something is not a reason to value it, as the beauty of something is. That beauty is a property of all beautiful things strikes me as a plausible thesis, even though nothing I say in this book depends on it. By contrast, if the arguments of this book succeed, we need not, to make sense of our normative discourse and evaluative practices, think of goodness as what all the things that are quite simply good have in common.

Chapter 2

Goodness before and after Moore

Moore takes goodness to be one of the principal subjects of moral philosophy or ordinary practical thinking. But he does not write as though he is discovering the existence of a property that has hitherto been unnamed and overlooked. Nor, in placing goodness at the center of moral philosophy, does he take himself to be giving this branch of philosophy an entirely new focus. He thinks he is talking about what many other philosophers and nonphilosophers, both his contemporaries and his predecessors, also refer to—although too many of them, he argues, have a defective understanding of what this property is.

But is he right to assume that in talking about *absolute* goodness, he is not assigning to moral philosophy a new subject matter? Obviously, *goodness* is a topic treated in the works of Plato, Aristotle, the many authors of the Hellenistic schools, Christian philosophy, the natural law tradition, classical utilitarianism, Kant and the Kantian tradition. But that does not answer our question: which of these authors and traditions is talking about *absolute* goodness— the *impersonal* goodness that must be distinguished from the property of being good *for* someone?

Because this study is not primarily a historical investigation, but a philosophical inquiry into absolute goodness, I will make little effort to answer that question—to decide which authors, other than Moore, have held that we should value things because they are, not good for someone or good of a kind, but, quite simply, good.[1] Nonetheless, because it seems so plausible, I will assume that Moore was neither the first nor the last philosopher to suppose that we should value things that are good *simpliciter* precisely because they have that property. This seems to be one traditional way in which philosophers of the West have thought about goodness, and that is reason enough to give it our attention.

It is tempting, in fact, to think that this is a tradition that stretches all the way back to Plato. Just as the form of beauty is not beauty in relation to anything (*Symposium* 211), so the form of good (*Republic* 505–510) can be understood as the property a thing has when it is good *simpliciter*.[2] Similarly, Aristotle's *Nicomachean Ethics*

---

1. In addition to the brief historical remarks of this chapter, see the antepenultimate paragraph of chapter 9 and my discussion of eight authors in appendixes B through F.

2. For this reading, see Julia Annas, *An Introduction to Plato's Republic* (Oxford: Oxford University Press, 1981), pp. 221 and 322; John M. Cooper, "The Psychology of Justice in Plato," *American*

begins not with a statement about what is good *for* someone, but with the observation that "every craft and every inquiry, and likewise every action and decision, seems to aim at some good" (1094a1–2). He makes a distinction, later in this treatise, between being good without qualification and being good for someone (1152b26), and most of his statements about what he takes to be good things (virtue, some pleasures, certain honors) seem to characterize them as good without qualification. So it can be argued that the kind of goodness that both he and Plato are talking about is the very same property that Moore calls absolute goodness. For current purposes, we need not decide whether that way of reading Plato and Aristotle can be sustained.[3]

The Platonic conception of goodness (if indeed he is talking about absolute goodness) is modified in familiar ways by some eminent Christian philosophers, who conceive of the highest instance of goodness not as an impersonal property or a relation but as a divine person who has every possible perfection.[4] Everything in the worldly realm that is a good thing is a mere image of divine goodness, who is the highest conceivable good object. God consists in infinite goodness, and we can acquire some dim understanding of what God is like and which finite, worldly objects are good by seeing how those transient beings are related to divine

---

Philosophical Quarterly 14 (1977), pp. 151–157, esp. pp. 154–155; Nicholas P. White, *A Companion to Plato's Republic* (Indianapolis, IN: Hackett), p. 35; and Talbot Brewer, *The Retrieval of Ethics* (Oxford: Oxford University Press, 2009), pp. 195–206, esp. p. 201. For opposition to this interpretation, see Terry Penner, "The Forms, the Form of the Good, and the Desire for Good in Plato's *Republic*," in *Modern Schoolman* 80, no. 3 (2003), pp. 191–234.

3. See appendix F for my doubts about whether Plato and Aristotle are talking about absolute goodness as Moore conceives it.

4. A theological conception of goodness along these lines is defended by Robert Merrihew Adams in *Finite and Infinite Goods: A Framework for Ethics* (New York: Oxford University Press, 1999). I discuss some of our differences in appendix C.

being. Since justice, for example, is reasonably regarded as a good thing, and all good things are images of God, we can be confident that God is, in some way, just—although the justice of God will presumably be a higher form of justice than ordinary, human justice. Furthermore, by studying sacred texts, we can learn about the ways in which God has been made manifest in human life, and by taking God's plans as exemplars of goodness, we will increase our understanding of what we should pursue because it is an image of God's goodness. Loving and worshipping God is good for us, but the highest object of our attention must not be what is good for us, or what is good for anyone, but Goodness itself—Absolute Goodness. Christian philosophers who think along these Platonic lines can agree with Moore that the concept of goodness (period) is the most important concept we have, even if they reject his thesis that no light can be shed on what goodness is. They say, for example, that we can better grasp what goodness is by conceiving of it as a person. That is a reason I more often use "absolute goodness" to name the concept we are exploring here than "impersonal goodness": I do not want my very words to exclude the possibility that whatever is good *simpliciter* is, in a way, personal, by being God or godlike. Even so, there is, I believe, a way in which attending to absolute goodness is "impersonal" in a pejorative sense: doing so depersonalizes relations, taking from them a humane concern that ought to be present. That will become an important element in my argument against absolute goodness (chapters 14 and 15).

It can also be argued that absolute goodness is not an abstruse notion dreamed up by philosophical theorists and unfamiliar to ordinary people. In fact, that concept seems to be employed on the opening page of a text that has had more readers than all of the treatises of Western philosophy combined. Recall the familiar words of the Book of Genesis: On the first day of creation, "God said, 'Let there be light:' and there was light. And God saw the light, that it was good" (1:31). Several lines later, after God has created the dry land and the seas, he again contemplates his creation, and sees that it was good—and he continues making this positive assessment, as one day of creation succeeds another. All of this occurs before the day on which God creates living things and subsequently makes man and gives him dominion over them. Genesis does not say that God saw that his work was good *for* someone. There was no one, just yet, for whom the light and the division of land and sea was good. The Bible depicts the newly created world as something that is, quite simply, good. It is, of course, no surprise that God saw that the light and his other products were good. God is supremely and absolutely good—not good in relation to something else, but just plain good. Little wonder, then, that what he makes will also be good (period).[5]

So it is plausible to suppose that Moore was not the first to assert or assume the existence of absolute goodness. Nor was he the last. In *The Right and the Good*, W. D. Ross argues that goodness is "an intrinsic quality of certain things,"[6] and he speaks of pleasure, knowledge, and virtue as things that are good (period)—not good *for* someone.[7] "What we ought to do," he says, "depends to a large extent... on the goodness or the badness of the things we can in our

5. Genesis 1:31 is cited by Panayot Butchvarov as evidence against the thesis (to be discussed in chapter 5) that Moore's use of "good" is meaningless. "Millions have thought they understood [it]." See *Skepticism in Ethics* (Bloomington: Indiana University Press, 1989), p. 17. That Genesis provides an example of Moore's absolute use of "good" was also suggested to me in conversation by Tom Hurka.

6. Oxford: Oxford University Press (1930), p. 103.

7. Ibid., pp. 65, 67. Note, too, his statement that when we call courage or pleasure "good," we are using it as "an absolute term" (p. 67). He occasionally uses the expression, "good *sans phrase*" (p. 102).

acts bring into being."[8] I take this to mean that pleasure, virtue, and knowledge should be valued *because* they are good (period), and for that reason alone.[9]

The concept of absolute or impersonal value—"intrinsic value," as it is often called—continues to be employed in much contemporary Anglo-American moral philosophy.[10] To take some representative passages: Noah M. Lemos writes that "according to the traditional view, intrinsic value is a *nonrelational* concept. When one says that something is intrinsically good, in the sense with which we are concerned, he means just that, that it is intrinsically good *period*. He does not mean that it is intrinsically good for me, for himself, for human beings, or for rational beings."[11] Ronald Dworkin says: "Something is intrinsically valuable . . . if its value is *independent* of what people . . . want or need or what is good for them. Most of us treat at least some objects or events as intrinsically valuable in that

8. Ibid., p. 102.

9. In *Foundations of Ethics* (Oxford: Clarendon, 2000), Ross says that "when . . . we describe a conscientious or a benevolent action as good we are ascribing to it a characteristic that we think it has in itself, apart from the reaction of any one to it" (p. 258). He later adds that "it is impossible to approve of anything . . . without thinking that it has a goodness of its own which makes it fit to be approved" (p. 261). I take these last six words to mean: "constitutes the reason why it should be approved." Here again he treats goodness as a reason-giving property. A framework for ethics that owes much to Ross is defended by Robert Audi, who writes: "Our experience reveals the good and the bad as basic practical reasons and counter-reasons . . ." See *Moral Knowledge and Ethical Character* (New York: Oxford University Press, 1997), p. 271; and *The Good in the Right: A Theory of Intuition and Intrinsic Value* (Princeton, NJ: Princeton University Press, 2004), pp. 122–134.

10. Warning: an author who speaks of what is "*intrinsically* good" need not have in mind what I am calling *absolute* goodness. Lemos and Dworkin, cited in this paragraph, *are* using "intrinsically valuable" to talk about absolute goodness, as is shown by the fact that they distinguish it from what is good *for* someone. But it is also possible to use the phrase "intrinsically good" as an abbreviation for "intrinsically good for someone," and in that case, it does not designate absolute value. What is intrinsically good for someone does not derive its being good for that individual from its causal relation to something else. More about this in chapter 7.

11. *Intrinsic Value: Concept and Warrant* (Cambridge: Cambridge University Press, 1994), pp. 3–4 (author's emphasis).

way: we think we should admire them because they are important in themselves...."[12]

Lemos and Dworkin are clear that the kind of value or goodness they are talking about is not relative goodness—it is not goodness *for* anyone. But Dworkin's statement goes further than that of Lemos. Dworkin speaks of the value (in other words, the goodness or importance) of something as the *reason* why a certain attitude toward it (admiration) is appropriate. We should take a stance toward certain things, he says, *because* they are valuable. That is precisely how Moore thinks of goodness. But Lemos does not go quite so far. He distinguishes (as Dworkin does) between the property of being good (period) and the property of being good for someone, but he does not say that the property of goodness is reason-providing. He does not commit himself to Moore's idea that we should take an interest in certain things precisely *because* they are good.

In fact, against Moore and in agreement with several other philosophers (Franz Brentano, A. C. Ewing, Roderick Chisholm[13]), Lemos proposes that goodness *can* be defined, and he endorses

---

12. *Life's Dominion: An Argument about Abortion, Euthanasia, and Individual Freedom* (New York: Vintage, 1994), p. 71 (author's emphasis).

13. See Franz Brentano, *The Origin of Our Knowledge of Right and Wrong*, English edition edited by Roderick Chisholm and translated by Roderick Chisholm and Elizabeth Schneewind (London: Routledge & Kegan Paul, 1969); A. C. Ewing, *The Definition of Good* (London: Macmillan, 1947); Roderick M. Chisholm, "Defining Intrinsic Value," *Analysis* 41 (1981), pp. 51–53. A similar approach can be found in Elizabeth Anderson, *Value in Ethics and Economics* (Cambridge, MA: Harvard University Press, 1993); and Michael J. Zimmerman, *The Nature of Intrinsic Value* (Lanham, MD: Rowman & Littlefield, 2001). For criticism, see Butchvarov, *Skepticism in Ethics*, pp. 35–36, 42–58, 82–122. He argues that such definitions of goodness are objectionable because they "fail to offer a phenomenology of the psychological attitudes in question, which at least seem to involve awareness of actual or apparent goodness" (p. 36). See, too, Chris Heathwood, "Fitting Attitudes and Welfare," in Russ Shafer-Landau, ed., *Oxford Studies in Metaethics*, Vol. 3 (New York: Oxford University Press, 2008), pp. 47–74; Wlodek Rabinowicz and Toni Ronnow-Rasmussen, "The Strike of the Demon: On Fitting Pro-Attitudes and Value," *Ethics* 114 (2004), pp. 391–424.

a definition of it that assigns it no reason-giving force. To be intrinsically valuable, he holds, is to be the object of a fitting attitude or emotion.[14] "Knowledge is good," according to this definition, is made true by the fact that one ought to love knowledge. Similarly, "pain is bad" is analyzed as "one ought to hate pain." So conceived, the goodness of knowledge and the badness of pain are not properties that give us a reason to have a favorable or unfavorable attitude toward these things. Rather, the goodness of knowledge consists in its being the case that one ought to have a positive attitude toward it, and the badness of pain consists in its being the case that one ought to hate it. (I return to this line of thought in appendix D.)

Moore's conception of goodness is deeply embedded in our everyday ways of thinking and speaking.[15] When God considered the world that he had made, he had a reason to think favorably of his handiwork: it was good. Its being good was not the same thing as the correctness of his attitude, but the basis that made his attitude correct. Similarly, we normally suppose that there is a reason why we should have compassion for people who are suffering: we think that what they are experiencing is a bad thing. We do not merely judge, without having a reason for such a judgment, that they ought not to have to endure such pain. There is something about pain (or much pain, at any rate) that makes it something to be avoided: its badness.

Those who side with Moore, agreeing with him that goodness is a reason-providing property, will be called "friends of absolute

14. *Intrinsic Value*, pp. 11–12.
15. I take Raz to be agreeing with Moore when he says that "valuing... is right or wrong depending on whether what is valued possesses or fails to possess the value property because of which it is valued, or at any rate some value property in virtue of which its valuation is right, or in the absence of which it is wrong" (*The Practice of Value*, p. 130).

goodness" in this study.[16] I do not include in this group philosophers who believe that we can give a reductive definition of goodness in terms of the fittingness of a mental attitude. It does not matter, for present purposes, whether the friends of absolute goodness are few or many. It does not matter who else besides Moore and Ross are members of this circle. Their thesis has enough initial plausibility to deserve a fuller hearing.

16. Moore assumes that goodness is *always* reason-providing. One might partly agree with him by holding that goodness is in some circumstances reason-providing but in other circumstances not. My principal target will be Moore's full thesis rather than the modification just mentioned, but I believe that if my arguments succeed, they will make that modification implausible as well. I return to this point in chapter 9.

Chapter 3

An Argument
for Absolute Goodness

It is easy to see why absolute goodness has had philosophical friends. It does not require a religious orientation or abstruse metaphysical reflection to arrive, in short order, at the conclusion that some things should be sought because they are good (period). Consider simple and innocent pleasures, for example—not wrongful pleasures, not the pleasures of a sadist, but the pleasurable sensations one feels as one sits in a nice, warm bath or the pleasure of eating a delicious peach for which one has developed an appetite. Do we not seek and welcome such pleasures because we look upon them favorably? Do we not look upon them favorably because we think a reason can be given in favor of pursuing them? Can we not subject them to some sort of evaluation, on the basis of which we pursue and welcome them? Yes—or so it is plausible to assume, at first. And having agreed that they should be favorably evaluated, would it be mistaken to express our evaluation of them by saying: these experiences are, quite simply, *good*? How else are we to convey our positive evaluation of these pleasures, if not by calling them good? Why suppose that anything else needs to be said of them, as an explanation of why they are to be valued, beyond affirming them to be good?

I believe that these thoughts, and others like them—after all, pleasure is not the only thing that seems to be absolutely good— have some initial persuasive power. But I will argue that second thoughts are in order. There are powerful reasons to doubt that we succeed in justifying our valuation of something by adverting to its goodness, plain and simple. We do have reason to welcome certain kinds of pleasures and many other sorts of things; that part of the argument just rehearsed is, of course, true. But if I am right, the reason is never that they are, quite simply, good things.

My discussion will proceed on the basis of entirely secular assumptions. Obviously, if God exists, and if God is absolute goodness, then there is such a thing as absolute goodness, and something's being absolutely good, by being godlike, is a reason to value it. I set aside, within this study, all questions about the existence and nature of God, and ask whether there is any *other* reason, drawn from assumptions widely accepted by common sense or secular philosophies, to suppose that there is such a thing as absolute goodness. Many friends of absolute goodness—within the twentieth century, Moore and Ross are excellent examples—have assumed that there is, and have done so without seeking support in theological premises. Against them, I argue that there are weighty reasons to demur. I do not address myself here to someone who thinks that we can have reason to believe in absolute goodness only by first recognizing the existence of God.

Chapter 4

Absolute Evil, Relative Goodness

The term I have chosen, in deference to Moore—"absolute goodness"—is not entirely devoid of the potential to mislead us. Its opposite is "absolute badness" or "absolute evil." So in questioning whether we should value anything because it is absolutely good, I am, of course, also questioning whether we should devalue anything because it is absolutely bad or evil. To some ears, it will sound as though I am calling into question the existence of absolutely evil people. Those who interpret what I am saying in this way will point to such mass murderers as Hitler, Stalin, and Pol Pot and ask me: aren't such people absolutely bad, or absolutely evil? My reply is that these individuals were, indeed, absolutely bad or absolutely evil *people*, or absolutely bad or evil *human beings*. But it would be an error to drop the words "people" and "human beings," when we express our condemnation of these tyrants, and to claim that they were bad (period). When we judge them blameworthy of horrible crimes, we are judging them as human beings or persons.

Their moral failure cannot be adequately expressed by saying merely that they were not good people. They were much worse than that: they were extremely bad, in fact, *evil*. So evil, in fact, that we might go so far as to say that they were *absolutely* bad and *absolutely* evil people. I have no quarrel with that designation. I merely point out that they were not bad or evil *simpliciter*. Rather, they were absolutely bad or absolutely evil people.

When we take notice of such phrases as "absolutely bad person," we can see that "absolute" and "absolutely" are often not used as I use them in this study. They are not always used as the English equivalent of *simpliciter* or *tout court*. Rather, they sometimes mean "in every respect," "without reservation or qualification," "completely," "purely," "perfectly." That is what would be meant by calling Hitler *absolutely* bad or evil: he was entirely and completely contemptible. To give another example of this use of "absolutely": when we call someone an *absolutely* loyal friend, we mean that his loyalty is unconditional, boundless, and pure. He is not loyal up to a point and no further, or loyal in some circumstances but not others. Similarly, we might say of an actor that he has achieved absolute perfection at his craft, meaning by this that he has attained, to the highest possible degree, every excellence of his profession. He is not merely good—he is absolutely good. But we would be trading on an ambiguity in the word "absolute" if we were to say, on this basis, that there is such a property as absolute goodness. The actor in question is not good *simpliciter*. He is not good absolutely in the sense that he has the property of being, quite simply, good. Rather, it is as an actor that he is absolutely good, just as it is as a person that Hitler was absolutely bad. The question we are asking here is not whether there are absolutely good or bad things of a kind—meaning by "absolutely" that they are completely, perfectly, purely good things of that kind. It is whether some things are to be valued because they are good (period).

Contrast between things

One reason to use the term "absolute" goodness in a study of goodness *simpliciter* is that "absolutely" brings to mind a contrast with "relatively," and the philosophical tradition that I am challenging characterizes the goodness it posits as something that does not have its goodness only in relation to something else. We can use the absolutely-relatively contrast to characterize the difference between being good (period) and being good *for* someone. If you say that a certain kind of food is good for horses, the word "for" indicates that you are not claiming that such food is good *simpliciter*, but good only in relation to horses. You are leaving it open that it might also be characterized as bad—in relation to other animals. Similarly, if you say that you own a good toaster, that use of "good" might also be characterized as relational rather than absolute: relative to the class of toasters, and judged by the standards appropriate to things of that kind, your toaster is a good one. But when Moore and like-minded philosophers call innocent pleasures good, they are not basing their evaluation of pleasure on its relation to something else: it is not being called good for someone or good as a member of some kind. Since it is a nonrelational goodness, and "absolutely" can mean "nonrelationally," the term "absolute goodness" is an appropriate designation for the sort of goodness this tradition posits. Even though "absolutely" has other uses (as we saw earlier in this chapter), it is a good choice of a term for what is good *simpliciter*.

The pleasurable sensations one feels as one sits in a nice, warm bath are available to us only by taking certain measures to produce and safeguard them. We first have to draw water from the tap; we have to fix leaky pipes, pay our water bills, and so on. Should we say that these measures also have the property of being absolutely good, when they succeed in producing the pleasant sensations that are absolutely good? That is not what Moore or other friends of absolute goodness say, and they have good reason not to do so. Drawing water from the tap is not good *simpliciter*; it is good only in relation to something else—it is a good way to get water into the bathtub.[1] Just as a good tennis player is not good (period), a good means to an end is not absolutely good but good only in relation to something else—the thing to which it is a means. Instrumental goodness is not a kind of absolute goodness, but a way to bring us closer to absolute goodness. More generally, I will be assuming that the things that friends of absolute goodness take to be nonrelationally good (that is, good *simpliciter*) are only those things that do not derive their goodness from a source external to themselves, as instrumental means do. In that sense, they have the property of goodness without the mediation of anything further. They have the property of goodness (assuming there is such a property) simply because it is part of their nature to be good.

There is one other possible way of way of using the phrase "absolute goodness" that needs to be set aside. Someone might say that he is "against absolute goodness" and mean by this that, as Hamlet puts it, "there is nothing either good or bad but thinking makes it so."[2] But that thought would be better expressed by saying that there is no *objective* goodness—that all goodness and, indeed, all evaluative and normative properties whatsoever (moral rightness, human well-being, human virtues) are subjective, human constructions, not "out there" in the world.[3] Much more than this needs to be said

---

1. "It would be a good thing to draw water from the tap" is, of course, a meaningful sentence. But that does not show that the goodness of drawing the water is nonrelational goodness. It is good only as a means, and therefore in relation to, something else—the pleasure to which it leads. In that sense, the goodness of drawing the water is not absolute goodness.

2. William Shakespeare, *Hamlet* II.ii.249–250.

3. For two opposed views about what the objective-subjective distinction amounts to, and for several other important ways of categorizing goods (intrinsic-extrinsic, final-instrumental, unconditional-conditional), see Korsgaard, "Two Distinctions in Goodness;" and Rae Langton, "Objective and Unconditioned Value," *Philosophical Review* 116 (2007), pp. 157–185. For another helpful study of some of these distinctions, see Julie Tannenbaum, "Categorizing

about what the objective-subjective distinction involves, but fortunately we need not enter that terrain, for my doubts about absolute goodness do not arise from any wider doubts I harbor about whether there are normative, or evaluative, or moral properties. I believe that there are such things and that they are not human constructions or projections of human subjectivity. To put my point metaphorically: I believe there is a landscape filled with normative and evaluative items, and it is our job to investigate that world. What is good for children, or one's friends, or human beings and living creatures more generally: that is something waiting to be discovered, and if we are sufficiently obtuse, we might all be in error about these matters. What I doubt is that one of the items in that landscape is a certain property whose instantiation gives us reason to value things—the property that is called, quite simply, "goodness" (and equivalent words in other languages). To doubt that there ever was a single individual whom we call Robin Hood, the sole subject of our familiar legends, is not to doubt that there have ever been human beings or bandits or to suppose that all human beings and bandits are figments of our subjectivity. Similarly, to ask whether there is such a property as absolute goodness is not to entertain the question whether there are properties in general or the sorts of properties referred to by the words that we systematically employ when we engage in practical reasoning.

Moral properties? yes

human creatures? no

No property of goodness

good, period

Goods," in Russ Shafer-Landau, *Oxford Studies in Metaethics*, Vol. 5 (New York: Oxford University Press, 2010).

Chapter 5

Recent Skepticism about Absolute Goodness

I am not alone in having arrived at a skeptical conclusion about absolute goodness, although the route by which I come to that conclusion is different from those that others have taken. Probably my doubts would not have occurred to me, had I not read these other authors, and I am eager both to acknowledge my debt to them and to call attention to the ways in which my approach to this subject differs from theirs.

One kind of skepticism among contemporary philosophers about goodness stems from a remarkable short essay of P. T. Geach, published in 1956.[1] Geach said: "There is no such thing as being just good or bad, there is only being a good or bad so-and-so."[2] Two of his principal targets were Moore and Ross, but rather than name them, he spoke disparagingly of a group of philosophers whom he called Objectivists. Here is how he characterized their way of thinking: " 'Forget the uses of "good" in ordinary language' says the Objectivist; 'in our discussion it shall mean what I mean by it in such typical remarks as "pleasure is good." You, of course, know just how I want you to take these. No, of course I cannot explain further: don't you know that "good" in my sense is a simple and undefinable term?' "[3]

---

1. *Analysis* 17, pp. 33–42. My citations refer to its republication in Philippa Foot, ed., *Theories of Ethics* (London: Oxford University Press, 1967), pp. 64–73.
2. Ibid., p. 65.
3. Ibid., p. 67.

Against this, Geach said: "How can we be asked to take for granted at the outset that a peculiarly philosophical use of words necessarily means anything at all? Still less can we be expected at the outset to know what this use means."[4] His suspicion that major figures in moral philosophy failed to signify anything by their theoretical claims was no doubt fed by the general philosophical climate created in England by Wittgenstein's approach to philosophy. Both his *Tractatus Logico-Philosophicus* and *Philosophical Investigations* hold that apparent meaningfulness can be merely apparent. In the latter work, meaninglessness is portrayed as an affliction that befalls philosophical discourse when it removes itself from the concrete practices that ground communication. Inspired by Wittgenstein's works, we might reject large portions of traditional ethical theorizing for its remoteness from concrete practical questions. We know how to answer such questions as "Is this a good car?" because there are familiar standards by which cars are to be evaluated. But in everyday conversation, we do not ask each other, "Is pleasure good?" It is by this route that Geach arrives at his conclusion that such a question is illegitimate or, at any rate, that we are not entitled simply to assume that it is legitimate.[5]

Geach's essay did not fall on deaf ears. Two of the most eminent moral philosophers of recent decades—I am thinking of Philippa Foot and Judith Jarvis Thomson—have been influenced by him. Citing his essay with approval, each defends a kind of skepticism about goodness that resembles his. Foot's aim, in "Utilitarianism

---

4. Ibid.
5. See, too, Paul Ziff, *Semantic Analysis* (Ithaca, NY: Cornell University Press, 1960), chapter 6. He claims that "pleasure is good" and "a charitable deed is something that is intrinsically good" (as well as some other sentences of little interest to moral philosophers) sound odd, and he proposes that their "deviance" derives from their failure to conform to a semantic rule: what is good answers to certain interests. See pp. 212, 216, and 236. He also notes that "pleasure is good for one's soul" does *not* sound odd (p. 217).

and the Virtues," is to cast doubt on whether we can understand what utilitarianism is talking about when it asserts that we should always strive to achieve the best state of affairs. She says: "We should begin by asking why we are so sure that we even understand expressions such as 'a good state of affairs' or 'a good outcome'; for as Peter Geach pointed out years ago there are phrases with the word 'good' in them, as e.g. 'a good event', that do *not* at least as they stand have a sense."[6]

Similarly, Thomson asks: "When philosophers ask, as many have done, 'Is knowledge, or pleasure, good?' what exactly do they mean? Geach said there is no good reason to think they mean anything at all."[7] She then adds that although he was too hasty in the way he reached his conclusion, a more careful attempt to find a meaning for their question confirms his verdict. "In the end," she says, "Geach was right: The philosopher who asks, 'Is knowledge, or pleasure, good?' is not asking an intelligible question—it is no more intelligible than the question whether the melon your grocer points to is (not a good melon, but all simply) a good thing."[8]

Although the doubts about goodness raised by these authors have certainly had a salutary effect on my own thinking, the conclusion I have come to, and which I defend here, is that they have

6. Her essay first appeared in *Mind* 94 (1985), pp. 196–209, and is reprinted in her *Moral Dilemmas and Other Topics in Moral Philosophy* (Oxford: Clarendon, 2002), pp. 59–77. The statement I cite (with the author's emphasis) is from the latter, p. 63.

7. *Normativity* (Chicago: Open Court, 2008), p. 14. For her earlier discussions of this topic, see "The Right and the Good," *Journal of Philosophy* 94 (1997), pp. 273–298; and *Goodness and Advice* (Princeton, NJ: Princeton University Press, 2001).

8. *Normativity*, p. 17. For discussion, see Charles R. Pigden, "Geach on Good," *Philosophical Quarterly* 40 (1990), pp. 129–154; Michael J. Zimmerman, "In Defense of the Concept of Intrinsic Value," *Canadian Journal of Philosophy* 29 (1999), pp. 389–400; Michael J. Zimmerman, *The Nature of Intrinsic Value*, pp. 15–32; and Walter Sinnott-Armstrong, "For Goodness' Sake," *Southern Journal of Philosophy* 41 (2003), Supplementary Volume: "The Legacy of G. E. Moore: 100 Years of Metaethics," pp. 83–91. Thomson replies to Sinnott-Armstrong in that same issue, pp. 92–94. I am grateful to Tom Hurka for some of these references.

not identified what is problematic about goodness, as traditionally conceived. Their idea, as I understand it, is that these traditional theories violate a linguistic rule—a rule that governs the proper use of the word "good" (and other words that have the same meaning). Speakers who talk in terms of what is good (period) are, of course, trying to form meaningful sentences, but they fail to do so, and therefore what they utter cannot be evaluated as true or false. Thus Geach, Foot, and Thomson.

My own diagnosis, by contrast, is that positing the existence of absolute goodness stands to ethical theory as positing the existence of phlogiston stands to physics. The problem with phlogiston is not that it is a *conceptual* impossibility whose nonexistence could have been recognized had its defenders been more clear-headed. Rather, as it turned out, its existence was not as sound a scientific posit as its competitors. Similarly, the kind of skepticism about absolute goodness that I defend does not charge the friends of absolute goodness with the sin of speaking unintelligibly. It proposes that they are mistaken in their assumption that absolute goodness is a reason-giving property. It grants that we can make sense of calling friendship, knowledge, pleasure (and the like) good things—if we mean by this merely that there is a reason to value these things. But if goodness is (as its friends hold) something more than that—if it is the common property these things share that gives us reason to value them—then it doubts that there is such a property.

To reach this conclusion, we have to take a stand about how we should live our lives—how we should arrive at conclusions about what to do, how we should feel about the various states of affairs that are important for us to evaluate, what our highest aspirations should be, how we should raise our children, and so on. Thinking about such problems by positing absolute goodness as a reason-giving property does not help us with them—in fact, it can lead us astray. That property does not do the work that a normative or evaluate property needs to do, and that is why we are justified in concluding that it does not exist. That is the proper way to determine which entities dwell in the normative landscape. We cannot exclude goodness from that territory simply by reflecting on how words are to be used in order to communicate with meaningful sentences. We also need to draw on our knowledge of which sentences containing the word "good" are *true* (not merely meaningful), as well as our understanding of what makes them true. So, I agree with Geach, Foot, and Thomson that we should not value something on the grounds that it is, quite simply, good. But the route I take to that conclusion takes me through different terrain.

Because of Geach's classic paper and the work of those who have been influenced by it, it has now become a familiar and widely accepted point that when we say that something is a good member of a kind (a good camera, for example), our claim cannot be decomposed into two independent subclaims, one of them adverting to goodness, the other to the kind in question. (A good camera does not have two separate properties: one that makes it a camera, and the other that makes it good *simpliciter*.) I will myself build on that point (chapter 6). But it does not take us all the way to the conclusion that goodness is not a reason-giving property, nor to the further conclusion that there is no such property as goodness.

Another author has raised doubts about whether a thing's being valuable or good provides a reason for having any of the various favorable attitudes toward it that constitute ways of valuing it: T. M. Scanlon.[9] Unlike Geach, Foot, and Thomson, he does not

9. *What We Owe to Each Other* (Cambridge, MA: Belknap, 1998).

entertain doubts about whether there is such a thing as goodness or value, but he denies that these are reason-giving properties. Before I discuss his contribution to this subject, I will explain why I believe that skepticism about absolute goodness is warranted. We have seen (in chapter 3) how tempting it is to be led to the conclusion that some things should be valued because they are good. It is time to look at reasons for resisting that conclusion.

Chapter 6

Being Good and Being Good for Someone

Before I raise doubts about the thesis that some things should be valued because they are absolutely good, I should state some premises I will be using—I hope they will be taken as obvious—about the relationship that consists in something's being good *for* someone and its opposite (something's being bad *for* someone).

First, I believe that there are these two relationships: being good for someone and being bad for someone; furthermore, some things are related in these ways; and in favorable circumstances, we can know that these relationships hold. To give an example: smoking tobacco is bad for some people. (It is bad for them because of its causal consequences, a point I will return to in the next chapter.) There is such a thing as smoking tobacco, there are people who engage in this activity, and those two things—the people who smoke and their activity of smoking—are related in a certain way: their smoking is bad for them. We know all of this to be true. Admittedly, not every philosopher agrees with what I have just said. I am thinking of Moore: he holds that it is unintelligible to speak of what is good for someone or bad for someone. If he were right, it would be nonsense to say that smoking is bad for people. I return to this issue in chapter 12.

Second, I believe that the relationship of being good for someone should not be defined, partly or wholly, in terms of something's being absolutely good.[1] Similarly, neither should being bad for someone be understood, partly or wholly, as consisting in something's being absolutely bad. It is obvious that B's being bad for someone does not consist *wholly and simply* in B's being bad (period). Smoking cigarettes, let us suppose, is bad for someone—call him George. His lungs are susceptible to cancer, and if he smokes more than a few cigarettes a day over the course of his boyhood, he will die prematurely. We can logically infer from the fact that smoking cigarettes is bad for George that it is bad for someone. But notice that we cannot simply infer from this that smoking cigarettes is bad (period).

What would it mean for it to be the case that smoking is bad *period*? That is a puzzle to which I will soon turn (chapter 8). For the moment, however, I leave that question aside. Let's suppose, provisionally, that this is a notion that makes sense. Let's allow, temporarily, that there is such a thing as being bad (period), and let's allow that smoking might have that property. Even so, we could not

1. Here I write in opposition to the theory defended by Robert Merrihew Adams in *Finite and Infinite Goods*, pp. 83–101. See appendix C for some reflections on his approach. I accept Talbot Brewer's characterization of the thesis I am defending here: "*goodness for* is not a species of goodness *simpliciter* but a *sui generis* and essentially person-relative evaluative property" (*The Retrieval of Ethics*, p. 211), although it is not relative only to persons.

establish that smoking is bad simply by establishing that smoking is bad *for* someone. Being bad for someone and being bad absolutely are two different properties. So being bad for someone should not be taken to consist simply in being bad (period). Similarly, being good for someone should not be taken to consist simply in being good (period). I doubt that anyone will deny this.

Might it be the case, nonetheless, that the relationship of being good for someone should be defined *partly* in terms of something's being absolutely good? The idea would be this: to be good for someone consists in having two properties, first, it is partly constituted by being good (period) and, second, it partly consists in having some further feature (as yet unspecified). Ditto for the relationship of being bad for someone.

That, I believe, is a suspect proposal. I will argue against it in chapter 13, but we can already see, by way of an analogy, why we should be on our guard against it. Being a good chess player does not consist in having two independent properties: first, being good; second, being a chess player. To be a good chess player is to be good-at-chess, not good (period) and at-chess. To call someone a good chess player is to compare her with other chess players; it is to say she is good-in-relation-to-them—not good (period) and something more. This shows that not all phrases constructed out of "good" and some other bit of language should be understood as having one component that refers to the property of goodness and then (as an independent matter) some second component. So we must not be predisposed to accept the idea that the phrase "good for" *must* refer to a relation constructed out of two separate elements—that when something is good for someone, that holds because, first, it is good (period) and, second, because of something else in addition. We know that phrases constructed out of "good" do not have to work that way.

We should not be misled by the fact that the word "good" appears within the phrase "good for." No doubt, that linguistic overlap brings with it certain commonalities: the word "good" has a certain meaning, and that has consequences for the meaning of "good for" and other phrases that contain the word "good." When something is evaluated as good (period), it receives a higher evaluation than does something that is evaluated as bad (period). Something that is called, quite simply, good is therefore said to be better than something that is called, quite simply, bad. That can be said to be true by virtue of the very meaning of these terms—"good," "bad," and "better." Correspondingly, what is good for someone is better for that person than what is bad for him. And again by virtue of the meaning of the words "good," "bad," and "better," a good tennis player is a better tennis player than a bad tennis player. Even so, the task of deciding whether someone is a good tennis player cannot be construed as the aggregation of two independent subtasks: first determining whether he has the property of being good and then determining whether he has the property of being a tennis player. Similarly, I want to say, something's being good for someone does not consist, first, in its being good (period) and, then, its being something else in relation to that individual (namely, whatever else stands behind the word "for").

Just as we learn how to decide whether someone is a good chess player or a good tennis player by becoming acquainted with these games and with those who have these skills (not with absolute goodness), so it is from our exposure to things that are good for human beings that we learn what is involved in something's being good for them, and from our exposure to what is good for cats, dogs, trees, and so on, that we learn what is involved in something's being good for them. It is not by learning about goodness (period), then learning about human beings, and then putting these two independent inquiries together, that we grasp what is good for human beings. To understand what is good for some particular human being, we must have some knowledge of human beings in general and also of that human being in particular.[2]

None of this presents us with a reason to doubt that there is such a thing as absolute goodness or badness, nor to doubt that these are reason-giving properties. Rather, the conclusion for which I am arguing is that, regardless of whether there is such a thing as absolute goodness, and regardless of whether it is a source of reasons, the relationship of being good *for* someone does not depend on absolute goodness for its existence. Therefore, it is not conceptually impossible for something to be good for someone but not absolutely good. Smoking, for example, might be bad for someone, without being bad (period). Similarly, if absolute goodness is a property that some things have, then it is conceptually possible for something to be good absolutely without being good for anyone. Justice, for example, might be good, without being good for anyone. Two independent inquiries, then, must be undertaken to determine whether something is good (period) and to determine whether it is good for someone.

2. I mean to leave open the possibility that there are significant differences in what is non-instrumentally beneficial among human beings. This issue will be more fully discussed in chapter 13.

Chapter 7

Noninstrumental Advantageousness

Are some things *noninstrumentally* good for individuals? I believe so, for the following reasons.

There is no longer any doubt that smoking tobacco (with some frequency over a long period of time) is bad for a great many people. It is bad for them because of its effects on them. That is an empirical claim. Now let us add a *conceptual* point: if this is bad for people because of its effects, then there must be something else—those effects, or the effects of those effects, or something else down a long causal chain—that is also bad for people, not because of something else it brings about, but because it is, by itself, bad for people. Instrumental disadvantages and advantages inherit their disadvantageousness and advantageousness from things that are noninstrumentally disadvantageous and advantageous. That is a point that can easily be overlooked, because "good for," "bad for," "beneficial," and so on are so often applied to mere means. So it is worthwhile to spell this out more fully.

The idea originates with Plato, who argues in the *Republic* that justice is by itself advantageous, apart from its consequences. We need not decide whether he is right to place *justice* in this category. For our purposes, what is important is the existence of the category of noninstrumental advantages. Although many things that are good for us are correctly so classified merely because they are tools for achieving further results that are good for us, not everything that is good for us need have that instrumental character. Something can, in other words, be good for someone without being useful. Suppose, for example, that it is good for people to feel the love of others or to enjoy participating in a sport. If these things are good for us, that need not be solely because they lead to something else that is good for us. In fact, it can plausibly be said about these particular items that they are good for us regardless of whether they lead to anything else. They are *noninstrumentally* good for us. (I will also say that that such things are noninstrumental *advantages* or *benefits*, since I use "good for," "advantageous," and "beneficial" interchangeably. Often I will omit "noninstrumentally" when the context makes my meaning clear.)

There is, near the beginning of Aristotle's *Nicomachean Ethics*, a well-known argument for the conclusion that there must be something that is good "because of itself," everything else being desirable because of it. It is a difficult argument to accept, because it seeks to show that there is one and only one ultimate goal at which all human beings should aim. But I believe that Aristotle would have been right, had he sought to argue for a far more modest conclusion. Suppose we agree that some things, A, B, and C, are good *for* us solely because they are effective means to something else, D. What can we say, based on this information alone, about the character of D? Can we say, for example, that it must be noninstrumentally good for us? Of course not. Like A, B, and C, it might be good for us to have only because it, too, is an effective means to something else, E. And the same point applies to E. But this chain of cause and effect cannot be infinitely long. At some point, if it is correct that A, B, C, and so on are genuinely good for us, then it seems that there must eventually be something, X, that they lead to and that is not good for us merely as a means to something further.

That conclusion does not quite follow, but it is close to one that does. The point we need to keep in mind to fix the argument is that the causal chain might lead to some X that is neutral in value— intermediate, in other words, between being noninstrumentally good for us and noninstrumentally bad for us. We call things good for us not only when they lead to further things that are good for us but also when they help us avoid further things that are bad for us. We take medicine, for example, to avoid the harms that might occur in its absence. The medicine is good for us simply because it prevents the occurrence of what is bad for us. It need not, in addition, promote something else that is good for us. It can leave us no better off and no worse off than we now are.

There is no way to prove by reasoning alone, and apart from any assumptions about which things are noninstrumentally advantageous, as well as assumptions about whether some people have those things, that in fact there are things we now have that are noninstrumentally good for us. Nonetheless, we can establish this much by reasoning alone: if some things are *instrumentally* good for us, then there is such a property (whether it is instantiated or not) as being *non*instrumentally good for us, a further property of being *non*instrumentally bad for us, and a still further property of being intermediate between *non*instrumentally good for us and *non*instrumentally bad for us. To classify something, A, as instrumentally good for us presupposes that there is some further thing, X, to which A leads. Classifying A as good for us can be justified only if that further thing, X, will be better for us than what is noninstrumentally bad for us. Medication, for example, can be good for us only if it either helps bring about a condition that is noninstrumentally good for us or helps prevent a condition that is noninstrumentally bad for us. Whether any existing medication is actually good for us is, of course, not a matter that philosophy alone can decide. That depends on not only what is noninstrumentally good or bad for us (a matter about which philosophy should have something to say) but also whether medicine as now practiced is effective in bringing us closer to those goals.

The effectiveness of something as a means to an end that some-one is pursuing is not by itself a reason to suppose that it is good *for him* that he so use it, even to a small extent. Suppose his end is one whose achievement is not good for him, and his failure to achieve it would not be bad for him. He pursues it, let us imagine, for the good of others and not himself. In that case, there is no basis for saying that it is good *for him* (where this means "beneficial to him") that he use those means. If he uses them, he achieves his end, but if that makes him no better off than he would otherwise have been, then it was not good for him to use those means.

Suppose, in a different case, the means someone uses do not bring about a goal whose achievement will be noninstrumentally good *for anyone*. Nor, let us further suppose, will his action help avoid anything that is noninstrumentally bad *for anyone*. In that case, the means he uses are not *instrumentally* good *for anyone*. So if we classify something as instrumentally advantageous, it must be effec-tive, to some extent, in bringing about either what is noninstrumen-tally good for someone or preventing what is noninstrumentally bad for someone.

Everyday practical discourse is filled with assertions about advantages and disadvantages. What we are committed to, when we use this discourse, is the assumption that some things are good for someone without their being good for someone as a means to a further end.

If there is such a property as absolute goodness, then the things that are useful in producing whatever has that property can be called good. They are, as I noted in chapter 4, good not absolutely but as a means. But it would be a misuse of terms to say of them, for that reason alone, that they are beneficial or advantageous. If what they lead to is not good for anyone, and if what they hinder is not bad for anyone, they themselves cannot be good for anyone.

Chapter 8

The Problem of Intelligibility

In chapter 6, I said that we should not infer from something's being bad for someone that it is bad *simpliciter*. My example was this: smoking cigarettes might be bad for George, but it would not follow that smoking is bad (period). I admitted that in addition to rejecting this inference, we should also ask a question about its conclusion: what would it even mean to say that smoking is bad? Let us now linger over this question. Doing so should make us realize that Geach, Foot, and Thomson have raised a legitimate question, and one that is not easily answered. Although I do not accept their diagnosis of what goes awry in talk about absolute goodness, it is a step forward to feel the force of their argument.

Suppose we hear someone say that people should give up cigarettes because smoking is bad, and we ask him to clarify: does he mean, we ask, that smoking is bad *for smokers*? Well, he replies, smoking does happen to be bad for smokers, and even for those within their vicinity who inhale their smoke—but that is not what he had in mind. He did not mean to say that smoking is bad *for* certain people, either instrumentally or noninstrumentally. We might then ask: are you saying that smoking is morally bad—that we are, in other words, morally required not to smoke? Not at all, he replies. What he means, he insists, is precisely what he has said: smoking is bad—period. Would we not be tempted to say that our interlocutor is confused, even if we have no ready-to-hand explanation of how he has fallen into this confusion? The problem does not seem to be that what he has said is *false*—it's not as though we feel certain that smoking is good (period) or intermediate between being good (period) and bad (period), rather than, as he asserts, bad (period). Nor does it seem accurate to describe our dissatisfaction with this interlocutor by saying that he has provided no argument for his assertion. Admittedly, he has not defended himself. But there seems to be a more serious defect in his utterance, namely, that we do not know what he is talking about. One way to explain what has gone wrong is to say that he has violated a rule that governs the use of "bad."

Things can be bad *for* us merely because what they lead to is bad for us. They inherit their disadvantageousness from the disadvantageousness of what they produce. One would expect, similarly, that if some things (pain, for example) are *absolutely* bad, there would be nothing puzzling about saying of the things that lead to them: "they are bad, regardless of whether they are bad *for* anyone." For example, if pain is absolutely bad, then "smoking is just plain bad, regardless of whether it is bad for anyone" should be accepted by anyone who sees that smoking leads to pain. But, in fact, "smoking is just plain bad, regardless of whether it is bad for anyone" is an odd thing to say. Why should it mystify us? Why doesn't smoking come to be just plain bad because of the just plain badness of the pain to which it leads?

The puzzling assertion that smoking is bad (period) is not unique. We can produce many similar puzzles, all of them resulting from talk about absolute goodness or badness. To take one more case, suppose someone tells us: "George is good." Unless the context of his utterance had already made his meaning clear, we would surely ask for elaboration. We might say, for example: "I know which George you are talking about, but what did you have in mind in calling him good? Are you saying that he is a good poet? Or good at chess? Or that he is a morally good person?" Suppose our interlocutor responds by denying that he has any of these claims in mind. What he means, he says, is precisely what he has already said: George is good—full stop. I think we would be tempted to say, in response, that our interlocutor is not making sense.

It can't be the case that George is just plain good.[1] Why not? Isn't that because *whenever* you use the word "good" (and words that mean the same in other languages), you must supplement it in some way? You might, for example, say that George is a good sailor, or that he is good to his aunt, or that he is good to talk to—but you cannot intelligibly say that he is good (period). At any rate, it seems plausible to suppose that there are rules that govern the use of "good" and that the reason we cannot understand our interlocutor lies in his failure to be guided by one of them. After all, the complaint we want to make is not that he has failed to defend his assertion that George is good. The problem is that we do not understand what he would be defending, were he to offer a defense.

If there is a rule regarding "good" that is partly or wholly constitutive of its meaningful employment and that these two speakers have violated, what is it? Obviously, it cannot be "do not say of people that they are good (period)" or "do not say of smoking that it is bad (period)." It will be a *general* rule, forbidding us to say of *anything* that it is good (period) or bad (period), on pain of lapsing into unintelligibility. If that is a rule we must observe to make sense, it is nonsense to say that pleasure is good or that pain is bad. Notice that if we refrain from saying of pleasure that it is good and pain that it is bad, we are not thereby deprived of any resources for evaluating these experiences. We can evaluate them by saying that they are

---

1. But can't it be the case that George is *valuable*? It's often said, after all, that *all* humans beings have intrinsic value. Switching back to the word "good," it might also be said that George's *existence* is a good thing—that his being alive makes the world a better place. I will have much to say about these questions in chapters 25 through 27 and appendixes A and B. I will argue that "George is valuable" is no improvement over "George is good" and that the mere existence of a human being is not a good thing.

good or bad *for* those who feel them. Speaking in these terms has a distinct advantage: it is intelligible.

Geach implies that it is only philosophers who have ever lapsed into talking unintelligibly by using the words "good" and "bad" absolutely. But that is not part of the argument just rehearsed for taking those uses to be unintelligible. Even if ordinary people untainted by philosophical speculation *frequently* told each other that pleasure is good and pain bad, that would not tell us how to interpret someone who says (in the circumstances just described) that George is absolutely good and smoking absolutely bad. It is not impossible that a large number of people, including many nonphilosophers, speak in ways that no one understands. After all, if it has sometimes escaped the notice of some philosophers that they are failing to make sense, surely this can also happen to people who are (for good reason) less reflective about the concepts they are using. The failure to grasp the rules that govern the use of "good" may be quite widespread, just as logical fallacies are all too common.

There is no doubt that in ordinary conversation people frequently use the word "good" without supplementing it with other phrases, because the context in which they speak makes it clear which further words are needed to make their meaning explicit. As they observe a performance, they will exclaim, "He's good!" meaning that he is good at what he is doing. They reward students who are performing well by saying "good," meaning that their essays are good essays. When their team loses, they say, "That's too bad"—bad, in other words, for their team. But none of this has any bearing on the philosophical issue we are discussing. It does not matter how frequently or infrequently "good" is used in the way it is used by those philosophers who say of pleasure or other things that they are good (period). The proper philosophical question is whether we can make sense of that usage.

After I examine more thoroughly (in chapters 29 and 30) the conjecture that a *linguistic* error is made when something is called absolutely good, I will reject it. I believe that we should count "smoking is bad (period)" as meaningful but false. Recall the analogy I proposed earlier in chapter 5: just as the science of today has rejected the hypothesis that oxidation is caused by the presence of phlogiston, but not because the concept of phlogiston is incoherent or because sentences about phlogiston are meaningless, so we should, after long and careful reflection, entertain doubts about whether there is such a thing as the reason-giving property of being absolutely good. That, I will argue, is not because "smoking is bad" and other such sentences are unintelligible, but because we have a better explanation of why we should not smoke or refrain from other kinds of activities—we should do so because they are bad *for* us.

Chapter 9

The Problem of Double Value

I will now explain why I doubt that we should respond affirmatively to the question with which I began: "Are there things we should value because they are, quite simply, good?" We saw in chapter 3 why it is reasonable to be tempted by a positive answer. Now it is time to see why second thoughts are in order.

Consider an excruciating pain that is not a component of a larger, complex, salutary experience. We are to imagine a long-lasting pain that is difficult for the person who feels it to bear, a pain, further-more, about which nothing favorable can be said. The question to be asked is this: is that painful experience itself bad *for* him? (It does not matter to me, for present purposes, whether the subject of this experience is human. But I will assume that we are talking about a human being rather than some other sort of animal.) I would like to suggest that the answer to my question is yes: this sort of pain is bad *for* the person who feels it. Furthermore, it is *noninstrumentally* bad for the person who feels it (regardless of whether it is, in addition, instrumentally bad).

In giving this answer to my question, I am not yet addressing the question whether we should say *both* that the pain is bad for the person who feels it *and* that it is absolutely bad. That is an important further question, and I will soon turn to it, but for now, I want to concentrate exclusively on the question whether this sort of pain is bad *for* someone to feel.

That question, I think, can be asked in different ways. For example: Is feeling such pain by itself contrary to someone's inter-ests? Is someone made worse off, to some degree, simply by virtue of feeling such pain? Does having this experience constitute a disad-vantage? Does this count as an injury or a harm? Is it in itself a dim-inution in someone's well-being? With these questions, we are not asking whether this sort of pain has later causal consequences that are bad for the person who feels it. (Presumably, the answer to that question is that sometimes pain has these further effects, and some-times not.) Rather, our question is whether it is always *noninstru-mentally* bad for someone to feel this kind of pain.

We should have a great deal of confidence that the answer to this question is yes. If someone's life enters a period in which he suffers from a very painful disease, we take that as already a personal misfortune—something that makes his life less desirable *for him*, regardless of whether it leads to further personal misfortunes (disabilities, diminished functioning, early death, and so on). We do so *simply* because of the painfulness of the disease; we think that we would be doing something that is good *for him* if we could alleviate his suffering. (Notice that both of these points are being made: his pain is bad *for him,* and it is *noninstrumentally* bad for him.) If we discovered that this disease had been deliberately caused by someone who hates him—his wife, for example—we would say that he has a complaint against her that differs in kind from the criticism that the rest of us can make of her. She has not wronged us, but she has wronged him. That is because she has not made the rest of us worse off, whereas she has deliberately made him so. We can find fault with her, as he can (regardless of whether the pain he feels leads to further problems), but he can go beyond mere fault-finding: he has been personally affronted because he was the target of her attack. Her goal was not merely to bring about a certain amount of pain, but to cause him pain and thereby to make him worse off. Whether to forgive her is a problem for him but not for us. We can ask ourselves whether he should forgive her, but the question "Should we forgive her?" does not arise, because what she did was not bad *for us.* We lose sight of these important distinctions if what we find objectionable in her action is only that she increased the world's sum total of disvalue.

Recall, too, the argument (chapter 7) that there must be a category of things that are *noninstrumentally* disadvantageous if there are things that are *instrumentally* disadvantageous. Smoking, for example, is harmful to many people. It is harmful because of its later causal consequences. What are those long-term effects? One of them, let us suppose, is that it becomes painful to breathe. Now, we cannot count smoking as bad *for* someone unless what it eventually leads to is bad *for* that person. So the painfulness of breathing is something that must be counted as bad *for* the person who suffers from this experience. It is precisely the painfulness of breathing that makes this the case. Therefore, pains of a certain kind, regardless of whether they are also absolutely bad, are bad *for* those who feel them.

Now, having agreed that some pains are bad for those who experience them, let us ask a further question about those same pains: should we also say that they are absolutely bad? I can think of no reason to suppose that, in principle, something cannot be put into both of these categories—that, having been put into one, it is a conceptual necessity that it not be put into the other. Something's being bad for someone does not by itself make it impossible for it to be bad (period). So for all we have said so far, it might be true of certain pains both that they are bad for those who feel them and that, in addition, they are absolutely bad. (We should, however, keep in mind a point made earlier, in chapter 6: we are not entitled to assume that when something is bad for someone, it must be the case that it is also bad *simpliciter*. Pain's absolute badness should not be *inferred from* its badness for someone. For all that, it might be absolutely bad.)

Nonetheless, it is implausible to suppose that pain has this double disvalue. That is because we never find ourselves attending to both features of pain when we are engaged with practical questions, and it is doubtful that all of us have for so long so completely overlooked its duality. We frequently ask ourselves whether some project or task we are considering is worth the risk of pain. Should we stop smoking? Should we climb a mountain when the risk of breaking a leg (or worse) is significant? Should a nation's resources be devoted to inoculating its citizens against a disease that is only mildly painful? In all such cases, we have to decide not only whether pain has some disvalue but also how much disvalue it has, in comparison with other things that might be worse and in comparison with certain benefits that might make the risk of pain worth taking. What we never do, and what no one ever has done, is to take into account two kinds of disvalue that pain has: first, its being bad *for* those who feel it and, second, its being bad absolutely. We are justifiably confident that doing that would be double counting—assigning pain more disvalue than it actually has, by seeing in it two features that count against it rather than only one. Either we should say that pain is bad (period) or that it is bad for us. Using the way we reason about pain as our guide, we can plausibly deny that it has both features and that both provide reasons for avoiding and alleviating it. Using that same guide, it would be implausible to insist that it has both features but that one of them (which would it be?) is reason-providing, whereas the other is not.

I have argued that certain pains are bad for us. If the further argument just offered—that pain is not both bad for us and bad absolutely—is correct, we can infer that it is not the case that pain is bad absolutely. It has just one kind of disvalue: it is bad for us. Nonetheless, now that we see more fully where our arguments have led, we should ask ourselves whether we wish to reconsider. So let's ask once again: when one person deliberately causes another to contract a painful disease, should we say, not that what has happened is bad *for* anyone, but simply that it is bad?

The answer must be no, because otherwise we would be overlooking a vital feature of the situation: injuring or disadvantaging *him* is precisely what the agent aimed at and achieved. She was not seeking to bring into the universe something bad (period); her act was personally directed against *him*. She wanted to make *him* worse off and did so by causing him to be in great pain. If we accept that way of describing her act and agree that she did not bring about *both* what was bad for him *and* what was bad absolutely, then we must not say the pain she caused in him was bad absolutely.

Furthermore, we have no reason to revise our commonsense assumption that smoking is bad *for* the person who smokes because of the pain or other harms to which it eventually leads.

Since we continue to have every reason to assume that pain is bad for people, and since pain's disvalue is not due to its being both absolutely bad and bad for people, we should reaffirm the conclusion we reached several paragraphs ago: it is not the case that pain is *absolutely* bad; it is *relatively* bad—bad for those who feel it and suffer from it.[1]

The argument just given has limited scope, but it nonetheless should lead us to ask whether other arguments of the same sort can be given against placing other items in the category of what is bad (period) or what is good (period). It has limited scope in that it depends essentially on the way we reason about *pain*—not the way we reason about all practical matters. We do not assign *it* a double disvalue, and we have no reason to suppose that we are mistaken about that. It does not follow, as a matter of logical or conceptual necessity, that certain other things besides pain cannot both be bad absolutely and noninstrumentally bad for someone. Nor does it follow that some things cannot both be good absolutely and noninstrumentally good for us.

Nonetheless, there seems to be nothing else that is doubly valuable or doubly disvaluable in this way. I have no proof that nothing can fall into both categories, but when I reflect on the way I reason about how I should act, or how I should feel, or what I should recommend to or demand of others in the way of action and

---

1. I add the last four words ("and suffer from it") for reasons that I will present in the penultimate paragraph of chapter 13.

feeling, I never find, about this or that value or disvalue, that it is doubly valuable or doubly disvaluable, being both good absolutely and noninstrumentally good for someone, or both bad absolutely and noninstrumentally bad for someone. Nor do I know of anyone else who reasons in this way. (The question, recall, is whether, in our everyday practical reasoning, we count it in favor of something that it is both absolutely good and *noninstrumentally* good for someone. It is not whether we ever count it in favor of something that it is both good absolutely and also good *as a means* to something else.)

We might turn to philosophical texts, rather than everyday patterns of practical reasoning, to find attempts to show that some things are doubly valuable or doubly disvaluable in the relevant way.[2] Moore and Ross do not help us here, because they do not concern themselves with the category of what is good for someone. They take pleasure to be good but not also good for someone, and they take pain to be bad but not also bad for someone.

What of Plato? On one reading of the *Republic*, he holds that the property of being good absolutely is to be distinguished from the relation of being good for someone.[3] Whether that interpretation is correct is not a matter that can be adequately addressed in this book, but this can be taken as common ground: not a single line in this dialogue affirms, let alone argues, that justice (or, for that matter, anything else) is both good (period) and noninstrumentally good for someone. Book II of this work proposes, as an exhaustive taxonomy, that there are three kinds of things that are good *for*

---

2. See appendixes B through F. So far as I can tell, the classical utilitarian authors (Jeremy Bentham, J. S. Mill, Henry Sidgwick) do not help us here, nor does the great ideal utilitarian, Hastings Rashdall. Bentham, for example, says that by "utility" he means that which "tends to produce benefit, advantage, pleasure, good, or happiness (all this in the present case comes to the same thing)." See *An Introduction to the Principles of Morals and Legislation*, chapter 1, paragraph 3.

3. See the works cited in Chapter 2 note 2.

someone: what is by itself good for someone but lacks good consequences, what is by itself good for someone but has good consequences, and what is good for someone only because of its consequences. Justice is placed in the second of these three categories. It is therefore doubly valuable, Plato thinks. The possibility that it might be *triply* valuable—because it is by itself good for someone, because it is good for someone by having good consequences, and because it is just plain good—is not mentioned anywhere in the dialogue. I find nothing in it that can be construed even as an unsuccessful argument for the conclusion that justice is valuable in all three ways. _Plato no here in this chapter

Even if, as I claim, there is no reason to believe that there are things that should be avoided both because they are bad and because they are bad for someone (or valued because they are good and good for someone), that conclusion is certainly not sufficient for my larger purposes. The possibility remains that there are some things that should be valued because they are good absolutely, though good for no one, and others that are to be disvalued because they are bad absolutely, though bad for no one. (We will consider some possible examples later: cruelty might sometimes be bad *simpliciter* but bad for no one; equality might occasionally be good *simpliciter* but good for no one. And there are more cases to consider than these.) Absolute goodness and badness, in other words, might be reason-giving properties in some circumstances but not others: the goodness of a state of affairs might be a reason to promote it only when that state of affairs is good for no one, and the badness of a state of affairs might be a reason against promoting it only when that state of affairs is bad for no one. That strikes me as an unlikely possibility. But it is a conceptual possibility, and at this point it would be premature to say that it never occurs. As we continue our discussion, we will find no reason to suppose otherwise.

For now, I will be satisfied if I have given some reason to be skeptical about whether things fall into both categories of value or disvalue—being both good and good for someone or both bad and bad for someone. Pain does not, as we can see when we look at the way we think we should reason about it. Nor do we think we should reason about other things in this way. When we reflect in general on the way we think we should reason, we evidently find no need to say of anything either that it is both bad for someone and bad period or good for someone and good period.

Chapter 10

Pleasure Reconsidered

In chapter 3, I offered an argument designed to make it plausible that we should give a positive answer to the initial question of this book: Are there things we should value because they are, quite simply, good? Let us now go back to that argument and ask how convincing it is. Consider such innocent pleasures as the sensations one feels as one sits in a nice, warm bath or the pleasure of eating a delicious peach for which one has developed an appetite. I suggested that we are favorably disposed toward these pleasures, that we have a reason to welcome and pursue them, and that we can justify giving a positive evaluation of them. How should we express that positive evaluation? My answer, on behalf of the friends of goodness, was that they are, quite simply, good.

It should be evident by now what the weakness of this argument is. We can agree with one part of it: such pleasures are apt for evaluation. We can ask whether there is a reason to welcome them, and answer this question by finding something positive to say about them. The problem, however, is that there are other terms we can use to evaluate these pleasures. We can say, not that they are good *simpliciter*, but that they are good *for* the person who experiences them. Of course, we can say that there are two reasons for welcoming these sensations, not just one: they might be *both* good (period) *and* good for us. But as we saw in the last chapter, we do not have this double reason to avoid or alleviate pain, and that should incline us to be suspicious of the hypothesis that we have a double reason to seek these pleasures. After all, the pleasures of a warm bath or a delicious peach are sensations, just as pain is a sensation. They are sensations that have opposite valences. Since, as we have seen, the negative feature of pain is that it is bad *for* the person who feels it, it would be a mystery if the positive feature of pleasurable sensations were anything other than their being good *for* those who experience them.

Let us consider a wider range of pleasures and ask how they figure in our everyday practical reasoning. If the pleasures that we think should be welcomed have a double value, being both good absolutely and good for the one who is pleased, we would expect that feature of these pleasures to be something that we are aware of when we make decisions. Or at any rate, if we are often insensitive to that double value, we should acknowledge that as a failure. So consider how we reason about pleasure when it is not a mere sensation. Suppose I am tempted to go to a museum to see the latest exhibition, and part of my reason for being so inclined is that I would enjoy looking at the pictures. But the price of admission to this special exhibit is unusually high, and because large crowds are expected, my pleasure will be diminished. I have to determine whether the pleasure I would experience is worth the trouble and the expense.

In such situations as these, no one thinks that pleasure should be counted twice, first because it is good and second because it is good for the museumgoer. No one supposes, for example, that when the absolute goodness of pleasure is taken into account, but its goodness for the museumgoer is bracketed, the case against going to the exhibition might be slightly stronger than the case in favor, but that when the fact that the pleasure of viewing the exhibit is good *for* the viewer is acknowledged, the scales tip in favor of attendance. We do not reason in this way, and when we reflect on the fact that we do not, our reaction is not that we have been missing something important all along. We are confident that pleasure should not be doubly counted as a reason, once because it is good for us and a second time because it is good.

So we must choose: either the absolute goodness of these pleasures (if there is such a goodness) is, in these circumstances, not a reason-giving property, or the fact that they are good *for* us is not, in these circumstances, a reason-giving property. Since pain, when it is to be avoided, is to be avoided because it is bad for the person who feels it (that helps explain why smoking cigarettes is bad for people), innocent (that is, permissible) pleasurable sensations are to be counted as good for those who experience them, and that makes it reasonable to assume that the pleasures of looking at paintings are to be sought, when they are to be sought, because they are good for those who view them. Therefore, they are not to be valued because they are good absolutely.

I have been speaking of what is good for someone as a "benefit" or an "advantage," and so it might be asked whether pleasures can be so classified. I believe that we do, in fact, put them into this category. We count them as noninstrumental benefits or advantages.

Suppose, for example, you are looking for a way to do something good for your friends, and you find that you can arrange an extended holiday for them—a long period of time in which they will enjoy doing the things they most like to do. If you make these arrangements and they enjoy their holiday, we would say that they have taken advantage of what you have provided them and that you have benefited them. Of course, the enjoyment they take in playing tennis and hiking need not be a means to further ends— they need not be instrumental advantages. But as we have seen (chapter 7), there is (in fact, there must be) such a thing as a non-instrumental advantage. Various pleasures fit comfortably into this category.

So here is where things stand, thus far: what initially seemed to be a persuasive reason to suppose that certain pleasures should be valued because they are absolutely good should now seem less persuasive. If a thing's absolute goodness is to count as a reason for valuing it, we should be able to find some convincing examples of things that are to be valued for that reason. So far, we have found none. That is also where things will stand when we have more thoroughly examined this subject.

Chapter 11

Scanlon's Buck-Passing Account of Value

For the sake of clarity, I should now say how my views accord with or depart from Scanlon's thesis (mentioned earlier in chapter 5) that when a thing has value, its being valuable does not itself constitute a reason for valuing it. He holds that whenever something is valuable, it has some further feature that makes it so, and *that* further feature is what provides a reason in favor of valuing it, not the mere fact that it is valuable.

Like many authors, he uses "valuable" and "good" almost interchangeably; if there is a difference between what these words designate, it is not clear what it is, and he does not distinguish them. He expresses no doubt about the existence of the property of being good or being valuable. But if he is right, they are far less important than philosophers have sometimes thought, because they are not reason-giving properties. As he says, goodness and value "pass the buck"—the work of specifying a reason in favor of something is done by other features, not by its goodness and value. The buck stops with those further features, whereas value and goodness pass the buck to them. Unlike Geach, Foot, and Thomson, he does not claim that assertions that something is good (period) lack sense. On the contrary, he offers a way to understand them: they are best taken to mean that there is a reason to value something. For a thing to have the property of being good or valuable is simply for there to be some reason or other to value it. Whatever that reason is, it is not goodness or value, but something else.

Here is an example of what Scanlon has in mind: as I pass a shop, I ask myself whether I should indulge in a cup of vanilla ice cream. Yes, I tentatively tell myself—and then (being a philosopher obsessed with justification) I ask whether I can find a reason to support my tentative practical proposal. I will have found a reason, Scanlon supposes, if I foresee that eating the ice cream will be pleasurable. The fact that doing something will be a pleasure is, at least in this situation, by itself a reason for doing it. It is true, Scanlon grants, that eating the ice cream will be valuable or good. But that is not a *further* reason in favor of my tentative decision, in addition to the pleasure it will give me. The work of providing a reason is performed by the pleasure of eating the ice cream, not the goodness of that pleasure.[1]

Scanlon's deflationary stance toward goodness has no doubt encouraged me to have my own doubts about it. In a way, the project I am undertaking here can be seen as a modified version of one of his ideas. After all, I claim that absolute goodness is not a reason-giving property; there is certainly a close kinship between that thesis and Scanlon's claim that something's being good is not a reason to value it. Nonetheless, there are differences and even some disagreements between us, and it will be useful to make these explicit.

The most important difference between us is that he speaks of value and goodness in general as buck passers. That might be taken to mean not only that when something is good (period), that is in no circumstances a reason to value it but also that when something

---

1. W. D. Ross is making a different point about goodness when he says that it is a "consequential attribute." See *The Right and the Good*, pp. 79, 88, 121–122. By this, he means that "anything that is good must be good either by virtue of its whole nature apart from its goodness, or by virtue of something in its nature other than goodness" (p. 79). Ross's idea is simply that whatever is good is such because it has some other feature as well. If a sensation is good, for example, that is because of a certain quality of the sensation—it's pleasantness. This is compatible with a further point that I believe he wishes to affirm: that the goodness of the sensation constitutes a reason to welcome it.

is good of a kind (a good play, for example), that is no reason to value it, and finally that when something is good *for* someone, that, too, is in no circumstances a reason to value it. With the first part of this thesis (absolute goodness passes the buck), I have only a small quarrel, but his second thesis (being good of a kind passes the buck) and third (being good for someone passes the buck), I reject.

The small quarrel is this: Moore would say that the pleasure of eating a cup of ice cream is a factor worthy of our attention because pleasure is good, and the goodness of that pleasure is the reason we should welcome it. Against this, Scanlon holds that the pleasure of eating the cup of ice cream itself constitutes a reason to eat it, whereas the goodness of that pleasure does not. But I think these are not the only two alternatives. A third possibility is that no pleasure provides a reason unless it is a pleasure that is good *for* someone. The idea is that it is not mere pleasure that should attract us, even to the slightest degree, but good pleasure—pleasure that passes some evaluative hurdle. (In the same way, we should not be fans of all films, but of good films; not lovers of all food, but of good food; and so on.) And it is not implausible to suppose that pleasures that are not even slightly good for someone to feel are pleasures that he has no reason to seek or welcome. (Were we to accept that plausible idea, that would not commit us to Moore's thesis that it is the absolute goodness of pleasure that provides a reason to pursue it.) But if pleasures that are not good for the person who feels them are ones that he has no reason to welcome or pursue, then we should reject Scanlon's idea that pleasure itself is a justification-provider—that the justificatory buck can stop with the mere fact that something is a pleasure.

To generalize: if Scanlon is right that value concepts (expressed by "good," "valuable," "good for," and the like) do not contribute to the project of giving reasons, whereas other concepts do, then those other concepts must be capable of bearing that justificatory burden in isolation from those value concepts. It is not clear that pleasure can play this role or that anything else can. What sorts of friendships do we have reason to develop and sustain? What sorts of honors are worth pursuing? What kinds of knowledge are worth acquiring? I reply: the good friendships, the meaningful honors, the valuable forms of knowledge. When we set aside the goodness of a pleasure or a friendship or an honor or a form of knowledge, what remains seems to provide a less weighty reason for valuing that pleasure, friendship, honor, or knowledge—and perhaps no reason at all.

I take Scanlon's general thesis that value and goodness do not themselves constitute reasons, but only reflect the presence of other factors that are reason-giving, to commit him to saying that when something is a good member of a kind, that fact is not a reason for valuing it—it is rather what makes it a good member of that kind that does so. That seems implausible. We recommend a play to a friend because when we saw it, our experience convinced us that it is a good play—although we may be uncertain whether it was the staging or the acting or the writing that made it good, and we may also be unable to say what it was about the staging, the acting, or the writing that was excellent. But we nonetheless are giving to our the-atergoing friend a reason to see the play when we assure him that, whatever it is that grounds our judgment, it is certainly a good play. (We can similarly recommend the soup to our dinner companion by saying that it tastes good. By so evaluating its taste, we give him an excellent reason to try it. The ingredients of the soup, perhaps unknown to us, explain why it tastes good, but their presence con-stitutes no further reason for tasting it.) To say that something is a good play goes far beyond saying merely that there is some reason to see it. After all, one might have a reason to see a play because it was written by one's mother, or because one promised one's wife that one would accompany her. (*Everyone* might have reason to see a certain play, without its being a good play: imagine that an early work of Sophocles is discovered, and although it is dramatically weak in every respect, it nonetheless reveals information about the author that transforms our understanding of his other works.) When we say that a play is good and that our friend should therefore buy a ticket to it, our use of "good" does not "pass the buck."

At this point, I can imagine an important objection to what I have said. (I will return to my discussion of Scanlon in a few paragraphs.) Let's assume, before I state that objection, that what we should look for in a good play is some combination of such specific factors as three-dimensional characters, dramatic interaction, plot development, credible dialogue, wit, and so on. The objection that can now be raised is this: it is precisely *these specific qualities* that are the reasons to read, see, and admire the play. That it is a good play, however, is not yet *one more reason* to do so.

There is something right about that last statement: that it is a good play does not add to the force of the argument that has already been made for seeing the play by citing the specific factors that make it a good play (characterization, plot, and so on). But it does not follow that a play's being a good play is no reason to see it. One kind of reason to see the play is that it is a good play; the specific characteristics just mentioned do not advert to reasons of a different kind, and so citing them does not add to the case in favor of seeing the play that is established by its being a good play. By referring to the rich characters, engaging plot, and well-crafted dialogue, we explain in some detail why someone should see the play. By saying that it is a good play, we also give, at a higher level of generality, a reason to see it. What we implicitly know we should not do is add these two considerations together (its being a good play, the features that make it so) when we decide how strong a case there is for seeing the play.

We might say that the interaction between these two reasons is "nonadditive." That something is a good play is a reason to see it, but it is not an "additive" reason—it does not add to the case for seeing it that is made by citing the features that make it a good play. Now, friends of absolute goodness might grab hold of this and ask, "Well, then, why cannot absolute goodness also be a nonadditive reason?" Their idea would be that there is always one extremely general kind of reason to do anything for which there is a reason—it's being a good thing—but that this highly general reason always leaves unchanged the weightiness of the reasons for action that are given by more concrete considerations.

I accept this much: whenever there is a reason to do something, doing it can be called "a good thing." (At any rate, it is a good thing *to some extent*; after all, by hypothesis there is *some* reason to do it.) But it certainly does not follow, and we must not assume without argument, that whenever there is a reason to do something, one of those reasons consists in the absolute goodness of doing it. In calling it "a good thing," we may merely mean to convey the thought that there is something to be said in its favor. For that point, I am indebted to Scanlon.

Furthermore, if friends of absolute goodness wish to defend themselves by saying that although it is a reason-giving property, it (like being a good play) never adds to the weightiness of more specific reasons, then they are admitting that for practical purposes we can ignore it, because we will never go astray if we direct our attention to those more concrete reasons. So I would not expect a true friend of absolute goodness to warm to the idea that it is related to all other reasons as "that is a good play" is related to the more concrete properties that make something a good play.

In fact, there is something silly in the suggestion that whenever there is at least some reason to do something, one reason for doing it—even though it is not a reason that can increase the force of any other reasons—is that it possesses the property of being good. Suppose you take a holiday, and your reason is that it will be good *for* you. Are we now to suppose that there must also be a second reason for you to take a holiday, namely, that it will be absolutely good, but that you can ignore the existence of this second reason because it does not add anything to the case that has already been made in favor of your holiday by its being beneficial? What is the point of positing the existence of this rather ghostly factor—a practical reason (a reason to do something) that can always be ignored by practical reasoning? By contrast, the idea that some plays are good plays and that their being such is a reason to see them is extremely useful, even though, after we have listed all the specific features of a play that make it good and have recognized them as reasons to see it, we do not become aware of an even stronger case to see it when we take note of the fact that it is a good play.

I return now to my discussion of Scanlon's buck-passing approach to goodness and value in general. Against him, I have just argued, using the goodness of a play as my example, that something's being good of a kind can provide a reason. Now I turn to a further difference between us. I take him to be committed to the thesis that adverting to what is good *for* someone does not, in any circumstances, give a reason for valuing it, but only points to the presence of a reason. I demur, and that is my most important disagreement with him. But to begin with, it should be granted that being good for someone is a supervenient or consequential property, and that when it is instantiated, that is because a further underlying property is also instantiated. (This is a point Ross made about absolute goodness.)[2] Accordingly, when someone proposes to justify what he is doing by saying that it will be good for someone, we can ask him not only whom it benefits but also to spell out more concretely what kind of benefit will be achieved.

To illustrate (and here I switch from "good for" to "bad for"): suppose I am trying to persuade a friend not to seek a divorce from his wife, and I claim that he should not do so because it will be bad for his children. It is reasonable for him to ask me to be more specific. If there is no kind of harm that his children will incur, then his divorce cannot be said to be bad for them. I might support my assertion that his children will be harmed by saying that his divorce will fill them with anxiety and diminish their self-confidence. If I am right that it would have these effects and that these psychological states are bad for his children, then I have stated a reason why he should not seek a divorce. It is implausible to suppose that when I claim that his divorce would be bad for them, I have merely said that there is a reason for him not to seek a divorce but have said nothing about what that reason is.

I suggest, further, that the claim "his divorce will harm his children" (here "harm" is equivalent to "be bad for") already *fully* states a reason against what he proposes to do. When he asks me, "What harm will it do them?" he is asking me to defend my claim. But it would be a mistake for him to say that even if it is true that his action harms them, that is, by itself, no objection to his divorce—that an objection has been made only when I spell out what kind of harm it will do. It does not take two sentences, working together as a unit, to give a reason: first, "it will be bad for them" and, second, "here is the harm it will do them." Rather, the first of these sentences fully states the reason, and the second gives a reason for accepting the first

2. See note 1, page 55.

sentence. If he asks me, "Why should I not make my children more anxious?" I can tell him why simply by saying that anxiety is bad for them. (Compare saying that the soup tastes good: in the right circumstances, that feature of it can be, by itself, a reason for trying it. Of course, there must be something in it that makes it taste good. But one does not need to advert to those ingredients to have given a sufficient reason to try it.)

Even though Scanlon says, indiscriminately, that value and goodness are buck-passing properties, what I take to be most important in his treatment of value is the idea that *absolute* goodness is not a reason-giving property. That thesis is twofold: first, when we say of something that it is good (period), that statement does not give a reason to value it. I agree. Second, that statement is not mere nonsense, because what it can be taken to mean is that there is a reason to value it, even though the reason has not been specified. I agree (for reasons I will give later) that such statements as "Pleasure is good (period)" are meaningful. And I also agree that sometimes when people say, "That is good," they simply mean that there is a reason to favor or value that which they call good. That is one common use of such words—although it is certainly not the way Moore intends to use them, when he says that "the only possible reason that can justify any action is that by it the greatest possible amount of what is good absolutely should be realised." Some people intend to pass the buck when they speak of things as good (period). Moore does not, and I believe that his thesis that goodness is a reason-giving property should not be rejected on the grounds that it involves a misuse of the word "good."

Scanlon might mean that the buck-passing nature of goodness in general and absolute goodness in particular is guaranteed by the very meaning of the word "good." Note how different that analysis is from the one proposed by Geach and Thomson. They hold that it is *unintelligible* to say that pleasure, for example, is just plain good. Scanlon, by contrast, would hold—according to the reading of him now under consideration—that it is *true* to say that pleasure is just plain good. Or perhaps, more cautiously put, his thesis would be that *if* the pleasure of eating ice cream is a reason in its favor, then it is true that eating ice cream is good (period).

There may nonetheless be less distance than that between Geach and Thomson on the one hand and Scanlon on the other. Geach and Thomson can be taken to mean that if we look at the way Moore, Ross, and others use "good," their statements are unintelligible: those statements presuppose that "good" names a reason-giving property, and that is a mistake. Scanlon, by contrast, reflecting on the way "good" and "valuable" are often used in ordinary discourse, observes that speakers do not take these words to name reason-giving properties but use them merely to advert to the existence of reasons. So read, he is free to agree with Geach and his followers that Moore and Ross are using "good" unintelligibly.

Geach, Foot, Thomson, and Scanlon have this much in common: some traditional moral theories, they claim, have assigned too large a role to absolute goodness. I think they are right about that. But we need to look at many more considerations before we can reach that skeptical conclusion.[3]

3. For further discussion of buck-passing accounts of value, see Roger Crisp, "Value, Reasons, and the Structure of Justification: How to Avoid Passing the Buck," *Analysis* 65 (2005), pp. 80–85; Roger Crisp, "Goodness and Reasons: Accentuating the Negative," *Mind* 117 (2008), pp. 257–265; Jonathan Dancy, "Should We Pass the Buck?" in Toni Ronnow-Rasmussen and Michael J. Zimmerman, eds., *Recent Work on Intrinsic Value* (Dordrecht, Netherlands: Springer Verlag, 2005), pp. 33–44; Sven Danielsson and Jonas Olson, "Brentano and the Buck Passers," *Mind* 116 (2007), pp. 511–522; Pamela Hieronymi, "The Wrong Kind of Reason," *Journal of Philosophy* 102 (2005), pp. 437–457; Philip Stratton-Lake and Brad Hooker, "Scanlon versus Moore on Goodness," in Terry Horgan and Mark Timmons, eds., *Metaethics after Moore* (Oxford: Clarendon, 2006), pp. 149–168; Pekka Väyrynen, "Resisting the Buck-Passing Account," in Russ Shafer-Landau, ed., *Oxford Studies in Metaethics*, Vol. 1 (New York: Oxford University Press, 2006), pp. 295–324.

Chapter 12

Moore's Argument against Relative Goodness

I have been assuming for some time now that speaking of what is good for someone is intelligible and that the relationship of being good for someone deserves to play an important role in our practical reasoning. Now let us pause and look more carefully at these assumptions.

Moore argues, in *Principia Ethica*, that to speak of something as being "my good" is at best misleading. We can make sense of it, he thinks, but only if we read it to mean "that is absolutely good, and it is mine." Its goodness is not a for-me sort of goodness, because there is no such thing as a for-me sort of goodness, or a for-someone sort of goodness. Rather, there are things that are good (period), and various individuals have some of those things. When, for example, I experience pleasure, that feeling is absolutely good. That particular pleasure is good, and it is my pleasure. No other sense can be made of the idea that when I am pleased, that is my good.[1]

One of the goals of *Principia Ethica* is to prove, against Henry Sidgwick, that egoism—the thesis that the proper ultimate goal of

---

1. See *Principia Ethica*, sections 59 and 60, and especially p. 150. He tries to show on that page that "my good" is a confused expression, but his target is also the egoist's use of "good for…" and kindred phrases. He says that "the addition of 'for him,' 'for me,' to such words as 'ultimate rational end,' 'good,' 'important' can produce nothing but confusion" (p. 153). For a defense of Moore's position, see Talbot Brewer, *The Retrieval of Ethics*, pp. 210–214; and Donald H. Regan, "Why Am I My Brother's Keeper?" in R. Jay Wallace, Philip Pettit, Samuel Scheffler, and Michael Smith, eds., *Reason and Value: Themes from the Moral Philosophy of Joseph Raz* (Oxford: Clarendon, 2004), pp. 202–230. For discussion of Regan's arguments, see Connie S. Rosati, "Objectivism and Relational Good," *Social Philosophy and Policy* 25 (2008), pp. 314–349.

each human being is to maximize his or her own good—is untenable and that our constant goal ought instead to be to promote the greatest amount of good (period).[2] That is one reason why Moore seeks a proof that absolute goodness is the fundamental concept of ethics and that such expressions as "my good" and "good for me" must either be translatable into a nonrelativized form or rest on a confusion. If he were right about that, egoism would not even be an intelligible doctrine. But we need not go to that extreme merely in order to reject egoism. Suppose we admitted not only that speaking of what is good for someone is intelligible but also that in certain circumstances the fact that an action will benefit someone (oneself or another) is a good reason to undertake it. Those admissions would not commit us to the egoist's thesis that we should exclude the good of others from our ultimate goals. We can agree with this small portion of egoism: there are times when I ought to aim at what is good for me, precisely and only because it is good for me. Sometimes, however, circumstances are such that I ought to aim at what is good for someone else, precisely and only because it is good for him or her. That is what egoists implausibly deny. We need not fear that if talk about what is good for someone is coherent and betokens no confusion, there will be no rational basis for rejecting egoism. (Is this what Moore fears? I am uncertain. Perhaps he thinks that other arguments against egoism succeed even were his to fail. But in *Principia Ethica*, he offers none.)

Moore holds, as we have seen, that the good-for relation is reducible to something else and that facts about what is good for someone therefore have no reason-giving force of their own. If he

---

2. Sidgwick discusses egoism in *The Methods of Ethics*, 7th ed., 1907, in book I, ch. 7; book II; and book IV, concluding chapter. His final chapter argues that reason is unable to choose between egoism and utilitarianism.

is right, philosophical clarity is not served by saying that smoking is bad for someone, because speaking in that way implies that there is such a thing as a for-someone sort of badness. He would say that the objection to smoking, properly expressed, is that what it leads to (pain and so on) is absolutely bad—not bad *for* someone. To explain why we should keep cigarettes away from children, using Moore's terms, we should say that if we fail to do so, there is a significant risk that certain absolutely bad things will arise. In whom will they arise? Only in those who are exposed to or inhale smoke for many years. For Moore, "smoking is bad for smokers" is false, if it is used to assert that what smoking leads to is not absolutely bad, but bad only in relation to certain individuals, or it is a misleading way to express the truth that the absolute badness of the pain created by smoking is present in some people and not others.

But testing Moore's views about absolute and relative goodness by applying them to smoking suggests that he has things the wrong way round. "Smoking is bad for smokers and people exposed to their smoke" does not seem false or misleading. Rather, it is "smoking is bad—period" that strikes us as a problematic assertion. At any rate, in our ordinary discourse, we have no trouble understanding each other when we use such interchangeable expressions as "that is good for you," "that benefits you," "that is advantageous for you," "that makes you better off," "that is in your interest," and their opposites. We do not think that to understand what we mean by such expressions, we need to translate them into a vocabulary that eliminates their relational nature. Of course, we sometimes argue about how to apply them. One parent thinks it does no harm for his child to play video games, but the other disagrees. Even so, we do not take such disagreements to be evidence that such terms as "good for" and "bad for" must be eliminated from our discourse. Still less do we suppose that our understanding of these disagreements would be enhanced by translating them into debates about whether watching video games is absolutely good or absolutely bad.

Can we find any argument on Moore's behalf for the thesis that "good for me" and kindred expressions rest on a confusion? Here is one possible route to his conclusion; it is the best argument I can construct for him: "Pain is bad (period). Therefore, pain ought not to be. So, we all have a reason to prevent or alleviate pain—anyone's pain. That is the right way to think about pain. But suppose we mistakenly conceived of pain as something that is relatively rather than absolutely bad—bad-for-someone, not bad (period). We could not in that case say that pain ought not to be, but only that pain ought-for-that-person not to be. That person in pain and that person alone would have a reason to prevent or alleviate his pain. That is an implausible conclusion, acceptable only to an egoist. Furthermore, it is nonsense to say that pain ought-for-someone not to be. The word 'ought' does not make sense if it is relativized in that way. It follows that 'good' and 'bad' should not be relativized either: there is no such thing as good-for-someone or bad-for-someone. There is such a thing as someone's pleasure, but no such thing as pleasure being someone's good."

Should we accept this argument? We might question whether it makes sense to speak of what ought to be or of what ought not to be, for it might be thought that "ought" cannot be attached to states of affairs but only to moral agents. According to this line of thought, it is meaningful to say that someone ought to call a meeting but not that a meeting ought to be called. But it seems to me that "a meeting ought to be called" makes good sense and can be true even if there is no one who ought to call that meeting. (There are many such sentences. Another example: "Weather like this should last forever.")[3] So I will not challenge the assumption made in the preceding paragraph that pain ought not to be.

The weakest components in the argument just rehearsed on Moore's behalf are the assertions that if pain were bad for someone, but not bad period, we could make no inference about what anyone ought (absolutely) to do about it, only about what someone ought-for-that-person to do and that we would have to say that only one individual (the person suffering the pain) has a reason to take action. To see how implausible those claims are, return to the example we have been using: when we say that smoking is bad for certain people, because the pain it will lead to is bad for them, we *can* infer that they ought (ought period: not ought-for-them) to stop smoking. And the claim that the pain they will endure is bad for them can be used as a premise that supports the conclusion that others—not merely those who will suffer—have reason to help them stop smoking. If smoking is bad for someone, that gives not only that person but also his friends, parents, children, doctors, and perhaps many others reason to help him stop.

I conclude that nothing can be found in Moore's writings or offered on his behalf to cast doubt on our commonsense assumption that it is intelligible to speak of what is good for someone.

3. Adam Ross, *Mr. Peanut* (New York: Alfred A. Knopf, 2010), p. 234.

Chapter 13

Goodness and Variability

Our examination of being good for someone and being absolutely good would be far simpler if we could give explanatory definitions of these two notions. We could then see more clearly what their differences are; we could more easily determine which things fall into these categories and the degree to which they overlap; we might be able to arrive at a more confident judgment about what importance they have for practical reasoning and whether one plays a more significant role than the other. Moore, however, thinks that absolute goodness is a primitive notion—a concept that cannot be decomposed into ingredients that are conceptually prior to and explanatory of it. Perhaps he is wrong about that, but he is not *obviously* wrong. It is not evident how the goodness he posited—goodness that serves as a ground for valuing things—should be defined. Plato agrees that the definition of goodness is far from obvious (*Republic* 505), although he does not assert, as Moore does, that it is indefinable.

The same definitional problem can be raised about the concept of being good for someone. It consists in being beneficial, advantageous, and so on—but these are just different words for the same thing, and they are not conceptually prior to and explanatory of the relation of being good for someone. Now, I believe that light can be shed on this relation if we think of it in terms of flourishing.[1] For G

---

1. See *What Is Good and Why: The Ethics of Well-Being* (Cambridge, MA: Harvard University Press, 2007), esp. chapters 1 and 3.

to be good for any living thing S, I hold, is for G to be a component of, or means to, that creature's development and the use of some of its natural powers. I find that looking at our lives from this broader biological perspective helps us see more clearly which things are good for us and what makes them so. My idea is not that the words "good for" mean the same as "flourishing," nor is it that the concept of being good for someone is the same concept as that of flourishing. Rather, I hold that a thing's making a contribution to someone's flourishing and its being good for someone are one and the same relationship. We can look at that single relationship in two different ways, just as the morning star and the evening star are conceptualized in different ways. Just as these are one physical object, so being good for someone and promoting someone's flourishing are the same relation.

But suppose we set that thesis aside. Suppose we treat both what is good absolutely and what is good for someone as primitive, undefined notions. I propose that we can learn something about how these concepts differ by reflecting more fully than we have so far on the fact that "G is good" is a one-place predicate, whereas "G is good for S" is a two-place predicate. Because of that difference, there is a conceptual truth about what is good for someone to which there is no corresponding conceptual truth about what is good absolutely. It is a conceptual truth about a type of thing that is good for someone that possibly that same type of thing is not good for someone else. To illustrate what I have in mind: possibly oats are good for a horse but not for a human being; possibly oats are good for this horse, but not good for that horse; and so on. Of course, when we empirically examine the actual properties of oats, human beings, and horses, we might discover that oats are good for all horses and all human beings. If oats were good for all living creatures whatsoever, and this were widely recognized, we could save some breath by saying quite simply and elliptically: "Oats are good." We would still be talking about a relationship and using a two-place predicate, but we would not need to specify for which creatures oats are good, and so we could leave one of the places blank.

The concept of what is good (period), however, does not leave space for this kind of variability. Friends of absolute goodness would be doing no violence to that concept were they to say that several (or many) different sorts of things are good, and some of them do take this position. Moore is one example: he holds that pleasure, friendly relations, beauty, and many other sorts of things are absolutely good. But he cannot say, and he has no wish to say, that there is another kind of a variability among goods, some of them being good *for* certain people, others being good *for* others. That is precisely what he rejects, because that is the kind of variability that is permitted only by the concept of being good for and not by the concept of being good absolutely. For the friends of absolute goodness, there is a single list of good things that everyone ought to have. They might put that point as follows: *these* things (here they name the things that are good: for example, pleasure, knowledge, friendship) ought to exist and ought to be valued, and whoever can lend a hand in bringing them about and valuing them should do so. We all have the same reasons to act; we all have the same goals and duties— namely, to value these good things as they deserve to be valued, to preserve them, and to do what we can to bring them into existence. (Friends of absolute goodness are, of course, entitled to point out that differently situated people must use different *means* of producing something from the list of good things.)

It might be thought that my identification of what is good for creatures with what promotes their flourishing forces me to deny that there is any diversity among what is good for individuals. It is true that, according to my thesis, all things that are good for some creature (whether human or nonhuman) belong to a single kind. They have more than a word in common, and they are more closely unified than are things that merely have what Wittgenstein calls a "family resemblance." In a sense, I agree that there is just one kind of thing that is good for someone: flourishing. But within that kind, there are many different species. What constitutes the good of the individuals who belong to one species of living things only partly coincides, or perhaps does not coincide at all, with what constitutes the good of individuals who belong to other species.

One of the accusations that can be made against hedonism is that it reduces all value to just one type of good, pleasure, and certainly some forms of hedonism deny that the classification of pleasures into different varieties has any bearing on the degree of goodness of those pleasures. That is not the sort of monism I embrace. I hold that there is a great variety within the category of things that are good for living things. And that variety is of great practical importance. To be properly attentive to the good of a human being requires attending to different sorts of things from those that we attend to when we consider the good of a horse or a bird.

But the point I wish to make about the concept of being good for someone (and the way it differs from absolute goodness) goes beyond that. The concept of being good for someone leaves room for the possibility that even within a single species what is good for some members will be constituted differently from the way what is good for other members is constituted. The emotional health of one person, for example, might be a different mix of psychological elements from the emotional health of another, presumably because of differences in their physiology. Not only *might be*, but probably *is*. It is, in other words, plausible that, in a way that matters to our personal relationships, no two human beings are precisely alike in their mental composition.[2] To understand how a child, for example, should be treated for his good, one should not follow a formula derived entirely from one's experience of another child. It is not simply that the means used to promote the good of each will vary; in addition, there are differences in what the good of each is. A literary education will be best for this child because of the kind of person he is, but for that other child, with different skills and proclivities, a musical education will be best.

The question whether there is at least some degree of heterogeneity in human well-being, from one individual to another, is partly an empirical matter. I find it plausible, as do many others. But for now, what is more important is that even if that empirical hypothesis is rejected, the concept of what is good for someone still leaves room for the possibility that the thesis is correct. In fact, the concept of being good for someone allows for the possibility that the types of things that are good for one individual do not overlap *at all* with the types of things that are good for another. It is possible that for George, the good things are just A, B, and C; for Harry, just D, E, and F; and so on. If my identification of being good for someone and flourishing is correct, that would mean that for George flourishing consists in one kind of life, for Harry a completely different kind of life, and so on. We know that this conceptual possibility is not realized. Human beings are not so entirely unlike each other that the sorts of things that are noninstrumentally good for George are *all of them* different from the sorts of things that are noninstrumentally good for Harry— and so on, for each human being. There is at least some overlap.

Here, then, is one important difference between being absolutely good and being good for someone—a difference that exists however

---

2. The causes of human individuality are the subject of debate among psychologists. See Judith Rich Harris, *No Two Alike: Human Nature and Human Individuality* (New York: W. W. Norton, 2006).

these concepts are defined and whatever is placed in these two categories: a certain kind of individual-by-individual variability is allowed by the concept expressed by the two-place predicate that is not allowed by the concept expressed by its one-place counterpart. Although friends of absolute goodness are free to hold that several or many different types of things are good and are free to hold that these things are not all equally good, they cannot propose, as one component of their theory of absolute goodness, that because you and I differ in some way, it might be the case that one mix of goods is good *for* you and a different mix good *for* me. Their theory has absolute goodness as its subject, not advantageousness. Insofar as they are theorizing about absolute goodness and proposing that the mere goodness of certain things (not their being good *for* someone) constitutes a reason for valuing them, they must give the same counsel to everyone: we are all to value these goods because they are good.

But suppose that there are so many types of absolutely good things that no individual can give to each of them the attention it deserves. The friends of absolute goodness will, of course, regret this limitation in our nature. "What a shame," they may say, "that we cannot fully devote ourselves to all that ought to be valued." And they are free to recommend that we pay attention to our individual circumstances and value only those among the good things that we can properly value, leaving aside the ones to which we cannot give the attention they deserve. What they cannot do, however, is to say of something that they take to be absolutely good: you have no reason to value it (that is, no *pro tanto* reason)[3] precisely because your psychological constitution is such that it is not good *for* you to

---

3. For those not familiar with this term, a *pro tanto* reason for valuing something is one that counts to some degree in favor of valuing it, regardless of whether that reason is a sufficient reason for doing so or a decisive reason for doing so, and regardless of whether, all things considered, the balance of reasons favors valuing it.

do so. Being friends of absolute goodness, they think that the absolute value of anything that has such value gives everyone a reason to value it. They cannot agree that one lacks a reason to value such a thing simply because it would not be good for one to value it. As they see it, the absolutely valuable things call on us to be as responsive to their value as we can be; they do not call on us to be responsive to them only if it would be good for us to do so. The appeal of what is good (period) cannot consist in its being beneficial for us valuers to value them. And all absolutely good things have this appeal; all of them call on all of us to intellectually acknowledge and emotionally respond to their value, insofar as we can.

By contrast, if we hold (as seems plausible) that what is good for one human being does not exactly coincide with what is good for another, that is no reason to think of this as a limitation in our nature or a cause for regret. The peculiar mix of emotions that is best for you to achieve is, let us suppose, different from the one that best suits my psychological profile, and as a result, what constitutes your good is not quite the same condition as what constitutes mine. I have no reason to regret that I cannot be in precisely the same kind of state that is good for you to be in. That is because I am not thinking of your kind of psychological condition as something that is good (period). It is good for you, and I may, in certain circumstances, have reason to help you achieve it. But I have no reason to want to be in the same kind of state of mind that you are in, if being in that condition would not be good for me.

These reflections about the differences between the concepts of absolute and relative goodness give us reason to affirm a point that was made earlier (chapter 6): it would be misguided to define the relation of being good for someone by analyzing it into two components: being good absolutely and something else. For example, it might be said that what it is for someone's experience of a type of pleasure to be good for him consists in the facts that, first, that kind of pleasure is absolutely good, and, second, he feels it. His feeling it—so this line of thought goes—is what makes it good *for* him; were he not to experience it, that type of pleasure would still be good, but it would not be a kind of pleasure that was good for him. The reason why he should experience it is that it is good (period)— not that it is good for him. He achieves what is good for him by doing what brings to himself something that is absolutely good.

That definition of what is good for someone in terms of absolute goodness would in effect eliminate a resource that is made available to us by our having the concept of relative goodness. When we think in terms of what is good for someone, we leave room for a kind of variability in value that would be closed off by this proposed reduction. Now, suppose we thought that the differences among us human beings have *no* bearing on the way we should interact with each other, because the similarities in our psychological and physical constitutions are such that invariably what we should do to promote what is good for any human being is precisely what we should do to promote what is good for any other human being. It would still be the case that being good for a human being does not consist in being good (period) plus something else. Recall my earlier remark that if it were well known that oats are good for every member of every species, we could speak elliptically and say quite simply that oats are good, but that would simply be an abbreviated way of saying that oats are good *for* all. Oats are not just plain good; they are good for this or that creature, and their being good for someone does not consist in their being good plus something else. So, too, for the things that are noninstrumentally good or bad for us—such things as pleasure and pain. Pain's being bad for all is not to be understood as a fact that can be derived from pain's being absolutely bad (plus some other premise). If it is bad for all who feel it, that is because of a similarity among all creatures.

⌈One further observation leads to the same conclusion: When a fungus invades a tree and interferes with its ability to draw nutrients from the soil and produce blossoms, we are not tempted to ask whether this is absolutely good. We say instead that what has happened is bad for the tree but good for the fungus—and in saying that, we do not suppose that we have evaded a more important question, the question whether this event is good (period). When we judge that what the fungus does to the tree is bad for it, we do not draw from a list of bad things and infer that since the tree has one of those bad things, what has happened to it is bad for it. Now, since human beings are like other parts of nature, in that we, too, are creatures for whom some things are good and others bad—although there is only a partial overlap between the sorts of things that are good for us and that are good for other living things—we should expect the point just made about trees and fungi to apply to our situation as well. It is not necessary, to draw conclusions about what is good for us, to begin with premises about what is good absolutely. That does not by itself show that there is no such property as what is good absolutely. But at any rate, the concept of absolute goodness is not presupposed by the concept of being good for someone. Pain can be bad for someone without being bad.⌋

In fact, there is some empirical basis for thinking that pain is not experienced in the same way by every human being and that lends support to the hypothesis that not only is it conceivable that pain is bad for some individuals but not for others but also that this conceptual possibility is realized. Some people characterize what they are feeling as pain, but they report that they are not averse to it, and they give no sign of minding what they are feeling. It seems that pain has a phenomenological component that allows it to be identified as pain and that this mark of pain is different from the one that causes so many people (but not all) to have an immediate antipathetic reaction to it.[4] It would be disadvantageous, on balance, for someone to have to do without the instrumental benefits that derive from a human being's normal aversion to pain. But it is plausible to say that in these unusual people, who do not mind the pain they feel, the experience of pain is in itself not bad for them. That is, unlike the pain most of us feel, it is not the case that the pain they feel is noninstrumentally bad for them.

That is another reason to deny that we should put pain into the category of things that are absolutely bad. If pain is absolutely bad, and the badness of something is a reason why it should be disvalued by anyone who is in a position to do so, then these unusual people, who do not mind pain, ought nonetheless to fight against their pain. If we think they have no reason to do so, we can explain why: the question to be asked about pain is whether it is bad for the person who feels it, not whether it is bad absolutely.

---

4. See Nikola Grahek, *Feeling Pain and Being in Pain*, 2nd ed. (Cambridge, MA: MIT Press, 2001). He discusses a syndrome in which pain occurs without painfulness, as well as one in which there is painfulness but no pain. L. W. Sumner also discusses such phenomena in *Welfare, Happiness, and Ethics* (New York: Oxford University Press, 1996, pp. 100–101). See, too, Valerie Gray Hardcastle, *The Myth of Pain* (Cambridge, MA: MIT Press, 1999), for a critique of common philosophical assumptions about pain. "What counts as pain processing as opposed to an emotional reaction to pain or a belief that one is in pain ... is difficult to determine, for they all shade into one another" (p. 108).

Chapter 14

Impersonality: An Ethical Objection to Absolute Goodness

I turn now to a further reason for doubting that absolute goodness is a reason-giving property (which should in turn induce skepticism about whether it is any property at all—whether there is such a thing as absolute goodness). The issue I consider in this chapter is, in a way, the converse of the problem of double value that I raised in chapter 9. There my idea was that in our ordinary reasoning about what to do, when we count it in favor of some option we have that it would be good *for* us because we would enjoy it, we do not think that furthermore pleasure is *absolutely* good and that therefore we have even more reason to choose that option. If something is both good for us and good, there should be more in its favor than there would be were it merely good for us but not good. That intensification of reasons is what normally happens when two reason-giving properties are present in the same situation. When no such intensification occurs, we must wonder why. The explanation, I suggested, is that absolute goodness is not a genuine reason.

In this chapter, I want to consider what happens when absolute value points us in one direction but relative value pulls us in the opposite direction—when, for example, there is a conflict between doing what is bad for someone and doing what is assumed to be absolutely good.[1] If absolute goodness is an important reason-giving property, we would expect that sometimes we should do something because it is absolutely good, even though we thereby bring about what is bad for someone. If the goodness (period) of an option we are considering is large enough, it should provide a reason that is sufficiently strong to justify undertaking actions that we recognize to be harmful. But, I will argue, it is doubtful that doing what is bad for someone can be justified in this way—and the explanation, I suggest, is that absolute goodness (and badness) are not genuine reasons.

If a friend of absolute goodness concedes that such goodness always provides a weak reason—so weak, in fact, that it always yields to reasons that advert to advantages and disadvantages (even small ones)—then in effect it can be either entirely or largely ignored in our practical reasoning. I suspect that no matter what our situation is, we can always find some option that might benefit someone or other or that might alleviate some condition that is disadvantageous to someone. At any rate, situations in which we cannot do so must be very rare. Accordingly, if absolute goodness need enter our deliberations only in such circumstances, it is not an important

---

1. An example that many people might find persuasive is the lawful punishment of a criminal act. A simple form of retributivism holds that punishment ought to impose on a guilty individual something that is bad for him and that the justification of such punishment need not advert to any result that is good for anyone; rather, it is a sufficient justification for punishment that it is a good thing (period). Against this, I believe that the most appealing theories of punishment are the ones that not only use the notion of desert (which I think is indispensable to ethical thought) but also point to the benefits of having a just system of law backed by the threat of punishment. But even if my doubts about simple retributivism are ill founded, that approach to punishment has no need of the notion of absolute goodness. What it needs instead is the thesis that the criminal should suffer some disadvantage because he *deserves* it. All the work of the theory is done by the concept of desert; it has no need of the further assumption that giving someone what he deserves is *good* (period). I will make a related point when I discuss whether equality is absolutely good (chapter 24). See, too, my discussion of the idea, closely related to simple retributivism, that when bad people get away with their crimes and live a life of ease, that is, quite simply, a bad thing (chapter 20).

reason-giving consideration, and someone who entirely neglected it would not be going seriously astray. An important kind of reason is one that sometimes can outweigh other types of reasons or justify setting other kinds of reasons aside. So if absolute goodness is in certain circumstances an important reason, then the opportunity to do what is absolutely good should at least occasionally justify doing less of what is good or more of what is bad for someone.

Let us imagine a situation in which benefiting someone conflicts with doing what is not good for anyone but is nonetheless allegedly of absolute value. Consider a mathematician employed by a university who devotes herself to proving theorems in a branch of nonapplied mathematics. We ask her why she is dedicating so much of her life to a matter that has no likely useful applications. She replies that mathematical knowledge is a worthwhile and excellent thing, even if it benefits no one. If she can find the proofs she is looking for, that will be good—period. It will make the world a better place. Her work, she believes, need not be good for her either instrumentally *or noninstrumentally*. Nor need her mathematical discoveries be good (instrumentally or noninstrumentally) for anyone else—members of the mathematical community, scientists, ordinary citizens, other living creatures, and so on. She thinks of her work as important. Her reason for pursuing it is not that it helps pass the time, that she likes it, or that it gives her pleasure—in fact, she may not enjoy it at all. Friends of absolute goodness would approve of her way of justifying her activities. By proving theorems, she is, as Ross puts it, making an "addition to the sum of values in the universe."[2]

To emphasize the point that she is not trying to do what is good for anyone—herself included—we might say that the good or value

2. *The Right and the Good*, p. 132. Cf. Moore, *Principia Ethica*, p. 77.

to which she devotes herself is impersonal. It is not the love of a human being or a person that drives her, but her dedication to a very different sort of object. As she sees it, mathematics and the knowledge of it deserve her *devotion*, just as some religious people think of God as an object that deserves their devotion and worship. But these religious people see themselves as expressing their love for a divine person, whereas she, in her dedication to mathematics, is not attached to a person of any kind, human or divine. Persons, she thinks, are not the only suitable objects of love. We should also love what is good, for no reason other than its being good.

She might have arrived at her conception of mathematical research as good (period) by making one or another of two questionable philosophical assumptions. I mention them only in order to set them aside. My complaint about her is of a different sort. First, she might have mistakenly assumed that to be good for someone is to be valuable merely as a means and decided that therefore certain kinds of mathematical knowledge, lacking instrumental value, are not good for anyone. Yet she is sure that such knowledge has noninstrumental value of some sort, so she says of it, not that it is good for someone, but good (period). That she would be making a mistake follows from the arguments I presented in chapter 7: as we saw, there is such a thing as being noninstrumentally good for someone. Mathematical knowledge might fall into that category, and our mathematician would be in error were she to overlook that possibility.

She might also have arrived at her conception of mathematical knowledge as absolutely good by making the assumption that to call anything good *for* someone is merely to make a statement about that person's psychological orientation toward it. More precisely, her idea might be that what makes something good for someone is the fact that she has a favorable attitude of a certain sort toward it:

she desires it and pursues it, or would pursue it were she able to do so. But she thinks that the value of mathematics is not the result of her attitude toward it. On the contrary, her love of mathematics arises from her belief that it deserves such devotion. On that basis, she might have inferred that mathematics is not good for her, but just plain good. Had she reasoned in this way, she would have relied on the questionable assumption that whatever is good for someone must be made so by that person's psychological attitudes. That assumption overlooks the possibility that we can develop a desire to engage in an activity by being brought to see that, because it would be good for us, we ought to want to undertake it.

So the mathematician I am describing has not come to the conclusion that mathematics is absolutely good by making doubtful assumptions about what is involved in being good for someone. I want to characterize her in that way because I do not want to assert or imply that no one could possibly arrive at the idea that some things are absolutely good except by making some error about the concept of something's being good for someone. I want to show that there is something *morally* problematic about the category with which she is thinking—absolute goodness.

Let us now characterize our mathematician more fully. To begin with, she must be pleased by and grateful to funding institutions that foster pure mathematical research and the teaching of pure mathematics. After all, she wants these disciplines to flourish, and they flourish when important discoveries continue to be made and new generations of students devote themselves to these areas of research. If mathematics enters a period in which no important discoveries are made, it languishes as a discipline; if too few young people learn pure mathematics, its ongoing success, even its existence, is threatened. But, to repeat, she is not grateful to institutions that support mathematical research because she believes anyone *benefits* from it. Her reason is that mathematical knowledge and instruction is an excellent thing.

She need not believe that mathematical knowledge has greater importance than every other branch of knowledge or that knowledge is the only absolutely good thing or the best among the things that are absolutely good. She does not want large numbers to study this subject even if they have no real insight into it. It is real mathematical understanding and skill that she believes should be fostered. She realizes that not everyone should study this subject, but she is eager to see that the mathematical talent of everyone who has it should be nurtured.

That will be the reason she devotes herself to teaching her subject: that, too, contributes to the flourishing of her discipline.[3] Some of her students may eventually do important new work in pure mathematics. But it is important to her that her students learn the subject properly even if they do not themselves make new contributions to it, because mathematics languishes or is endangered as a field when too few people understand it (just as a language is threatened when too few people speak it). Of course, she might have to decide, in certain circumstances, whether to spend her time increasing the mathematical knowledge of her students or instead to occupy herself with her own mathematical research. But in any case, it is not *her* acquisition of such knowledge that she values; it is mathematical knowledge as such. Note, then, that her devotion to

---

3. She would receive the applause of Roger Scruton, who writes: "True teachers do not provide knowledge as a benefit to their pupils; they treat their pupils as a benefit to knowledge. Of course they love their pupils; but they love knowledge more. And their over-riding concern is to pass on that knowledge by lodging it in the brains that will last longer than their own. Their methods are not 'child-centered' but 'knowledge-centered....'" See *The Roger Scruton Reader*, compiled, edited, and with an introduction by Mark Dooley (London: Continuum, 2009), p. 153. The passage is taken from Roger Scruton, *Culture Counts: Faith and Feeling in a World Besieged* (New York: Encounter, 2007). He does not speak of "absolute goodness," but his statement suggests that he is among its friends.

mathematics is impersonal in two ways: First, as I have been emphasizing, she does not think of it as good for anyone. Second, she does not favor her acquisition of mathematical knowledge over that of others, but treats any person's mastery of this discipline as something that she and everyone else has a reason to endorse and support. It is *anyone's* acquisition of mathematical knowledge that is good, not just hers; anyone's extension, not just hers, of that knowledge through discovery is constitutive of the flourishing of this subject.

Note that she is not someone who thinks that absolute value in general, or the absolute value that resides in knowledge of mathematics, should be *maximized*. She subscribes to the commonsense moral assumption that our pursuit of value should be constrained by the usual moral rules that tell us not to murder, steal, lie, cheat, and so on.

Some further details must be added, and then I will be able to formulate the difficulty that I think this example raises for friends of absolute value. Suppose our mathematician is the mother of a young child, and she must decide what sort of education he should have. Let's imagine, further, that her child has great mathematical talent, and so he can easily acquire knowledge of many theorems of pure mathematics. Just as she does not undertake her research because it is good for her to do so, but because she takes such research to be absolutely good, so let us suppose that if she teaches her son the mathematics to which she is devoted, she will be doing so not because it is good *for him* to learn these theorems, but because it is good for there to be mathematical knowledge in him and because he might contribute something to the subject's advancement. The question I want to ask is this: can any objection be made to her imparting this knowledge to her son on these grounds? It seems to me that there is. I think there would be something chilly about her, were she to do so.

[To be clear: when I voice this objection, I am certainly not saying or assuming that parents who impart useless mathematical knowledge to their children are wrong or mistaken to do so. I believe, on the contrary, that mathematical studies are worthwhile because, when they are loved and enjoyed, they are noninstrumentally good *for* those who undertake them. But the mother we are imagining is not teaching her child mathematics because it is good *for* him. The question I am raising is whether the reason *she* gives for teaching her son mathematics is a good reason, not whether there is some good reason for teaching mathematics to children.]

As a parent, she ought to love her child and to supervise his development with a view to his good—that is, with a view not to what is impersonally good, but to what is good *for him*. She must encourage him to engage in activities that are good for him. But mathematical knowledge, she believes, is not good for anyone. If she encourages him to study pure mathematics, the time he spends doing so will not be good for *anyone*, she believes, and it will displace other activities that would be good not only for him but also for others. So she ought to agree that there is at least this to be said against his acquisition of mathematical knowledge: he would be better off doing something else instead.

In fact, she should ask herself whether she can be fairly accused of using her son as a mere means when she encourages him to spend his time on mathematical research. Her motive in doing so is not a concern for what is good for him. Rather, she hopes that he might contribute to the flourishing of mathematics by making discoveries, but even if he does not make original contributions to the field, she thinks he can serve it by being one of the people who understands it and thus makes it thrive as a discipline. His understanding of mathematics will be a valuable thing and will make the world a better place. But by thinking in these terms, she is in effect viewing her child as a receptacle in which mathematics flourishes; he is, in her eyes, a site at which more mathematical knowledge enters the world or a device by which it is produced. Surely that is not the kind of relationship she should have with him. Nor is it the sort of attitude she should take to the other people in her life—her students and colleagues, for example. Her interactions with them, like those with her son, should be guided by a desire to benefit them. In fact, I believe that there is even an objectionable coldness in our mathematician's way of thinking about herself, and not just about other people. She has chosen a career with no thought of what is good for anyone—including herself. If that indifference to what is good for people in general is objectionable, as I think it is, that is partly because she is one of the people to whose good she ought to be attentive.

My complaint about her does not presuppose that a parent must never ask a child to make a sacrifice—to accept less of what is good for him than he might have had. On the contrary, it is obvious that, like everyone else, children should accept a lower portion of what is good for them to allow others to have their fair share of benefits. Rather, my complaint is that *this* does not seem a good reason to ask a child to make a sacrifice: to serve mathematics.

As a contrast, imagine a second mother who, like our first, is a devoted mathematician but, unlike her, has *two* sons. They are equal in mathematical talent, let us suppose, but the younger brother, unlike his older sibling, thoroughly and passionately enjoys this subject. This second mother, let us further suppose, trains her second son in mathematics because she wants to educate both of her children in ways that are good *for* them, and she thinks that it is non-instrumentally good for her younger son to spend his time expanding his mind through activities that he enjoys—and these happen to be mathematical activities. Because her first child does not enjoy studying mathematics, despite the fact that he has mathematical talent, she thinks that it is not good for him to spend his time learning theorems, and so she trains him in some other activity—music, let's suppose—for which he not only has some talent but which he thoroughly enjoys. This second mother, we can imagine, is, like the first, a mathematician and teacher of mathematics, but, unlike the first, she does not think of mathematical knowledge as something that is absolutely good and to be advanced for its own sake. Mathematics, she thinks, is good for some people to study—those who have a talent for the subject and derive pleasure from it—but it's not for everyone. It's good for her, she thinks, because it enjoyably expands her mind, and that is why it is also good for her younger son. But although she is unequivocally devoted to this subject, she does not think of it as, quite simply, a good thing. So she has no temptation to insist that her older son dedicate himself to mathematics regardless of whether he likes doing so. She believes that it is not mathematical knowledge that she is to serve, as she plans the education of her children. Rather, her education of her children is guided by her commitment to what is good for them.

This second mother, I believe, has the right attitude toward the education of her children; it is far more appealing than the pedagogy of the first mother. I suggest, further, that these contrasting examples have an important bearing on the question we have been pursuing in this study from the very start: are there some things we should value because they are, quite simply, good? The first mother answers that question affirmatively—mathematical knowledge is one such thing, she believes—and as a result, she takes an objectionable approach to the education of her son. She would have done better by him had she, like the second mother, not taken mathematical knowledge to be, quite simply, a good thing.

What has led the first mother astray, I suggest, is precisely her belief in absolute goodness. She regulates her relationship to others by her devotion to something that she takes to be more elevated than any person or group of individuals. Her dedication to goodness is akin to a sense of reverence for a divinity. What Goodness (the upper case is apt), as she conceives it, has in common with God, as many think of God, is that because it is far superior to human life (not to mention animal and plant life), human interests must sometimes be sacrificed for its sake. In her interactions with others (not only her children but also her students and colleagues), insofar as she acts as a mathematician and a devotee of mathematical knowledge, she is guided not by her conception of what is good for any of them, but by her conception of a goodness whose value has nothing to do with its being good for anyone. In taking absolute goodness to be her guide, she depersonalizes her relationships with others and even with herself.

Notice that I have not portrayed her as someone who *never* acts in the service of what is good for others or herself. If that were her predicament, she would be a moral monster. Rather, I have merely described one part of her life—the part in which she imparts, acquires, or in some other way expresses her dedication to mathematical knowledge. My claim is that this portion of her life is disfigured by her commitment to doing what is good even when it is not good for anyone.

The first mother's son, as I described him, has a great talent for mathematics. But I did not say either that that he enjoys the subject or that he does not. What is important, for our purposes, is that his mother does not care whether he enjoys it, just as she does not care whether learning the subject is good for him. For her, all that matters, when she considers whether to teach her son mathematics, is that mathematics is absolutely good.[4] Now, I can depict the first mother as an even chillier parent than I have done so far: let us add that although her son has great mathematical talent, not only does he derive no pleasure from studying the subject but also, on the contrary, it causes him to have painful headaches. Medical examinations, let us further suppose, reveal that when her son studies mathematics, certain neurons in his brain fire in a way that will eventually cause his health to suffer and may even shorten his life by a few years. Studying mathematics is, for these reasons, instrumentally bad for him. When we add these further details, it becomes all the more evident that it would be wrong for his mother to have him study mathematics, precisely because she would be doing what is bad for her child. But I also believe that it was already sufficiently clear, before we took the study of mathematics to be painful to this child, that there was a serious defect in his mother's way of approaching the question of how to educate him—namely, she was not being guided by thoughts about what is good for him, but only by thoughts about what is good *simpliciter*.

---

4. Objection: "If the first mother's son does not enjoy mathematics, then as a matter of fact he will be unable to understand it and will not be able to make any original contributions to the subject. So mathematics will not actually be served by the way she educates her son. The example therefore has no force." I am skeptical of the universal empirical generalization on which this objection rests. But even if we accept that generalization, it remains the case that she has the wrong sort of reason for not teaching her son mathematics.

Chapter 15

Further Reflections
on the Ethical Objection

I hope readers will grant that the example used in the preceding section has at least this much force: the mother who educates her son without regard to what is good for him, but who is instead guided by her conviction that mathematics is absolutely good, together with her conviction that he has mathematical talent, and that she therefore has sufficient reason to have him learn this subject, is making some kind of mistake. That much I take to be obvious. But it is not obvious, or at least not equally obvious, what her mistake is. I suggested that what leads her astray is her very belief that absolute goodness is a reason-providing property. The very fact that she thinks in these terms, in other words, is already an error. To reach that further conclusion, more needs to be said.

A friend of absolute goodness might claim that the case of the mathematical mother has no force as an objection to absolute goodness; what the example shows, he might say, is that mathematical knowledge is not absolutely good. But, he adds, it hardly follows that *nothing* is absolutely good, nor does it follow that absolute goodness is not a reason-providing property.

But it is implausible to suppose that we would react differently to this kind of example were we to change it by portraying the mother not as a devotee of mathematics but of some other branch of knowledge instead—history, for example, or science, or literature. No one could reasonably say that it is because *mathematics* figured in the example rather than one of these other subjects that the mother's attitude toward the education of her child could be faulted.

A friend of absolute goodness, granting this, might next say that what the example of the mathematical mother shows is only that *knowledge* is not absolutely good, not that there is nothing at all that can be put in this category. Pleasure, he might say, and pleasure alone is absolutely good. Alternatively, he might hold that several kinds of things are good—pleasure, virtue, and perhaps several others—but that knowledge is not on this list.

There are two reasons why this would be an ineffective way of depriving the example of the mathematical mother of its force. First, it is not apparent why knowledge should be left off the list of things that are absolutely good, if there is such a thing as absolute goodness. The idea that knowledge or, more generally, being in an excellent cognitive condition is in some way noninstrumentally desirable, and no less so than pleasure, has a long history. Plato, for example, says in the *Philebus* that the two leading answers to the question, What is good? are knowledge and pleasure (11b-c). Ross holds that both of them are absolutely good.[1] So if knowledge is to be omitted from the category of absolutely good things, whereas other items are to be put in this category, some argument must be found for this differential treatment. I conjecture that the only sort of argument that could establish this conclusion is one that claims that pleasure and pleasure alone is absolutely good. Some eminent philosophers (Epicurus, John Locke, Jeremy Bentham, John Stuart Mill, Henry Sidgwick) believe as much—assuming, for the sake of argument, that they are properly interpreted as friends of *absolute* goodness—but it is now generally accepted that their conception of what is valuable is too limited and that many different types of things are

---

1. *The Right and the Good*, pp. 134–135.

good. I am assuming throughout this study that if there is such a thing as absolute goodness, several kinds of things have this property, and that knowledge is one of them. (My arguments apply with equal force against the claim that only one type of thing is absolutely good. But the friends of absolute goodness have a more appealing theory if they are pluralists rather than monists. So I criticize the more plausible version of their theory.) The example of the mathematical mother should therefore be taken to indicate not that she goes astray in her idea that knowledge is good (or her more specific conviction that mathematical knowledge is good) but in the very fact that she thinks in terms of absolute goodness.

There is a second reason why it would be implausible to hold that the example of the mathematical mother shows merely that knowledge is not absolutely good and that it is ineffective as an objection to the whole category of absolute goodness. What is problematic about her way of thinking about the education of her son is that it is impersonal. The problem is not that it is mathematics in particular that she is devoted to, nor that what she counts as good is a branch of knowledge rather than some other type of thing. The problem, as we saw, is that in her education of her son, she sees him not as an individual whose needs and interests may differ from those of others, but as a medium in which something absolutely good is to be valued. All theories about which things are absolutely good have that same element of depersonalization: what they are theories about is conceived as something the value of which does not reside in its being good for anyone.

To see more clearly that it is the impersonal nature of absolute goodness that makes it objectionable for the mathematical mother to look to it as a guide, rather than her conviction that mathematical knowledge is absolutely good, we should look for a different sort of example. Let us now imagine a doctor who devotes himself to the alleviation of physical pain in human beings, not because he cares about what is good or bad *for human beings*, but because he thinks that pain, being a bad thing, should not exist. The pain in an animal is something that he is equally concerned to alleviate or eliminate— although he feels no more love or affection for animals than he does for human beings. He is a cold-hearted enemy of pain itself. Physical suffering, he thinks, is an ugly stain on the universe, a quasi-demonic force that takes up residence in sentient beings, and so he sees himself as making the world a better place by diminishing the amount of pain in it. People and animals are for him only the battleground on which the war against pain must be fought, because pain requires for its existence a host in which it resides. He need not deny that pain is, in addition to being absolutely bad, bad *for* those who suffer from it. But it is the absolute badness of pain that serves as his reason for opposing it. If he believes as well that people benefit from his efforts, he views that as an incidental side effect of his fight against pain.

The doctor just described is as chilly a person as the mathematical mother—and that criticism of him is justified even if he is as effective in his efforts to alleviate pain as are doctors who have more humane motives. The defects both of them exhibit consist in their impersonal way of interacting with others. She sees her son as someone in whom something that is absolutely good can be inserted; he sees his patients as creatures in which what is absolutely bad takes up residence. She is guided by the assumption that there is such a thing as absolute goodness, that it deserves to be valued, and that mathematical knowledge has this property; he by the assumption that there is such a thing as absolute badness, that it deserves our enmity, and that pain has this property. It would be implausible to suppose that what is defective in the cold-hearted doctor is not his conviction that absolute badness is to be opposed but rather his assumption that pain is absolutely bad. If there is such a thing as absolute badness, pain is as plausible an example of it as any. Similarly, if there is such a thing as absolute goodness, knowledge is not an implausible example of it. So the lesson we should learn from the case of the mathematical mother is that what has gone astray in her education of her son is the fact that she looks not to what is good for him but to what is good absolutely.

Why should she look to what is good for her child when she educates him rather than to what is good *simpliciter*? There is no reason to think that it is only when she *educates* her child that she should be guided by what is good for him rather than what is good. She should also be guided by what is good for him, rather than what is absolutely good, when she fosters his physical health, his emotional well-being, and so on. *All* her interactions with him should be governed by reasonable assumptions, not about what is good absolutely, but about what is good *for* him.

Now, although there are ways of interacting with a child that are peculiarly appropriate to the parent-child relationship, it would be implausible to suppose that her child is the only person with whom her interactions should be governed by reasonable assumptions about what benefits others. It would be difficult to believe that although positing absolute goodness and making assumptions about what is good (period) are out of place when a parent interacts with a child, when adults interact with each other they need to invoke the existence of absolute goodness and make assumptions about which things are absolutely good. The cold-hearted doctor I described is just as chilling a figure as the mathematical mother, and he can easily be imagined as someone whose opposition to pain brings him into frequent contact with adults, as well as children. But he is equally in error in his attitude to both groups. He ought to realize that the pain of human beings is to be alleviated because it is bad *for* human beings, whether they are children or adults. It would be crazy to suppose that a child's pain should be alleviated because that is bad for him, but that an adult's pain is to be alleviated because that is absolutely bad.

The conclusion to which I am drawn, then, when I try to say what lesson should be learned from the example of the mathematical mother, is quite general in scope: it is that in *all* our interactions with *all* other human beings, we should be guided by our conception of what is good for them rather than by any conception of what is good absolutely. In fact, I believe that we should go one step further, since I think it would be odd to suppose that whereas human pain is objectionable because it is bad for humans, animal pain is objectionable not because it is bad for animals but because it is absolutely bad. So I believe that in all our interactions with *all* other animals (in fact, all creatures) we should be guided by our conception not of what is good period, but of what is good *for* them.

That does not mean that our interaction with other creatures should be governed by no other concepts aside from those of benefit and harm. In our dealings with others, we need to keep track of all sorts of considerations—not only benefit and harm, but also justice, respect, desert, obligation, duty, responsibility, and so on. My thesis is that we do not need, in addition to these familiar sorts of considerations, the concepts of absolute goodness and absolute badness.

There is a still more general thesis that I am proposing: not only should our interactions with *others* be guided not by absolute but by relative goodness but also *all* practical thinking should be so guided. Some of my practical problems are self-regarding and do not concern my relationship with others. When, for example, I decide whether to stop smoking, that is a question that concerns my health, not, at least in most circumstances, a question of how I should interact with others. But as we saw in our discussion of smoking (chapter 8), the concept of what is absolutely bad or absolutely good plays no role in guiding this decision. In fact, as I noted there, if someone insists that smoking is, quite simply, bad, we would be puzzled about what he could mean. If I should not smoke, that is simply because doing so is likely to be bad for me, not because it is bad. More generally, my hypothesis is that when one makes decisions about what pertains only to oneself, one ought to be guided by a reasonable conception of what is good for oneself, but one does not need to be guided, in addition, by a conception of what is absolutely good.

Chapter 16

Moore's Mistake
about Unobserved Beauty

Moore's principal examples of items that are absolutely good are "the pleasures of human intercourse and the enjoyment of beautiful objects."[1] To agree with him, he says, one need only think clearly about this matter: "if we consider what things are worth having *purely for their own sakes,* [it does not] appear probable that any one will think that anything else has *nearly* so great a value as the things that are included under these two heads."[2] He recognizes, nonetheless, that his thesis is a bold one and that its truth has not been

1. *Principia Ethica,* sec. 113, p. 237.
2. Ibid., sec. 113, p. 237 (author's emphasis).

generally recognized. "That it is only for the sake of these things—in order that as much of them as possible may at some time exist—that any one can be justified in performing any public or private duty; that they are the *raison d'être* of virtue; that it is they . . . that form the rational ultimate end of human action and the sole criterion of social progress: these appear to be truths which have been generally overlooked."[3]

I will discuss Moore's claim that the pleasures of human intercourse are absolutely good in the next chapter. Here I will focus on the enjoyment of beauty. The question I want to pursue is whether we should be convinced that the enjoyment of beauty has the property of being, quite simply, good. If we find that idea appealing, then we will be committed to saying that there is such a property as goodness. Moore makes a stronger claim: not only is the enjoyment of beauty good (period); it is—along with "the pleasures of human intercourse"—one of the most valuable things we can have. It is, in other words, not a small good, but one of the greatest. But I will set aside that thesis about how good the enjoyment of beauty is. Moore will have established something quite important if he can convince us that the enjoyment of beauty is just plain good.

Moore's claim that the enjoyment of beauty is a great good is put forward in the sixth and final chapter of *Principia Ethica*, which concerns the ideal state of the universe. But he had already advanced a striking thesis about beauty in chapter 3, which contains his attack on hedonism (the thesis that pleasure alone is good). Sidgwick defends this doctrine in *The Methods of Ethics*, and he is one of Moore's principal targets. Sidgwick holds that beauty unobserved and therefore unappreciated does not "possess the quality of goodness"; rather, what is good is the pleasant consciousness

3. Ibid., p. 238.

of beauty.[4] That is one reason he thinks that what is good is always some pleasant state of consciousness. To cast doubt on the thesis that beauty isolated from consciousness is not good, Moore asks his readers whether they would accept Sidgwick's statement: "No one would consider it rational to aim at the production of beauty in external nature, apart from any possible contemplation of it by human beings."[5] "I, for one, do consider this rational," Moore comments, and to induce his readers to agree, he describes two worlds, one of them beautiful—"put into it whatever on this earth you most admire"—and the other "the ugliest world you can possibly conceive." Now, Moore asks: even if no human being is present in either world to observe the beauty of one or the ugliness of the other, would it not be "better that the beautiful world should exist, than the one that is ugly? Would it not be well...to do what we could to produce it rather than the other?"[6]

It would be a mistake, I think, to be supremely confident that Moore is wrong about this, and no less a mistake to be certain that he is right. The practical assumptions that we are entitled to be most confident about are the ones that we use in everyday decisions, provided they can survive critical scrutiny. But when we ask whether we would produce or sustain a world of natural beauty that no one would ever appreciate, we are asking a question no

4. *Methods of Ethics* book I, chapter IX, section 4, p. 113. Moore refers to this section at *Principia Ethica*, p. 133.

5. *Methods of Ethics*, p. 114. Moore quotes Sidgwick at *Principia Ethica*, p. 135.

6. *Principia Ethica*, p. 135. If you are not already familiar with this treatise, you might at this point be puzzled. As I just noted, Moore claims that one of the greatest goods is the *enjoyment* of beauty (not the mere existence of unobserved beauty). You might ask: doesn't Moore have to hold that the enjoyment of *anything* is a great good, and isn't that a large concession to hedonism? The answer is no. Moore also believes that two goods, each small in value on its own, can, when combined, have more value than the mere sum of their separate values. So enjoyment, considered in isolation from its object, can have a small value, and beauty, isolated from observers, can also have a small value; but the enjoyment of beauty can be a great good.

human being has ever encountered, and to which we are unlikely ever to need an answer. My own (hesitant) reaction is that I would choose the beautiful world over the ugly one, but how do I know that in reacting this way I am not letting myself be influenced by the illegitimate but nonetheless persistent thought that perhaps, despite the way the example is described, someone might someday behold the universe I choose?[7]

What is important for present purposes, however, is that whether we think Moore is right or wrong to claim that we should choose the world of beauty, what he needs to show is not this proposition alone, but furthermore that the reason we should choose beauty over ugliness is because beauty "possess[es] the quality of goodness," in Sidgwick's phrase. We have to keep in mind that, according to Moore, goodness is a reason-giving property; he claims, in fact, as we saw in chapter 1, that it is the *only* property that gives us reason to act. So he must deny that by itself the beauty of a world is a reason for creating or sustaining it. What he must hold is that whatever has the property of beauty necessarily has the further property of goodness and that it is the goodness of beauty, not beauty itself, that should ground our choice of the more beautiful world. Otherwise, this fanciful example cannot be offered as a case in which our choice of one alternative over another is grounded in absolute goodness and badness.

But is there any reason to suppose that whatever is beautiful must also have the property of being absolutely good—not good *for*

---

7. The beautiful but unobserved world is not good *for* anyone, because it contains no individuals for whom it is good. If I were confident that I ought to choose such a world over an ugly but unobserved world, then I would have to acknowledge an exception to the general rule (which is attractive to me) that what we should choose should be chosen, at least in part, because doing so is good for someone. My principal goal in this study is not to argue that that general rule is exceptionless. It is to cast doubt on the thesis that absolute goodness is a reason-giving property. That is why I can leave open the possibility that a world of unobserved beauty should be chosen. That choice need not rest on the goodness of such a world.

anyone to behold, but good *simpliciter*? Moore gives none. Perhaps he simply assumes that the only reason to choose the beautiful world and reject the ugly one is that the first world is one in which there is goodness and the second is one in which there is badness. But if that is what he is doing, he is simply assuming what he needs to prove.

When Moore posits that in one universe there is great beauty and in the other great ugliness, he has already evaluated those two alternatives. To think of something as beautiful or ugly is already to assess it; "good" and "bad" are by no means our only evaluative terms. From these evaluative judgments—one universe is beautiful, the other ugly—we can straightway move to the conclusion that one should choose to bring the beautiful world into existence rather than the ugly one. (After all, these are assumed to be the only evaluative differences between them; one receives a positive, the other a negative evaluation.) We do not need the further evaluative judgments that beauty is a good thing and ugliness a bad thing.

There is another way in which Moore might have arrived at the conclusion that whatever is beautiful must be good. Surely he is asking his readers to believe that if the beautiful world is created, that is a better state of affairs than the one that would exist were the ugly world created. Now, suppose he made the further assumption that whenever one state of affairs is better than another, the explanation must be that the first has either a higher amount of goodness (period) than the second or a smaller amount of badness (period). (Goodness, so understood, is like color: what makes one patch greener than another is the presence of a more saturated greenness.) Obviously, once this assumption is granted, it becomes plausible to suppose that the reason the existence of the beautiful world is a better state of affairs than the existence of the ugly world is that the beautiful world has the property of being absolutely good, and the ugly world has the property of being absolutely bad.

But it is not true that the comparative judgment that one state of affairs is better than another must rest on a noncomparative judgment having to do with the presence of absolute goodness or absolute badness. Consider an analogous case: six is a larger number than five, but our confidence in that arithmetic truth does not rest on any prior judgment we have made about one or the other of these two numbers being a large number or a small number. The question "Is five a large number, a small number, or intermediate between being large and small?" is not one that can be answered, unless some context is provided. In comparison with a trillion, it is small; in comparison with 0.001, it is large. But that is just a way of saying that it is smaller than one and larger than the other. Similarly, if I point to two boxes on the table and ask you whether you think they are large boxes, you would not yet know how to answer my question, because I have not told you by what standard their size is to be judged. You would have no such trouble, however, if I asked you whether one box is larger than the other. That shows that we can come to a conclusion about which of two physical objects is larger without having first decided whether either of them has the property of being large. (One more example: which, among all the objects in the universe, are the ones that are close to you in space? There is no determinate answer, in the absence of some standard of proximity. The objects close to you are made such by being closer than that standard. But we can determine which of two objects is closer to you without having to decide first whether one or both of them is close to you. The answer to the comparative question "which is closer?" does not turn on whether one or the other is close.)

We are entitled to draw a more general conclusion from these examples: comparative judgments do not need to rest on noncomparative judgments. To say that one state of affairs is better than another is to make a comparative statement. We should not assume that it must rest on the premise that there is such a thing as absolute goodness or absolute badness. Accordingly, even if the existence of a beautiful world is a better state of affairs than the existence of an ugly world, that judgment need not rest on the premise that it is the goodness of the first world and the badness of the second that grounds that comparison. The first world may be better than the second simply because the first is beautiful and the second ugly, and the existence of a beautiful state of affairs is better than the existence of an ugly state of affairs.

We can arrive at this conclusion by a different route. Suppose we can create either of two situations. In the first, we can do what is equally beneficial for each of ten people. In the second, we can provide those same benefits to those same people, and furthermore, we can provide each of them with an equal amount of other benefits as well. The first state of affairs contains much that is good for everyone (and equally so); the second contains even more of what is good for everyone (again equally so). Which is the better state of affairs—the state of affairs we should choose, if we can? Obviously, the second. Is that because the second state of affairs contains a higher degree of the property of goodness (*simpliciter*)? No, nothing in my description of the two alternatives implied that any individual possessed something *absolutely* good. The second state of affairs is better because the only difference between it and the first is that everyone in the second has more of what is good for him. Just as the two universes Moore describes can be compared with respect to their beauty and ugliness, and one of them can be chosen over the other simply on that basis, so the two social scenarios I imagined can be compared with respect to the benefits they involve and the equality of those benefits.

Chapter 17

Better States of Affairs
and Buck-Passing

The point just made deserves to be repeated for emphasis, and it should be connected with our earlier discussion of Scanlon's buck-passing account of value (chapter 11). It is indisputable that in making decisions, we compare alternative options, and we ask ourselves, "Which of the states of affairs between which I must choose is better?" Here, "better" need not be relativized. I need not be asking, "Which is better for me?" But I must be asking, "Which is better—period?" And that may make it seem as though the basis on which I must decide is absolute goodness.

Suppose I must decide between two options, one of which is good for A but bad for B, and the other of which is good for B but bad for A. Obviously, I cannot reach a conclusion about what I ought to do without deciding which of these two alternatives is better than the other. But the question "Which is better?" must not be interpreted as an ellipsis to be completed by the specification of one of the two individuals involved. It does not mean "which option is better for A?" because I already know the answer to that question. Nor does it mean "which is better for B?" for the same reason. Nor does it mean "which is better for both?" because there is no such option. Even if I put the amount of good and harm I might do for A and B together on a single scale, and choose the option that produces the greatest sum (harms being subtracted from benefits), I must still admit into my way of thinking about my dilemma the notion of one thing being *simply better* than another, and this is not the same thing as one thing being *better for someone* than another. The better option, says the friend of absolute goodness, is the one that has a higher degree of the property of absolute goodness.

I agree that in resolving my problem, I put my options into a relation: one of them I assess as the better alternative. But that does not mean that the *basis* on which I decide between them is my determination of which is better than the other. The grounds of my choice can rest instead on any from among a wide variety of reason-giving factors, for example, the different *relationships* I have with A and with B (one is a friend, the other a stranger), or my judgment about which of them is most *deserving* of help, or differences in *how much* I can help each. Suppose I choose to help A because he has helped me in the past, and furthermore I can do more good for him than I can for B. On these grounds, I decide that I have stronger reasons to help A than B. As a result, I judge that my helping A is a better state of affairs than my helping B. But the *grounds* on which I choose one alternative over the other is not that one state of affairs is better than the other, and so there is no reason to say that the basis for choosing one option over the other lies in the difference between the amounts of absolute goodness that each alternative possesses.

The moral we should draw is that one state of affairs can be better than another without that betterness relation being grounded in differences with respect to absolute goodness. To use Scanlon's phrase, when we say that one state of affairs is better than another, we pass the buck of justification: we do not thereby reveal the basis for choosing one over the other, but merely advert to the existence of some such basis. So there is such a relation as one state of affairs being absolutely better than another. But we need some independent argument for the thesis that absolute goodness is a reason-giving property before we can reach the conclusion that whenever one state of affairs is better than another, the explanation must be that this property is more fully present in one case than the other.

I have granted (in chapter 11) that "it is a good thing" is used by *some* speakers—although not the friends of absolute goodness!—to mean merely that there is a reason for valuing that thing. Doing so is not an abuse of language. Evaluative language *can* be meaningfully employed in a buck-passing way. Here I exploit that possibility, in holding that on one reading of "this is a better state of affairs than that" (the reading we should adopt), the phrase "is better than" passes the buck. We can, in other words, decline to construe this relationship as one that is reason-providing. (We could also stop using the expression "a better state of affairs" without loss; instead, we could speak of "a state of affairs for which there are better reasons.")

When one state of affairs is judged better (absolutely better) than another, that fact can be expressed (somewhat awkwardly) by saying one of them is good (period) to a higher degree than the other. That strained way of speaking can easily lead us astray, but it is not devoid of meaning; such statements can be true or false. But we must be careful not to slide from this to the conclusion that goodness is a reason-giving property (or a property at all) or that what grounds this comparison is precisely some difference in the degree to which our alternatives possess the property of goodness. If we rank one above the other because we believe that there are better reasons to pursue the one than the other, and those reasons are not themselves the difference between the absolute goodness of our alternatives, then absolute goodness is not doing the important work that Moore and others believe that it does. It is not functioning as a reason-giving property.

In fact, for reasons already given, it should not be thought of as a property of any sort. Recall my earlier point (chapter 16) that when one box is larger than another, that is not because, first, it has the property of largeness (period) and because, second, it is a box. It is not by being large (period) that a box is a large box, for there is no such property as being large (period). There is, of course, a certain ordering among boxes of different sizes—one is larger than another—but not because either of them instantiates the property of being, quite simply, large. In the same way, when we say that one state of affairs is better than another, we should not infer that in order for this to be so, there must be such a thing as the property of goodness (period), the possession of which is what makes it so.[1] (We will return to this theme in chapter 30, when I discuss Geach's notion of an "attributive adjective.")

1. Compare with this the thesis of John Broome that "goodness is reducible to betterness." See "Goodness Is Reducible to Betterness: The Evil of Death Is the Value of Life," in his *Ethics out of Economics* (Cambridge: Cambridge University Press, 1999), pp. 162–174. For my purposes, the main lessons of this essay are (a) philosophers should frame their evaluative questions by using the comparative term "better than" rather than the noncomparative term "good" because (b) goodness is reducible to betterness. I take him to mean that propositions using "better-than" are more perspicuous than the corresponding propositions expressed in terms of "good." In any case, if we distinguish, as we should, properties from relations, then Broome's position can be expressed by saying that there is no such *property* as goodness.

Chapter 18

The Enjoyment of Beauty

To return to Moore: although he holds that the very existence of a thing of beauty is absolutely good, he adds that when someone becomes conscious of a beautiful object, appreciates its beauty, and enjoys contemplating it, the amount of absolute goodness thereby brought into the world is far larger than that which exists simply by virtue of the presence in the world of that beautiful thing unobserved. The emotion felt by someone who observes a beautiful thing has some small value, he believes, as does the very existence of that beautiful thing. But when these two elements—the emotion and the beautiful object—form a single "organic whole" (as Moore calls it), there comes into existence far more absolute goodness than is present by virtue of the two elements of that whole when they are considered separately. The goodness of the whole is not merely the sum of the separate values of the parts.

For our purposes, what is important is not this principle regarding the nonadditive value of organic wholes, but Moore's thesis that the reason we should enter (and help others enter) into situations in which we (and they) appreciate and enjoy things of beauty is that doing so is good *simpliciter*—that, in doing so, we add to "the sum of values in the universe," as Ross would put it.[1] One objection to this thesis is the same in form as the one raised in chapter 16. There, I argued that if unobserved beauty is something worth protecting or creating, that by itself is no reason to posit the existence of absolute goodness. We can say that a certain kind of world is worth preserving simply because of its beauty; our efforts to preserve it need not be grounded in its being good as well as beautiful. Similarly, we explain why we should, for example, walk to the lake to look at the spectacular sunset by saying it is beautiful, and we enjoy looking at the beauties of the natural world. Why should the enjoyment of beauty have to be absolutely good for there to be a reason to enjoy something beautiful?

1. *The Right and the Good*, p. 132.

Here is a further reason to doubt that the enjoyment of beauty must be thought of as something that is absolutely good. Suppose you are not aware, as I am, that tonight there is a spectacular sunset over the lake, and because you are a friend who lives nearby, I phone you to tell you about it and to make plans to see it together. I am not merely seeking companionship—not acting solely because I enjoy the pleasure of your company. I would have phoned you to tell you about it even if I myself could not go to the lake to see the sunset. What I've done is a small act of friendship. Viewing the sunset is something I know you would enjoy, and that is why I am phoning you. Now, it is far from obvious that *everything* that someone enjoys is good, even to the slightest extent, for that person. Some enjoyments may be noninstrumentally bad for us; the objects of those enjoyments may make such experiences a waste of time. But it would be crazy to suppose that the enjoyment of beautiful sunsets and other beautiful things is noninstrumentally bad for us. In fact, if someone has no emotional reaction to the beauties of the natural world, that would be a deficiency in his feelings and attitudes toward the world. It would detract from the richness of his life. It would also be a personal misfortune if someone whose capacity to respond emotionally to the beauty of the natural world is intact had no opportunities or occasions to exercise that capacity. He would have failed to take advantage of his possession of that psychological power. Accordingly, we can say that when I phone you to tell you about the beautiful sunset, I am doing something that is good *for* you. Your capacity to respond with joy to the beauties of nature ought to be exercised, if it is going to do you any good to have that capacity. When I phone you, I am calling your attention to just such an opportunity. Obviously, part of the explanation for my phoning you is that tonight's sunset is beautiful. But the other part of the explanation is my desire to do something for you. Moore would have done better, then, to say, not that the enjoyment of beauty is good absolutely, but that it is good *for* someone to have and to exercise the capacity to enjoy things of beauty.

When we reflect on how we educate our children or how we think children should be educated, it is again plausible to construe the enjoyment of beauty as something that is good for the person who has such experiences. It is to the good of our children that we look, when we plan their education. When we take them to beautiful parts of the world and call their attention to that beauty, we are enlarging and training their responsiveness to their natural environment, and in doing so, we are being attentive to their well-being—to what is good for them. We are also doing something noninstrumentally good for them if we give them an appreciation of the beautiful products of architects, painters, musicians, novelists, and so on.[2] (I return to these ideas in appendix C.)

2. These ideas play a leading role in the aestheticism of such figures as William Wordsworth, John Ruskin, Walter Pater, and Oscar Wilde. For a fascinating study of these and later authors, see Douglas Mao, *Fateful Beauty: Aesthetic Environments, Juvenile Development, and Literature, 1860–1960* (Princeton, NJ: Princeton University Press, 2008). That sensitivity to beauty is *beneficial* is a point on which Plato insists (*Republic* 401), as Wilde is aware. A more recent author who speaks of the "intrinsic value" of our experience of beauty and artworks as a noninstrumental *benefit* is Malcolm Budd, who writes that "many of what are thought of as benefits of the experience of art are intrinsic to the experience, not merely products of it. The experience a work of art offers can involve the invigoration of one's consciousness, or a refined awareness of human psychology or political or social structures, or moral insight, or an imaginative identification with a sympathetic form of life or point of view...; it can be beneficial in these and countless other ways.... Such benefits contribute to making the experience intrinsically valuable...." See *Values of Art* (London: Penguin, 1995), p. 7. Budd's appeal to the benefits of our encounter with the arts is part of a long tradition. As Paul Guyer notes, many authors (he mentions Friedrich Schiller, John Ruskin, William Morris, and John Dewey) value aesthetic experience "because of the benefits the development of [our] capacities can bring to the rest of our lives." See his "History of Modern Aesthetics," in Jerrold Levinson, ed., *The Oxford Handbook of Aesthetics* (Oxford: Oxford University Press, 2003), pp. 25–60. The passage cited is on p. 31. Much of the work of Noël Carroll is a critique of those philosophies of art (called "aestheticism" or "formalism") that seek to insulate aesthetic experience from all other human interests. See, for example, his "Art and Alienation" in *Art in Three Dimensions* (Oxford: Oxford University Press, 2010), pp. 143–162; the first thirteen essays collected in this volume explore this theme, as do many of the essays in his *Beyond Aesthetics: Philosophical Essays* (Cambridge: Cambridge University Press, 2001.)

Consider an art auction: a beautiful painting that had been displayed in a private home has gone on sale, and several people are bidding for it, each wanting that painting to be displayed in his home, because each wants the enjoyment of its beauty to be part of his everyday life and the lives of his family and friends. Moore would say that each of them is confused. He thinks that the only reason for each to place a bid is to produce as much good in the world as possible, and so each should want the painting to be placed where the largest number of people can see it. In that way, the amount of absolute good in the universe would be maximized. But the motivation of each person who places a bid is perfectly coherent, and it would be implausible to suppose that there should be no private collections of art or that people should not put on the walls of their apartments and houses beautiful paintings that they will enjoy. We find it natural to suppose that when the participants in the auction compete for ownership of the painting, each is acting partly in his own interest. The enjoyment of beauty is something that we plausibly take to be good—not absolutely, but for the person who has that experience.

There can also be times when we should refrain from bringing beauty into existence because, however many people such beauty would please, our act would be harmful to just a single individual. Suppose a husband and wife are able to manipulate the genetic endowment of their next child, and doctors can ensure that they could produce a baby girl who will eventually become a woman of stunning physical beauty. Were we persuaded by Moore that bringing beauty into existence and sustaining such beauty should be one of our principal projects because beauty is good, and the more beauty there is, the greater amount of absolute goodness there is, we would have to advise this couple to arrange for the birth of an exceedingly beautiful child. Furthermore, we may suppose, the enjoyment of looking at this beautiful woman could be shared by many millions of people. But the responsibility of these parents is to their future child, and they may, for good reason, fear that being extraordinarily beautiful will not be (instrumentally or noninstrumentally) good for their daughter—in fact, that her great beauty will have consequences that are extremely bad for her. They would be entirely justified, if these assumptions are correct, in seeing to it that their child is only as attractive as would be good for her.[3]

3. Novels are an excellent source of examples of the harm that physical beauty can bring to those who possess it. To take one, in Anthony Trollope's *The Way We Live Now*, Felix Carbury is undone in part because his beauty attracts the daughter of a man of immense wealth. His good looks are such a great resource that he develops no others.

Chapter 19

Is Love Absolutely Good?

I turn now to a feature of human life that no comprehensive ethical theory can ignore: the love and affection that human beings normally develop for one or more of their fellow humans. Moore certainly does not ignore this topic; as I noted (chapter 16), he considers "the pleasures of human intercourse or of personal affection" to be one of the greatest of goods.[1] The question I want to raise is not how great a good the love of human beings is, but whether it is good at all. More precisely, my question is whether love (or affection or friendship) is good *simpliciter*.

1. *Principia Ethica*, p. 251.

Sometimes love, friendship, and affection are bad for people. A father may watch a friendship form between his daughter and a schoolmate and worry that this new friend will be a bad influence. Or his daughter may fall in love with someone who, as it seems to her father, will treat her badly throughout her life. Parents themselves may love their children in harmful ways. Wanting to stay close to their children and fearing for their safety, they can smother their children's independence. All of these familiar points about the harm that love and friendship can do employ the concept of what is bad *for* someone.

But Moore has an ethical theory that urges us to look not to what is good for people and avoid what is bad for them—he takes these to be confused notions—but to what is absolutely good or absolutely bad. We are to make the world a better place by increasing the amount of good in it, and since "the pleasures of human intercourse or of personal affection" are among the greatest goods there are, we are to enter into relationships in which these pleasures are felt, and we are to help all others to do likewise. That commits Moore to saying that a father should set aside as unintelligible the question whether his daughter's relationship with her lover will be good for her and ask only whether the world will become a better place, should that relationship develop and endure.

Suppose that a friend of absolute goodness rejects Moore's belief that the notions of what is good for someone and of what is bad for someone should be banished from practical reasoning. Such a friend, let us imagine, wants to develop a theory about the value of human intercourse by using both the notion of what is good for someone and the notion of what is good absolutely. What form can such a theory take?

One option would be to say that *all* love, friendship, and affection is absolutely good. But since some of these relationships and feelings are harmful—to one of the individuals involved or both—such a theory will need to ask whether the absolute goodness of love can sometimes be great enough to outweigh the harm that it does. The answer such a theory should give, if it is to have any credibility, is no. At any rate, I cannot imagine any situation in which someone should, despite his recognition of the harm his relationship is doing to himself or to another person, continue to participate in it on the grounds that this love is adding to the amount of good in the universe.

The more attractive option, for a friend of absolute goodness who also uses the concept of what is good for someone, is to say that only some forms of love, friendship, and affection are absolutely good. Other forms will be absolutely bad or intermediate between these extremes. But such a theory will have to have some basis for making this distinction. It will have to explain why some forms of love are absolutely good whereas others are absolutely bad. And its explanation cannot be that a form of love is made absolutely good by the fact that in such a relationship each individual aims at and achieves what is good *for* the other person. If absolute goodness is to be an important factor in practical reasoning, it must be a property that is not a mere shadow of relative goodness. It must be defined without using the concept of what is good for someone, and it must be a factor that enters into our practical thinking as an input that is independent of considerations of what is good for someone.

Moore wisely notes that "the study of what is valuable in human intercourse is a study of immense complexity."[2] The question is whether we need to use the concept of absolute goodness, in addition to that of what is good for someone, to carry out this project successfully. That we do need to speak of what is good for people,

2. Ibid., p. 253.

when we consider the ethics of love and friendship, is obvious. Part of the role of being a good friend to someone is to hope that what he does and what happens to him is good *for* him, to be glad when things go well *for* him, to be willing to lend a hand, and to be willing to give up some of what is good *for* oneself to do what *benefits* him. When friendship and love are missing from someone's life, we take it for granted that this is to be regretted because it is bad *for* that person. These are central assumptions of our commonsense ethics of friendship. By contrast, it is not clear whether we need to invoke the notion of absolute goodness to explain "what is valuable in human intercourse."

If we look to Moore himself for guidance on this matter, what we find in *Principia Ethica* is a remarkably aesthetic approach to the phenomenon of friendship. Moore places his treatment of "the pleasures of human intercourse" after his discussion of "the enjoyment of beautiful objects" because his treatment of affection borrows heavily from his discussion of the value of being conscious of beautiful things.[3] He says that when human intercourse is at its best, there is an enjoyable and veridical appreciation of the beautiful and admirable features, both physical and mental, of the person toward whom one feels affection and that it is this aspect of these relationships that makes the enjoyment of human intercourse absolutely good. What is good in the best friendships, on this account, is very similar to what is good in the contemplation of beauty: it consists in enjoyable acts of appreciation. The "sum of values in the universe" increases when human intercourse is at its best, because it contains greater amounts of pleasant acts of appreciation.[4]

---

3. For his discussion of beauty, see ibid., pp. 238–251; on friendship, see pp. 251–253.

4. "Sum of values in the universe," it should be recalled, is Ross's expression (*The Right and the Good*, p. 132), but it corresponds to Moore's way of talking about the amount of good and evil "in the world" (*Principia Ethica*, p. 77).

What is both striking and at the same time dubious in Moore's theory is its thesis that personal affection has greatest intrinsic value when it is directed at those whose "admirable mental qualities... consist very largely in an emotional contemplation of beautiful objects."[5] He insists that *corporeal* beauty and the appropriate physical expression of mental qualities play a large role in accounting for the great value of friendship.

But let us leave this aspect of his theory aside, because there is a deeper problem with it. Suppose you and I have great affection for George, but unfortunately he has time to be with only one of us and, as it happens, you are the one who is lucky enough to see him and interact with him. The natural way to describe this situation is to say that this turn of events is good for you but bad for me. I noted some time ago (chapter 10) that just as pain should be taken to be not simply bad but bad for the person who feels it, so, too, pleasures are best understood as not absolutely good but good for those who experience them. Just as the participants in an auction are in competition with each other, as they bid for the possession of a painting they will enjoy looking at, so you and I are in competition for the pleasure of George's company. Moore is right to think that the enjoyment of interacting with and seeing our friends is one reason friendship is valuable, but throughout his treatise, he is blind to the fact that enjoyment is not absolutely good but good for someone. What he calls "the pleasures of human intercourse" are good for us, not good *simpliciter*. So if we want to show that we need the concept of absolute goodness to explain how we are to treat our friends, we must look not to *Principia Ethica* but elsewhere. But so far as I know, no other friend of absolute goodness has succeeded where Moore failed.[6]

---

5. *Principia Ethica*, p. 252.
6. To account for the goodness of friendship, Thomas Hurka proposes that it embodies other, more basic goods, namely, pleasure, knowledge, achievement, and virtue. See *The Best*

There is no doubt that we need to use the concept of what is good for someone to guide us in our affectionate relationships and to explain why we should welcome them. But must a satisfactory account of this moral phenomenon also make use of the notion of absolute goodness? We have discovered no reason to think so.

Things in Life: A Guide to What Really Matters (New York: Oxford University Press, 2011), pp. 141–161. I am doubtful that this reductionism can succeed, as I note in my review of this work (*Notre Dame Philosophical Reviews*, January 2011). In any case, Hurka is not a straightforward example of a friend of absolute goodness. I discuss his conception of value more fully in appendix D.

Chapter 20

Is Cruelty Absolutely Bad?

When Kant asserts, in the *Groundwork*, that "it is impossible to imagine anything... that can be called good without qualification except a good will," he is not saying that having a good will is good *for* anyone.[1] He does not think of moral virtue—the determination to act in accordance with the principles of a good will—as an *advantage*, whether instrumental or noninstrumental, enjoyed by good people. Moral virtue is always and necessarily a good *thing* without having to be good *for* anyone—either the agent or anyone else. The usefulness of a good will—its success in producing that for which it strives—is

---

1. *Groundwork for the Metaphysics of Morals*, translated by Arnulf Zweig (Oxford: Oxford University Press, 2002), p. 4:393.

no part of its intrinsic worth. "Like a jewel," he says, it "glistens in its own right, as something that has its full worth in itself."[2] Someone who has a good will need not actually achieve anything that is good for others; his good will remains a good thing, without being good for anyone. To fail to recognize the goodness of a good will, apart from its being good for the moral agent or the people with whom the moral agent interacts, is, according to Kant, to miss the most essential element of the moral life. (Notice that Kant is not claiming that there is only one sort of good thing—a good will. Rather, his thesis is that this alone is *unconditionally* good, that is, good in all conditions. Other goods are good only when combined with a good will.)

Similarly, when Ross writes that "the first thing for which I would claim that it is intrinsically good is virtuous disposition and action,"[3] he does not mean that virtue is good *for* anyone, but that it is absolutely good, or as he sometimes says, good "*sans phrase*."[4] He takes this to be obvious, but if anyone doubts it and says that pleasure alone is good, this doubt can be assuaged, Ross thinks, by conducting this simple thought experiment: consider "two states of the universe holding equal amounts of pleasure." In one of them, everyone is "thoroughly virtuous"; in the other, all are "highly vicious."[5] Would we not think that the universe full of good people is better than the one full of bad people?

Has Kant or Ross succeeded in showing that there is such a thing as absolute goodness? That is not quite the question I want to ask, because it is not their intention to produce such an argument. Rather, they take it for granted that there is such a property. They think that this assumption, and the further assumption that virtue

2. Ibid., p. 4:394.
3. *The Right and the Good*, p. 134.
4. Ibid., p. 102.
5. Ibid., p. 134.

has this property, is embedded in the ordinary moral consciousness of all human beings. Ross's thought experiment is merely meant to elicit our realization that this is something we already believe.

If one is already convinced, as Kant and Ross are, that there is such a property as absolute goodness, and one has already put other sorts of things into this category—pleasure, for example—then it would be reasonable to add virtue to the list of items that one takes to be good. Ross's thought experiment operates in this way: he is not arguing that we should accept the category of absolute goodness but is claiming that it would be a mistake to put pleasure but not virtue into this category.

We can come to the same conclusion he does by means of a different thought experiment, one that concerns vice (rather than virtue) and pain (rather than pleasure). Imagine a cruel person who deliberately inflicts pain, just for the fun of it. And suppose—in spite of what I have been arguing (chapter 9)—that pain is bad *simpliciter*, not bad for anyone. Accordingly, the cruel person we are imagining is creating a state of affairs in which something bad (period) happens: the pain he inflicts. But notice that the pain he brings about might have occurred in any case, without his intervention. If he starts a fire that causes his victim great pain, that terrible injury might have occurred through purely natural causes. Lightning might have started the fire that caused so much pain. That naturally caused state of affairs would have contained a bad thing: pain. But the state of affairs that consists in a cruel person deliberately causing pain is worse than one in which that pain occurs as a result of a lightning storm. How should we explain why it is worse? The obvious answer, for anyone who is already convinced that there is such a thing as badness (period), is that there is an additional bad item in the state of affairs that consists in a cruel person's infliction of pain. That additional badness consists *more badness within the thought*

Double value argument

in the cruelty of the man who set the fire. His aiming at what is bad (period) is itself bad (period).[6]

That seems to be undeniable. After all, we want to pass judgment on someone's cruelty; it is appropriate to evaluate this character trait and not merely describe it. With what terms should we evaluate his cruelty? By saying that this trait is bad *for him*? Perhaps it is, but perhaps it is not—it would take much careful thought to answer that question. In any case, it is not because his cruelty is bad for him that we feel confident that it should be condemned. Should we say, therefore, that our negative evaluation of the cruel person should be expressed by saying that what he does is bad *for others*? That cannot be right either, because we would think no better of him had his plan to torture his victim failed when some stroke of good luck saved his intended victim. Kant is right that we praise and blame people, or find them praiseworthy or blameworthy, because of the quality of their moral will, even when their efforts are unsuccessful. So, it seems best to say that the negative evaluation deserved by cruelty is simply that it is bad (period). Since (for purposes of this thought experiment) we have already assumed that there is such a thing as absolute badness, and we have put pain into that category, we have good reason to add cruelty and other vices to our list of bad things and to say, correspondingly, that the moral virtues are, quite simply, good.

If, however, the doubts I have been sowing about absolute goodness are reasonable, then the question we face here is rather different. Our evaluation of pain, I have argued, should be: it is bad *for* people and various animals (not: it is bad), or, more precisely, it is bad for most people and various animals. In fact, we have not yet

6. An example of this sort is given by Graham Oddie in *Value, Reality, and Desire* (Oxford: Clarendon, 2005), p. 198.

found *anything* about which there is a convincing reason to say that we should oppose it because it is absolutely bad or favor it because it is absolutely good. We are examining virtue and vice to find out whether here, at last, we can find good reasons to accept into our ethical theory the category of absolute goodness and badness, even though we have not found good reasons to put other sorts of things into these categories. So let us look carefully at the argument I have just given, which, by beginning with the premise that pain is absolutely bad and then making other assumptions, reached the conclusion that cruelty is absolutely bad. Suppose we reject the claim that pain is bad and substitute for it the premise, which I find more plausible, that pain is bad *for* people (that is, for most people). Should we be convinced by the argument rehearsed in the preceding two paragraphs that cruelty is bad *simpliciter*? No.

The weak link in the argument lies in the way it handles the point that someone might carry out an act of great cruelty and would therefore deserve to be blamed and in some cases punished, even if what he does is not bad for anyone. That is true. But the argument moves from this correct point to the conclusion that our criticism of the cruel person should not be expressed in the language of "bad for" but should instead condemn his cruelty on the grounds that it is, quite simply, bad. That inference might be justified, if we were already convinced that the pain that the cruel person is trying to inflict is bad (period). If pain is a bad thing, it seems natural to say that when someone tries to inflict it precisely because he takes it to be bad, his motive and endeavor are also bad. But now that we have rejected that way of talking about pain, we can say instead that when someone intends or tries to inflict pain on another human being (or animal) just for the fun of it, he is aiming, for no good reason, at what is bad *for* someone, and regardless of whether he succeeds, his state of mind and what he endeavors are blameworthy. He realizes or should realize that if he succeeds he will be doing something that is harmful—that it will be bad for the target of his attack. His reason for planning or trying to inflict pain by itself makes him subject to criticism. Intentions and attempts can be classified as impermissible, even when they are not successfully executed and therefore do no harm. So we must not be misled by the fact that someone is blameworthy even when his efforts to harm others bring about no actual harm; that does not show the concept of being bad (period) has a reason-giving role to play in our thinking. We do not need the concept of absolute badness to explain why we should be disturbed by even unsuccessful acts of cruelty. We can, instead, say that we must not aim at what is bad for others for its own sake; to do so is impermissible. There is no reason to suppose that there is yet another demerit of acts of cruelty, namely, that they are, quite simply, bad. (It is also possible for someone to seek to cause pain because he conceives of it as bad *simpliciter* and because his goal is to increase the amount of badness in the world. That, too, would be a motive that merits condemnation. But we can justify our criticism of it without ourselves believing, as he does, that pain is absolutely bad.)[7]

7. The issue I am discussing here can also be posed by means of examples in which one can prevent either a natural harm or that same kind and amount of harm maliciously produced. For example, suppose we can invest our resources in preventing deaths caused by destructive natural events (tornados, hurricanes, lightning) or in preventing the same number of deaths caused by malicious human beings. Some might say that we ought in this case to prevent the malicious harms, and their explanation might be that wrongdoing is itself absolutely bad. That people are killed is bad *for* them, but the two options are tied in that respect. The decisive factor, it might be said, is the absolute badness that would be added to the world were we to allow some to kill others maliciously. Against this, I believe that we need not posit absolute badness to support the intuition that it is malicious harm that should be prevented in such dilemmas. The rule of law is an enormous benefit, and it is not threatened by hurricanes and the like. But it would threatened were we to refrain from using our resources to enforce it. (If we are asked to consider a case in which there would be no threat to the rule of law, the example then becomes too remote from the world as we know it to serve as a test case in which we can have some confidence.)

There are other mental states, in addition to plans, endeavors, and intentions, that are open to assessment on the basis of their content and apart from their causal effects. If a belief is false, the mental condition of the believer is defective, because the truth or falsity of what we believe is one of the dimensions along which beliefs are subject to criticism. Similarly, we have several standards of correctness that we bring to bear on the assessment of intentions, aside from the causal consequences those intentions have when they are put into effect. They must not be incompatible with one's other intentions; if they are, one is already subject to criticism. What they are intentions to do must have some point. If they are contrary to the good of the agent, that counts against them. One's intention is already defective if it fails to meet these standards, regardless of whether one carries it out. It is no surprise, then, that we subject intentions to moral tests as well. That is, we assess them from the point of view not only of the agent himself but also from the point of view of others. One of those tests is this: it is wrong to seek, just for the fun of it, to inflict pain on others, when doing so is bad for them. The pleasure one would feel because one would know that they are suffering is not a reason, even a weak reason, to seek that goal.

A corresponding point can be made about a good will and good intentions. In our dealings with others, we must always take into consideration what is good for them, and it is often praiseworthy to aim at their well-being and work as effectively as we can toward that goal. Someone who meets this standard can be said to have a good will, and his efforts will be praiseworthy even if he encounters obstacles that could not have been foreseen and, as a result, nothing good for others is accomplished. Kant describes this situation by using the notion of absolute goodness: the good will is not good for anyone; it is simply good, and is good in all circumstances. But it is gratuitous to posit absolute goodness for no better reason than this. What is praiseworthy about the good will is not the absolute goodness it supposedly has, but the way it favorably orients itself toward what is good for others and is repelled by what is bad for them.

When, for example, a decent person reads about the terrible sufferings of people in some distant part of the world, we expect him to react sympathetically rather than with cold indifference. It is to his credit that he has such fellow feeling. What is bad for others is something we should have feelings about; of course, we should also do something about their misfortunes, when we are in a position to do so. But when we have such feelings, we are not bringing into the world something that is good—we are not, in Ross's words, "adding to the sum of values in the universe." In fact, that way of thinking leads to paradox: if millions of good people read about the suffering that takes place in a distant land and react sympathetically, might the universe become, as a result, a better place on balance? Might the proportion of absolute goodness to absolute badness become higher than it was before, because so many people are reacting to the suffering of a few and are doing so in a way that expresses their virtuous character? Something has gone wrong in our thinking if we suppose that the answer to that question might be yes.

How should the paradox be avoided? We would be hard put to do so, if we admit into our moral philosophy the categories of absolute goodness and badness. Kant and Ross are not making a mistake in supposing that once we acknowledge the existence of these categories—goodness and badness—we should put virtue into the first and vice into the second. Moore and Ross are not making a mistake in supposing that once we acknowledge the existence of these categories, we can say that some states of the universe contain more goodness than others. The cleanest way to avoid this road to paradox is to steer clear of the categories of absolute good and bad. The good people who feel bad when they learn of the suffering of others are not thereby adding to the value of the universe. They are reacting as they should, because they are concerned, as they ought to be, about what is bad for others. Events have occurred, they see, that make the world a worse place *for* others. But nothing has happened, by virtue of their sympathetic reaction, that is good for anyone. Their reaction can go no way toward making up for the occurrence of what is bad for others.

Just as many people are justifiably upset (and show their humanity) when they read or hear that others are suffering terribly because of floods, earthquakes, and other natural disasters, so, too, many rightly become indignant when they learn in vivid detail of those who live a life of luxury and ease as a result of their terrible crimes against innocent victims. It is tempting to say, in these cases, that the life of comfort and opulence that these people lead is good *for them*, but it is nonetheless a bad thing (period). Or to put the point in other terms, we might say that the world is made a worse place not only because others have suffered at their hands but also because these horrible people have benefited from their deviltry.

But is it really the case that riches and comforts are good for anyone who has them, regardless of the psychological state of the person who enjoys them? I doubt it, but let's set that difficult question aside, because in this book I am not defending a theory about what is good for human beings. There is a more obvious point to make for present purposes: These bad people do not deserve the wealth they have acquired. They did not earn it in morally acceptable ways; on the contrary, they acquired it through their dishonesty and cruelty. They are not sorry for what they did but are reveling in what they take to be their success—the very opposite of what they should feel. So we have all the reason we need to feel indignation when we reflect on their attitudes and their way of life.

We can express this point rather blandly by saying, "It is a bad thing that these people are enjoying their lives and priding themselves on their exploits." But we need not understand this to mean that the property of badness has been more fully instantiated in the world because of their crimes and that the grounds of our indignation is the existence of that added quantum of badness. We can instead treat the statement just made, "It is a bad thing that these people are enjoying their lives..." as a way of saying that we have reason to feel negatively about the way they live—to condemn them and feel indignation toward them. Our reason is that where there ought to be contrition and restitution, there is smugness and arrogance. Why ought there to be contrition and restitution? Because they owe it to others to make amends and to confess their crimes. These are the terms that do the real work of explaining why we ought to find these people blameworthy or even repulsive. It does not *add* to the case that we want to make against them to say that they made the world a worse place by doing a bad thing. If we use the expression "it is a bad thing" to describe such a case, that should be treated as a mere placeholder for the more concrete terms with which we spell out the reasons for our indignation and should not be puffed up into a phrase that names the very property that grounds our attitude toward them.

Chapter 21

Kant on Suicide

In Kant's hands, the absolute and unvarying goodness of moral virtue figures importantly in his subsidiary thesis that it would be wrong to commit suicide merely out of the conviction, however well founded, that one is and always will remain unhappy. His idea is that so long as one remains a rational agent, one will continue to possess and exercise the will to perform moral acts, and the goodness (not its goodness *for* anyone) of having this moral power is so great that it can compensate for any unhappiness one might experience, however large and however long in duration. Kant does not assert, as an underived first principle, that it would be wrong to commit suicide because of one's unhappiness. Rather, he has a reason for taking it to be wrong: the goodness of moral personality is not only unconditional (it remains good in all circumstances) but also unsurpassable. No matter how large and enduring the dis-value of being unhappy, it must always take second place, in our deliberations—or be given no place at all—when it competes with the goodness of exercising the power to perform acts of good will. To commit suicide out of the recognition that one will always be unhappy would not be a well-reasoned decision, even if it could be made (as it often is not) with utmost dispassion and foresight, because it would give more weight to a lesser good—one's own happiness—than to the incomparably superior good that consists in moral willing.

To use the terms by which Kant expresses this point: I ought not to "dispose of a human being in my own person" because "a human being is not a thing—not something to be used *merely* as a means."[1] One page earlier, he had drawn a contrast between goals that have a "value *for us*" with the "*absolute value*" of personhood.[2] Nothing that merely has value *for* us can be substituted for or given priority over personhood, which is *absolutely*, not relatively, valuable. As I read him, he means that one's capacity to will in accordance with the moral law is unsurpassably good (period), whereas one's happiness or unhappiness merely has relative value—it is good for us because it is the summation of our desires.

Kant's views about suicide should make us realize, if we have not appreciated the point until now, that the question whether there are things we should value because they are absolutely good is not a purely theoretical or academic matter without practical consequences. If goodness is a reason-giving property, as Moore and others have claimed, then we will go astray if we fail to recognize it and give it appropriate weight in our everyday lives. If something is not good for anyone, it might still have value and be worthy of choice by being, quite simply, good. I take this to be, in effect, what Kant believes about moral personality: because its activation in good willing is so great an absolute good, it should not be destroyed merely on the grounds that it fails to bring about what it strives to achieve. Recall his striking image: the good will "like a jewel, glistens in its own right, as something that has its full worth in itself." It must not be destroyed, so long as one can "summon...every means in [one's] power" to abide by the moral law, even if "with...its utmost effort it still accomplished nothing."[3]

1. *Groundwork for the Metaphysics of Morals*, p. 4:429 (author's emphasis). Kant also writes disapprovingly of suicide in his *Lectures on Ethics*. See the index to the edition edited by Peter Heath and J. B. Schneewind, translated by Peter Heath (Cambridge: Cambridge University Press, 1997).
2. *Groundwork for the Metaphysics of Morals*, p. 4:428 (author's emphasis).
3. Ibid., p. 4:394.

Let us, at least for the sake of argument, concede this much truth to Kant's claim that one's own happiness is not a sufficient grounds for suicide: a person who is living through a period of deep unhappiness, and who is justifiably confident that his suffering will not end while he remains alive, will be ignoring a powerful reason to remain alive if he fails to ask himself whether he might, in spite of his deep unhappiness, yet still be able to bring about much that is good for other people, were he to remain alive. He might also have reason to believe that if he is still able to exercise such virtues as compassion, kindness, and intelligence in his service to others, that would be good not only for others but also for himself. His virtues, in other words, and not merely his happiness are items that should figure in his judgment about whether anything in his future life will be good for him or others.

But Kant would not be satisfied if we affirmed only this much and no more. His thesis is that so long as we foresee that we will continue to *try our best* to abide by the moral law, then, whatever the likelihood of our thereby *achieving any results*—results that will be good for others—we ought not to commit suicide, because in doing so we will have destroyed something that is, in all circumstances, a good thing. The more plausible position, I believe, is that if one foresees that one's sincere moral efforts will accomplish little or nothing that is good *for* others or *for* oneself, perhaps because one's physical capacities are and will always be severely limited, and if one is justifiably confident that one will continue to be deeply unhappy for the rest of one's life, then the reasons to end one's life outweigh those that favor remaining alive. In these circumstances, one's rationality remains intact, but one's agency is nonetheless so ineffectual that one cannot actually produce what is good for others or for oneself. If, in addition, one's mind is filled with pain and anguish, life ceases to be worth living, even if one's moral will—one's sincere wish to be a moral person—is intact.

As we will see later (chapter 26), an argument similar to the one Kant gives against committing suicide on the grounds of one's own unhappiness has been used by justices of the U.S. Supreme Court to rule in favor of legal prohibitions of euthanasia. According to these judges, human life has intrinsic value and retains that value even when someone's continued existence, in an incurable vegetative state, does him no good and is costly to others. Absolute goodness, as we saw in our discussion of the parent who makes her child learn mathematics regardless of whether he will ever enjoy it (chapter 14), is an insidious category. It can be used, and has been used, to condemn acts that are entirely beneficial and in no way harmful. Of course, every concept employed in practical reasoning can be used to bad effect by someone who does not adequately understand it. But the seemingly innocent assumption that some things should be valued because they are, quite simply, good is inherently insidious, because we are so easily tempted to think of goodness, like beauty, as a reason-giving property. Goodness looks like a property that some things have and others lack; further, it seems as though it is always a reason in something's favor that it is good. Careful philosophical reflection is the only thing that can save us from these errors.

FOAG → don't committe suicide

Kraut → doesn't matter

Chapter 22

Future Generations

Let us turn now to the ethics of creating rather than destroying life. Suppose a man and a woman ask themselves: should we have a child? It would not be wrong or mistaken for them to take into consideration whether having and raising a child would be good for each of them. On the contrary, they ought to think in those terms—but not in those terms alone. It would be monstrous of them to pay no attention to the question whether any child they might have would live a life that would be good for *him* or *her* to live. It would be utterly selfish for them to raise a child whose life was likely to have little or nothing in it that is good for the child— even if being the parents of such a child were good for *them*. And it would be socially irresponsible for them to ignore the burdens and harms they would be imposing on their fellow citizens by bringing into the world a child who requires extraordinary medical attention or other social services. All of these factors pertain to what is good or bad *for* someone.

But is there still another consideration that they ought to take into account? Not what is good for them, or what is good for the child, or what is good for anyone, but what is good—period? They *must* include this value in their deliberations, if there is such a reason-giving property. And if absolute goodness provides reasons of more than negligible weight, then its production can be expected to compensate for the creation of much that has negative value—including the pain and suffering of the children they bring into the world. But it would, once again, be monstrous for a couple to think that they ought to have a child even though his life would, on balance, be bad for him, on the grounds that since much that is good (period), although not good for anyone, would be produced were they to have this child, that would compensate for the negative value of his unhappiness. A child is not to be brought into the world as an instrument to be used for the purpose of adding to the amount of absolute goodness in the world. The production of absolute goodness is not something to be thrown into the balance of considerations, as one factor among others, when we make decisions about whether to have children. Once that point is accepted, we must ask ourselves, why is that so? Is there something peculiar about the decisions we make about whether to have a family—something that would explain why factoring in absolute goodness is inappropriate in these circumstances, but otherwise appropriate? That seems unlikely. If there is no reason to think in terms of absolute goodness in planning a family, that is because there is no reason ever to deliberate in these terms.

A friend of absolute goodness might reject my argument on the grounds that it involves an incoherence and that the only way to think sensibly about the pros and cons of having a child is to use the concept of absolute goodness. The idea behind that objection is this: if a couple is merely thinking about having a child, then there is as yet no one whose good or bad they must consider, and there may never be (because they may decide not to have a child or they may be unsuccessful in their efforts to do so). No subject can be identified about whom it can be said: it is his or her good that is being talked about. So the only coherent question for a couple to ask, when they are thinking about having a family, is this: what are the various good things or bad things that would occur, were we to have a child? There is no one, as yet, for whom these things are good, and there may never be. But they can nonetheless ask, Would there be more pleasure in the world, were we to have a child? Would there be more pain?

So the friend of absolute goodness says, to coherently formulate the questions we ask about future generations, we need to think in terms of what is good or bad, but not good or bad for anyone.

To elaborate, suppose our couple resolves, after much reflection, not to have children for the sake of their own well-being. Further suppose that had they had children, those children would have had full and rich lives very much worth living. We cannot coherently say that it is bad for those children that they were never born. It is not as though there are potential children hovering over our world who are made worse off for not having been transferred from their shadowy, unreal world to that of flesh-and-blood human beings. Yet it is coherent to ask whether those parents were mistaken in their decision. Those who criticize our couple will say that they should have accepted a small loss in what is good for them to create a state of the world that has more good (period) in it. They failed to create as much of what is good (period) as they should have. If there was some reason for them to have children, it might seem that the only way in which this reason can be expressed is in terms of absolute goodness.

But an error is being made here. A couple that is uncertain about whether to have a child can nonetheless decide to undertake or refrain from certain actions because doing so would be harmful or beneficial to any child that they might have. A woman can, for example, refrain from taking certain drugs because, should she get pregnant, that would be bad for any child she would then have. Here her thought is not that the world would be a worse place, since it would contain less good. Rather, her thought is that should she have a child, it would be bad *for him or her*, were she to take this drug.[1] In having that thought,

---

1. In the case I am imagining, the effects of the drug on any child she might have are *entirely* bad: it has no good effects on a child at all, only bad ones. Of course, more complex cases are also possible. A woman might need to take a drug in order to get pregnant, but that drug might produce certain disabilities in any child she has. In that case, the drug has bad effects but

she cannot fairly be accused of positing a shadowy world of potential children waiting to be born and being subjected to injuries or favored with benefits. There is no one currently in existence whom she would be harming, were she to take the drug. She is not deluded about that. She is thinking of the condition of a child that *would be* born, were she to lead her life in a certain way, and since it would not be good *for* any child who would be born to her, were she to take this drug, she refrains. She can make her decision and coherently explain it without thinking in terms of absolute goodness and badness.

Similarly, if we think (correctly or incorrectly) that a couple we know should have accepted a small sacrifice in their well-being to have children because children brought up by such parents would have lived rich and happy lives, we can express our criticism by using the language of "good for" and do not have to posit the property of absolute goodness. We can say, "Had they had children, those children would have had many advantages, so many advantages that the slight disadvantages incurred by the parents would have been outweighed". There would, in other words, have been much that would have been good *for* any children they would have had. Our thought is not that the world would have contained more good in it. Rather, we are imagining the kind of children they would have had, and we are saying about them, "So much that is good for such children would have been given to them, and they would have done so much that is good for themselves." Admittedly, there is and will not be anyone for whom their decision is bad. But criticism often takes a subjunctive or counterfactual form: about someone who has died, I can say, I wish I had done so much more for him. Similarly, I can design a

---

might also have good ones as well: the disabilities are its bad effects (bad *for* the child), but these might—or might not—be outweighed by any components of her child's life that are good for him or her.

course with a view to the future good of any students who take it, even if I am uncertain whether anyone will enroll. (Among the students who might someday enroll are those who do not exist when I develop it. I ought not to lack interest in that potential audience.) And couples uncertain about whether to have a family can be careful about what they do, because should they have children, they want what is best *for them*.[2]

We believe that girls can be so young that they ought not yet have a child—that they should wait, for the good of any child they have, as well as for their own good, until they are mature enough, physically and emotionally, to have children. But suppose a girl does not take our advice and has a child when she is too young. We cannot say that it would have been better for that child, had her mother waited several more years before having a family. But we can say that had she waited, any child of hers would have had an advantage that her actual child lacks. It is not because we want there to be more of what is absolutely good in the world that we discourage young girls from having children. It is because we want whoever comes into the world not to be missing certain advantages.[3]

---

2. Similarly, we should assess our current energy policies by looking to future generations and asking, not whether they make it impossible for whoever is alive to have a quality of life that is just barely above the point at which a life is worth living, for this is too low a standard, but whether whoever is alive will have to endure, because of our policies, highly unfortunate conditions (premature death, disease, blindness, and so on)—conditions that would be bad *for* them even if on balance their lives would be worth living. We do not need to say that their premature death would be absolutely bad but not bad for them. I therefore believe that Derek Parfit does not need to posit absolute goodness to arrive at his conclusions in part 4 of *Reasons and Persons* (Oxford: Clarendon, 1984, reprinted with further corrections 1987). See, for example, his discussion of "The 14-Year-Old Girl" (p. 358) and "The Risky Policy" (pp. 371–372). My position is in accordance with the one proposed by Nils Holtug in "Who Cares about Identity?" in Melinda A. Roberts and David T. Wasserman, eds., *Harming Future Persons: Ethics, Genetics, and the Non-Identity Problem* (Dordrecht, Netherlands: Springer Verlag, 2009), pp. 71–92.

3. I take no stand here on this question: should parents who wish to do what is best for any children they might have in the future look to the total amount of what is good for their

Biodiversity

The existence of a great diversity of species seems to be a desirable thing. How much diversity? Perhaps the greater, the better. But it looks as though there is no creature, human or nonhuman, for whom this diversity is good. The cardinal I see in my garden is not benefited, instrumentally or noninstrumentally, by the fact that the number of biological kinds scattered around the globe and the differences among them are vast. Nor is any other creature. Animals, plants, and organisms are instrumentally benefited or harmed only by the specific features of the local environment they happen to occupy, not by general facts about the diversity of biological kinds throughout the world. Yet the diminution that has taken place in recent decades of the world's variety of living things is widely regarded as a matter of concern. Why so? One reason among others might be that the universe is simply a better place for having within it a great diversity of living kinds, even if there is no one for whom that diversity is

---

children or instead to the average amount? For example, a couple might have to choose between having twins soon or just one child later. What if each twin is likely to have slightly fewer benefits than that one child (but their combined benefits exceed that of the one child)? To say merely that the parents should consider what is good or best for their children does not answer the question. But what is needed to answer it is not the positing of a further kind of reason, namely, absolute goodness. Instead, the couple must decide which of two considerations is a weightier reason: having a family with the largest aggregate of good *for* their children or having one child who has as much of what is good *for* him or her as possible.

beneficial. It is a better place because biodiversity is, quite simply, a good thing.[1]

So it might be said, but I suggest that skepticism about this thesis is in order. One problem is that biodiversity might have instrumental value for human beings, and it is difficult to be confident that we can bracket our awareness of those potential benefits and still maintain our conviction that biodiversity is noninstrumentally good. Medical advances often come in the wake of our investigation of biological kinds, and the wider array of natural laboratories there are in the world, the better our chances will be of using plants and animals to provide medical, nutritional and other sorts of benefits to human beings.

Even from the point of view of theoretical knowledge pursued for its own sake, we have reason to regret that a smaller variety of subjects is available for students of the natural world to study. If scientific knowledge is good for human beings, the diminution of objects for us to study is bad for us. Students of the ancient Greek world lament the fact that so many texts have been lost to us, and in the same way, we are reasonably concerned that there are so many fewer species of living things to which our intellectual curiosity might lead us. Future generations of human beings who will, we hope and reasonably expect, take a direct interest in studying other species will have a smaller array of fascinating things to learn about.

Furthermore, we should not lose sight of the obvious fact that the lives of animals and plants can be (and in favorable circumstances are) good for those plants and animals. When a species reproduces itself, it brings into existence new individuals who are

1. See Dworkin, *Life's Dominion*, p. 75, on the intrinsic disvalue of the extinction of a species. He does not claim that the value of *diversity* explains why such extinction is to be avoided and regretted. But if one asks what is intrinsically bad about the death of an entire species, the distinctiveness of each species seems to have some bearing on the answer.

benefited (instrumentally and noninstrumentally) in many ways. And of course, when those offspring have more offspring, who in turn reproduce, and so on, the chain of creatures who are benefited goes on and on. All that comes to an end when a whole species dies out. There is nothing incoherent in the thought that this is regrettable. As I argued in the previous chapter, if a couple decides not to have children, it is not meaningless to say, "That is a shame, because the lives of any children they had would have been very good for them." Similarly, it is intelligible to say that the extinction of a species is regrettable on the same grounds: never again will there be creatures of this type, and so never again will good lives of this sort—lives good for those creatures—exist. We may express this idea by saying that the world will be a more impoverished place, because it contains within it less of what is good for its creatures. That thought uses the concept of what is good for someone, not the concept of absolute goodness. This is a reason to be worried about the extinction of a species that has nothing to do with diversity. But it is a reason to hope that a species will not become extinct and to take measures to keep that from happening. (All of this is compatible with the obvious thesis that some missed opportunities are more regrettable than others. For example, someone's refusal to benefit a large number of already existing creatures might be more regrettable—and more blameworthy—than his refusal to stop a chain of events that will keep a much larger number of creatures from coming into being.)

Someone might nonetheless say that he does not care whether an endangered species contains individuals whose lives are good or bad for them. He does not care whether any human being benefits from the existence of those individuals. He does not care whether anyone enjoys studying that species because it is fascinating. Rather, he believes that the species should remain in existence for this reason alone: there should be many different kinds of living things, the more, the better.

I find that an unappealing thesis. After all, we cannot plausibly say that the universe is a better place because it contains a variety of metals, inert gases, or semiconductors. If all the boron in the world were destroyed, that would not matter—unless boron has some instrumental value for some creature or other or is a fascinating object of human study. It would not be a matter for concern that because there is no more boron, the world contains a smaller variety of semiconductors. Variety in all its manifestations is not something that ought to exist. It would be arbitrary, then, to say that biodiversity should exist but semiconductor diversity should not, unless there is some reason why biological kinds, but not other kinds, should be various.

The more confident we are that the extinction of a species would or might involve a loss of what is good for someone—especially for humans but also for other living things—the more our confidence should grow that there is reason to prevent that loss. Variety for its own sake should not be our concern. In fact, we would have reason to be glad about the extinction of a species, if we could be confident that the members of that species would otherwise have had painful lives in which nothing good for them could be experienced. (Suppose a mad scientist has created a new form of life in order to torture the members of that new species. It would be best for those new creatures were their species to become extinct.) So we should reject this attempt to show that we need to think in terms of absolute goodness. It is not true that biodiversity is, quite simply, a good thing.

Chapter 24

Is Equality Absolutely Good?

Some philosophers hold that it should be a matter of concern or regret that human beings are unequal in certain respects, and they think that we should strive, with the help of laws and political institutions, to diminish these inequalities—if possible, to eliminate them. Not every inequality is troublesome, of course. If one person weighs more than another, they are unequal in one respect, but no egalitarian would be concerned just by that kind of difference between human beings. But when some people, through no fault of their own, are *worse off* than others, we might say, not implausibly, that this kind of inequality should not be and that, if possible, we should do something about it. So, at any rate, says the so-called luck egalitarian.[1]

The term "worse off" that I have just used must be understood in terms of differences in well-being, that is, differences in the degree to which people have what is good for them and bad for them. Someone who is born into extreme poverty, let us assume, is not only worse off than he would have been, had he been born with

---

1. See, for example, Larry S. Temkin, *Inequality* (New York: Oxford University Press, 1993), pp. 11–12. He proposes that, according to the most defensible form of egalitarianism, undeserved inequalities in well-being are in themselves objectionable; therefore, there is a reason to reduce them even when doing so is not good for anyone. See, too, his "Equality, Priority, and the Leveling Down Objection," in Matthew Clayton and Andrew Williams, eds., *The Ideal of Equality* (New York: St. Martin's, 2000), pp. 126–161; also Richard Arneson, "Luck Egalitarianism: An Interpretation and Defense," *Philosophical Topics* 32 (2004), pp. 1–20; G. A. Cohen, "On the Currency of Egalitarian Justice," *Ethics* 99 (1989), pp. 906–944. For criticism, see Elizabeth Anderson, "What Is the Point of Equality?" *Ethics* 109 (1999), pp. 287–337.

more material resources; he is also worse off than other people who exist. The resources those more fortunate people have are instrumentally good for them to have. The poor person, through sheer bad luck, has too few of those instrumental benefits, whereas those who are not poor have, through sheer good luck, much more that is instrumentally good for them. It is *that* kind of difference—a difference in what is good for or bad for people—that is thought by some to be objectionable. It is not merely that the poor have so little of what is good for them. What disturbs a certain kind of egalitarian, in addition, is that the poor have so much less of what is good for them than others do.

What bearing does this issue have on the question we are investigating here: should we value certain things because they are, quite simply, good? None, I think. But that answer needs defense, because we might be tempted to suppose that if the egalitarian I just described is right, then equality of well-being is, quite simply, a good thing.

Notice that this sort of egalitarian claims that there is a reason to favor certain measures—namely, those that make well-being more equal—even when they are good for no one, for there are two ways to put people on the same level. First, we can level up. That is, we can make those worse off than others less so by giving them more of what is good for them. Alternatively, we can level down. That is, we can make those better off than others less so by taking away some of what is good for them. So far as *equality* of well-being is concerned, both measures achieve the same result. Suppose that circumstances are such that the only way to achieve equality, or to reduce inequality, is to level down. One kind of egalitarianism holds that there is a reason to level down. That thesis leaves room for the concession that, all things considered, we should not level down when doing so takes away too much of what is good from those who are better off. But at any rate, says this form of egalitarianism, there is a reason to do so.

It must be emphasized that were we to level down, no one would become better off than he was before. The only change that would occur, with respect to what is good or bad for people, is that some will have less of what is good for them. So it might seem that the luck egalitarian must press his case for equality by asserting that equality of well-being is intrinsically a good thing. We do not produce what is good *for* anyone when we level down, but, he says, equality is a good thing (period). What is the reason we should level down? Because we must attend not only to what is good for people but also to what is absolutely good, and because equality is absolutely good. Since I am doubtful that absolute goodness is a reason to value anything, it seems that I must deny what this sort of egalitarian affirms.

I do not find egalitarianism of this form to be a plausible doctrine. There is no reason, I believe, to make some people worse off merely to bring their level of well-being somewhat closer to that of others. But I will not defend that claim, or argue against this form of egalitarianism here, because the more important point, for my current purposes, is that it is not the absolute *goodness* of equality that this doctrine must insist on, but rather the *justice* of equality. Egalitarianism, after all, is in the business of telling us what just distributions and just relationships involve. It starts from the assumption that institutions ought to be justly arranged and that people are obligated to treat each other justly, and it then proposes a theory of what justice consists in: equality of well-being. The egalitarian might be tempted to say, "Justice is a good thing (period). It consists in the equal distribution of what is good for people. Sometimes it requires taking away what is good for some, even though doing so is not good for anyone. That is, sometimes we must do what is good (absolutely) even though doing so is not good for anyone." But that temptation can easily be resisted because the claim that justice is absolutely good is doing no real work in this argument.

To call an act, law, institution, or person unjust is already to make a negative evaluation, just as to call a painting hideous is already to speak of it unfavorably. As I argued earlier (chapter 16), we do not need the assumption that beauty is a good thing to have a reason to look at beautiful paintings. Similarly, I add here, we do not need the assumption that justice is a good thing to have a reason to seek it. To acknowledge that a social ordering is just is to acknowledge that there is at least that much reason to favor it. It would be a mistake to suppose that there is, in addition, a second reason to favor it, namely, that, being just, it is also absolutely good. One can say, if one likes, "Justice is a good thing." But if one speaks this way, one must be careful not to suppose that this sentence identifies a reason in favor of justice—namely, its goodness. If one does make that supposition, then one must say either that the justice of an arrangement is by itself no reason in its favor or that there are two reasons in favor of any just arrangement: its justice and (by virtue of its being just) its goodness.

If I stop smoking cigarettes because smoking is bad for me, I already have all the reason I need for what I am doing. I do not have to show that by doing what is good for me, I am doing something that is absolutely good. It would be a mistake to say that my attempt to justify my action has not begun, or has not been completed, unless I ground what benefits me in absolute goodness. Similarly, if a parent notices that he has recently been favoring one of his children over another, he ought to alter his behavior because unequal treatment is unfair, and he ought to be fair in his distribution of benefits to his children. He ought to do as much good for one as for the other because that is what justice requires. In some circumstances, he might, on grounds of fairness, stop giving a benefit to one child, even though this does not make the other child better off. Similarly, a certain kind of political egalitarian thinks equality of well-being is so important that it requires us, in some circumstances, to favor a social arrangement that makes some worse off but no one better off. If there is any basis for accepting that policy of leveling down (and I doubt that there is), it is that what is good for people ought to be justly (and therefore equally) distributed, not because an equal distribution of what is good for people has a further feature, namely, that it is good.

Chapter 25

The Value of Persons and Other Creatures

Friends of absolute goodness might say that *persons* are among the items that are valuable, not as means to something else, but in themselves. (For simplicity of expression, I will write as though all human beings are persons, and all persons human beings.)[1] It is widely accepted that not all living things have the same moral status because persons are, in some sense that needs to be elucidated, more precious and more worthy of our devotion, respect, and con-

---

1. I am using "human being" in the nontechnical sense employed by ordinary speakers of English. The closest term used by anthropologists refers to the only extant species within the genus *Homo*, namely, *Homo sapiens*. The human beings discussed in this chapter have the enlarged conceptual repertoire that is typical of creatures that are full-fledged language users.

cern than certain other forms of life. It would be misleading at best to express this point about our moral status by saying that every person is good (or absolutely good) because that might be taken to mean that every one of us is a good person—and no one can reasonably believe that. That problem can be avoided by saying that every person is valuable and that persons are valuable to a higher degree than are certain other living things. A friend of absolute goodness might think that just as certain *states of affairs* are absolutely valuable—someone's knowing mathematics, someone's feeling pleasure, someone's having as much well-being as another—so certain *objects* also have absolute value: persons.[2] These different kinds of values call for different sorts of response: pleasures are to be sought and welcomed in recognition of their absolute value, whereas the value of persons (including bad people) calls for respectful attitudes and actions that fulfill our moral duties to them. Nonetheless, according to this way of thinking, there is a single property that is shared by both pleasures and persons: both are, quite simply, valuable. And that is not the same property as their being good *for* someone.

If all persons have the property of being valuable, what accounts for this? An answer that finds favor among many philosophers, and is emphasized by the Kantian tradition, is that we, unlike the rest of the natural world, are self-governing beings. You and I and other readers of this book can recognize the cogency of reasons and can be moved by them, whereas other creatures are governed by instincts, passions, and passing desires. Of course, those other living things have all sorts of other powers, but however impressive we may find them, we should not make the mistake of thinking that

---

2. Joseph Raz, for example, speaks of sensual pleasure, perceptual pleasure, beautiful sunsets, human freedom, and persons as "valuable in themselves," although I am not sure whether he writes as a "friend of absolute goodness" in my sense. See *The Practice of Value*, p. 34.

those animal powers are *absolutely* good. They are often good *for* the animals that have them, not good period. We alone have reflective freedom—the freedom to shape our lives in the light of reasons— and this makes us special because, regardless of whether that freedom is good *for* us, it is, quite simply, good.

The idea that we are special and that other forms of living things, including sentient creatures, belong to a lower moral category is reflected in what we tolerate in the treatment of animals but would not tolerate in the like treatment of persons. Many people, for example, favor carefully controlled experiments on mice, even if those experiments are bad for those animals, provided that they are well designed to alleviate or prevent a great deal of human suffering. Injecting cancerous cells into mice and thus shortening their lives seems to be justified, if such experimentation is likely enough to benefit us and if the benefit it provides is large enough. But we would never tolerate such experimentation on people. Why so? It seems plausible to reply that there is a valuable property that belongs to persons that entitles them to protection against being used in this way. That property is their capacity for reflective freedom. It must be a valuable property; otherwise, it would not play a justificatory role. If human beings were merely different from, but not in some way better than, other creatures, our differentiating features would have no moral significance. So it might be thought that we need the concept of absolute goodness for this purpose. Reflective freedom, or whatever it is that places us into a higher moral category, must be something that is good *simpliciter*.

Many of us kill insects because we want to avoid being bitten by them. To keep ourselves from being stung by a wasp, we would take its life. But when I kill a mosquito or a wasp, I bring about one of the worst things that could happen to it. Were I to allow myself to be bitten, that perhaps would have been bad for me, but only slightly so. The sting of the wasp would have been quite painful, but in a day or two, the pain would have been gone. How can I justify doing something so bad for the wasp when this averts something that is not very bad for me, something that is far from being the worst thing that could happen to me? Again, we may be tempted to find an answer in the idea that an insect is not an intrinsically valuable entity, whereas a human being is. We might suppose, in other words, that there is something that persons have but insects lack, a property whose value does not consist in its being good for us, but simply in its being good. We guide our interactions with our fellow human beings by properly valuing that property; since a wasp lacks it, we are free to kill it merely to prevent ourselves from being stung.[3]

But we need to be careful here, because the reflective freedom that we possess and other living things lack does not entitle us to treat them in any way we please. We must be attentive to what is bad for them and how bad it is for them, and we must take steps, when we can, to avoid or minimize the harm we do them. If, for example, I could, with a little effort, open the window and let the wasp out of the room rather than kill it, it would be wrong for me not to do so. Even though it lacks the capacity for rational freedom, I must consider

3. It is unclear whether bees, wasps, and other insects (there are several million species in this taxonomic class) have some form of phenomenal awareness or can feel any form of pain. Do they process sensory information without having conscious experience? If they lack any form of subjectivity, the loss that befalls them when they die may not be as great a loss as occurs to those nonhuman animals that do have some conscious awareness of the world. For discussion, see Sean Allen-Hermanson, "Insects and the Problem of Simple Minds: Are Bees Natural Zombies?" *Journal of Philosophy* 105 (2008), pp. 389–415. I thank Jon Miller for this reference. I assume that if we can easily protect ourselves against the harms of bees and wasps without killing them (by opening our windows and letting them out of our houses), we should do so for their sake. But readers who disagree because they think that such animals lack subjective awareness should change my examples. We can agree that when squirrels and raccoons are nuisances and we can easily rid ourselves of them without killing them, we should do so.

what is good or bad for it. Similarly, if experiments designed to alleviate human suffering could be performed without using laboratory animals or without causing them pain, they should be, even if they are more costly or time-consuming. Sometimes our treatment of farm animals makes them suffer greatly, and what it provides for human beings, aside from corporate profits, is harmful to us—poor nutrition and disease. In these cases, the way human beings treat animals is unjustified because the benefits we reap are too small to justify the harm we do them. But in other cases, we justifiably inflict some harm on them because in doing so the benefits we can offer to human beings are large enough (and cannot be achieved in less harmful ways). So it is undeniable that in considering our treatment of each other and of other creatures, we must use the concept of what is good *for* someone: we must attend to what is good for human beings, as well as what is good for nonhumans, and we must use good judgment in balancing these factors against each other. The question we must ask, then, is whether, to treat human beings and other living things properly, we need to advert to absolute goodness as well.

In our interactions with other people, it would be morally wrong to treat them in ways that ignore the fact that they are beings who respond to reasons. We owe it to others, in many circumstances, to offer a cogent case, one that addresses their rational faculties, for the things we do that have consequences for their lives. Why is that? I do not find illuminating the answer "because self-governance is quite simply good." A more promising answer, I suggest, will build on the idea that it is good *for* people, both instrumentally and non-instrumentally, to fashion their own lives in accordance with their knowledge of their distinctive personalities and circumstances. Often the best judge of what is best for an adult is that very adult, because whether something is good for him frequently depends on the specific details about his situation that he is specially qualified to know. (When, however, we foresee that they will be poor judges, we have reason to nudge them away from their errors.)[4] So the moral requirement that we offer justifications to others when our actions impinge on their lives is a way to make it more difficult for people to impose on others, out of benighted good will, a conception of what is good for them that is unsuitable to their situation. It also puts an obstacle in the way of those who set out to harm others: when an explanation must precede adverse action and must be offered to those who would be injured, the potential victims have a forum— not necessarily an effective one but nonetheless one worth having— in which they might lead those who have power over them to reconsider. Even when coercion is justifiably used against someone, he is better off when he is given some explanation of why he is being so treated than he would be were he coerced but given no reason. He is thereby included in the community of those whose reasonableness is recognized, and because that sincere acknowledgment from others, when perceived as such, is a form of friendship, however attenuated, it is something that is noninstrumentally good for people to receive. The message conveyed in such interactions is that "you are someone worth my while to address." It is good for people to receive that message, even when it is not made explicit but is tacitly conveyed by the way they are addressed.

Needless to say, we do not treat other animals in this way because it would be of no use, to them or to us, even to attempt such a thing. They cannot shape their own lives or be given assurances that they are part of a larger interactive community that includes human beings. Explanations offered to them would fall on deaf ears. But we can and should treat other living things in a way that accords with

---

4. I use the word "nudge" to bring to mind the social policies advocated by Richard H. Thaler and Cass R. Sunstein in *Nudge: Improving Decisions about Health, Wealth, and Happiness* (New Haven, CT: Yale University Press, 2008).

their nature and is attentive to their good. To treat many kinds of animals properly, we need to know what makes them suffer or ill. That is the analogue, for those animals, of treating human beings in a way that is mindful of their reasoning capacities and the benefits of exercising those capacities.

I do not mean to deny that people have a greater value than do other living things. The problem is how to explain what it means to talk of greater value here and how to defend that claim of superiority. Here, too, I believe that no light is shed by employing the concept of absolute goodness. A friend of that concept might say, "We, by virtue of our reflective freedom, have absolute value, and since no other living thing has that capacity, they all lack absolute value." But we have already seen that nonhuman creatures cannot be treated as though they were mere things. They, like us, have interests. When we can easily avoid killing the wasp by opening the window and letting it out of the house, we should. If there are methods for developing new drugs that benefit human beings without making animals worse off, we should adopt them, even if we would save money by instead experimenting on animals in ways that make them suffer. These ideas about what we may or may not do to nonhuman creatures rely on comparisons we make between what is bad for human beings and what is bad for those other lives. We say that this disease is so bad for human beings that the harm done to these animals is an acceptable cost. Or we say the opposite: the prospect that good would come to us as a result of these experiments is so low that the harm done to animals would be an unacceptable cost. In either case, we believe that we are not talking nonsense. We assume that meaningful comparisons between what is bad for us and what is bad for other types of creatures can be made. But that common assumption can be questioned, and so we must look more carefully at these interspecies comparisons of benefits and harms.

Let's begin with the simple and undisputable assumption that the benefits that belong to a single individual admit of degrees. Some things that are good for me are not as good for me as other things that are good for me. That point applies no less to noninstrumental than to instrumental benefits. To give an example of a meaningful comparison of noninstrumental benefits: it would be less bad for me to lose the ability to enjoy the taste of carrots than it would be for me to lose the capacity to enjoy the worlds of sound and color. For our purposes, what matters is that such a statement is intelligible, not that it is true, but if it is true (as it seems to me), then it must also be intelligible.

But can we also meaningfully compare, with respect to the size of benefits, not only two items within a single life but also two items that belong to two different individuals? Let's stay with the same sort of example. Suppose one person loses the ability to enjoy the taste of carrots. That is bad for him. A second person loses the capacity to enjoy the worlds of sound and color. That is bad for him. Is what is bad for one worse than what is bad for the other?

Someone might protest: "That question makes no sense. There is no such thing as what is bad for one person being quite simply worse than what is bad for another person. Talk of 'worse' must be relativized. What is bad for the first person is worse *for him* than what is bad for the second. Similarly, what is bad for the second person is worse *for him* than what is bad for the first."

The grain of truth in this protest is that each individual might prefer that, should misfortune occur to one or the other, it befall the other rather than himself. But it is wildly implausible to suppose that we cannot make meaningful interpersonal comparisons between the size of benefits and harms. Smoking cigarettes might do no harm at all to one person, might be only slightly bad for a second person, and might be extremely injurious to a third. Here we are speaking about the instrumental effects of a single type of activity. But what lies behind these statements are further judgments about what is noninstrumentally bad for people. Suppose smoking causes one person to lose his ability to enjoy the taste of carrots but causes another to lose his capacity to enjoy the worlds of sound and color. One of them has suffered a greater loss than the other. Something bad has happened to the first, and something bad has happened to the second. But there is a difference: what is bad for one is not so bad for him when it is compared with what is bad for the other. Bad things that happen to different people can be compared with each other with respect to how bad they are for the ones to whom they occur. More simply put, some human disadvantages are worse than others. Likewise, some human benefits are greater than others.

But do comparisons between the sizes of benefits and disadvantages cease to make sense when they involve individuals who belong to different species? So it might be supposed. The idea would be that to speak of what is good to a certain degree for a human being presupposes a standard of well-being for human beings, whereas to speak of what is good to a certain degree for a wasp (for example) presupposes a different standard of well-being. From this, it might be inferred that although we can say how good something is for a human being and how good something else is for a wasp, we cannot ask whether one of these benefits is larger than the other. We can say that the death of a wasp is bad for it, in comparison with the many other sorts of things that might happen to a wasp. Similarly, we can say that the death of a person is bad for that person, in comparison with the many other sorts of things that might happen to him or her. But can we meaningfully say that one of these deaths is a worse harm than the other? Not according to this way of thinking.

Two points can be made in reply, one small, the other large. The small point is that comparisons can be meaningfully made even when two different standards are used. For example, we can make sense of this statement: "this watermelon is a better watermelon than that poet is a poet." A watermelon might be the best-tasting watermelon ever, and a poet might write nothing but bad poetry. Its distance from the top, when judged by the standard appropriate to watermelons, is zero. His distance from the height of poetic excellence is huge. That does not mean that the watermelon is a better object than the poet is; there is no such thing as being a good object. But it meets the standard of watermelon excellence more fully than he meets the standard of poetic excellence. Similarly, we can meaningfully say, "This wasp has a more flourishing life for a wasp than that human being has a flourishing life for a human being." That would be the case if the wasp is doing as well, for a wasp, as a wasp can, and the human being is faring very badly, when its life is assessed against the standard of flourishing for humans.

But that leads to the larger point, which is that we can meaningfully ask not only how well an individual member of a species is faring in comparison with other members of that species but also how good a life any member of that species can have in comparison with the lives of the members of *other* species. It makes sense to say, "It is living as well as a wasp can, but the advantages it has are not as good for it as are the advantages of a human being who is living as well as a human being can." The idea expressed by this sentence is that the advantages that can accrue to a lucky wasp might be small in comparison with the advantages that can accrue to a fortunate human being, even if they are large in comparison with the advantages that are possessed by some less fortunate wasp. That thought does not deny that when we speak of what is good for a wasp, we must have in the background some standard of what it is for the life of a wasp to go well. But according to my way of thinking, our need to make such judgments against the background of a standard applicable to wasps does not make it impossible to understand what is being asserted when cross-species comparisons are being made.

When we ask whether a wasp is a large wasp, we compare it with other members of its species and invoke a standard of physical size that is appropriate for that kind of creature. Our doing so does not keep us from comparing the size of that wasp with the size of other types of living things or physical objects. It can be a smaller physical object than a human being, even though it is large for a wasp. What is true of assessments of physical size is also true of assessments of the quality of a life. It is meaningful to say that the capacities of some species are impoverished in comparison with those of other species. How desirable a life is for a creature, how good for it its natural capacities are, is determined not only by how fully it uses its inherent capacities but also by the richness or poverty of those capacities. (A creature whose affective life is inevitably thin and shallow has a less rich experience than does a normal adult human being and so lacks a good available to us. Its life is diminished by the meagerness of its experiential world.)[5] Not only is it intelligible to say but also it seems true that there is more to be gotten out of the life of a typical human being than there is to be gotten out of the life of a wasp. So even if a wasp fully uses its capacities and we use ours much less fully than we might, our lives can be good for us to a higher degree than the lives of wasps are good for

---

5. See Jerome Kagan, *What Is Emotion? History, Measures, and Meanings* (New Haven, CT: Yale University Press, 2007) for an extended discussion of the dissimilarities between many human emotions and those of many (perhaps not all) animal species. "The possible sounds that varied musical instruments can produce might be a useful metaphor to capture the different capacities for emotions across animal species. Pianos can generate many more patterns than kettle-drums" (p. 38). I take him to be making an empirical point about the experience of different species (just as a comparison of the sound waves made by pianos and by kettle-drums would be an empirical description). To say that the piano has the richer sound is both to describe and evaluate that instrument; in the same way, to speak of the greater richness of human experience is both a description and an evaluation.

them. What we are born with is better for a creature to be born with than what a wasp is born with.[6]

When a wasp dies, that, in comparison with much else that can happen to it, is quite bad for it. But how bad for it is it, when that is compared with the badness of human pain for the human being who feels it? Are we too quick to kill other living things merely to avoid the small inconveniences that tolerating them would bring us? It may be difficult to answer these questions. But what matters most, for our current purposes, is that these are not meaningless questions.

There is, as I have said, something to the idea that human beings are special and that other forms of living things, including sentient creatures, belong to a lower moral category. But to speak meaningfully about the distinctive value or preciousness of human life, we do not need to make use of the concept of absolute goodness. We can instead compare what is good for us and what is good for other sorts of living things and meaningfully say that the things that are good for us—love, friendship, civility, respect, music, poetry, science, philosophy—exemplify the relation of being good for someone more fully than do the things that are good for wasps, mice, or mosquitoes. What is best for them is not as good for them as the best things in human life are good for us. If we have to choose between the two, there are reasons to work for the good of our own species rather than that of another. Our interest in human well-being

---

6. I am not here addressing a question raised by Jeff McMahan in *The Ethics of Killing: Problems at the Margins of Life* (Oxford: Oxford University Press, 2002), chapter 2, section 5 (pp. 145–165). He wants to know by what standard we should assess how well the life of a particular human being or any other animal is going. Should we compare that individual's fortune with the norm that prevails for members of that same species? Or should we instead compare the individual's fortune with the fortunes it would possess were it to live up to that individual's full potential (regardless of how its life compares with that of other members of the same species)? My question is different: does it make sense to say of some human beings that they have better lives than some (or all) members of some other species? I think the answer is yes but that does not answer McMahan's question.

can be justified and is not a mere bias that results from our membership in the human species. It is the relation, good for, that stands behind this comparison, not the property, good.

Imagine that a pilot realizes that her plane will soon crash. It is headed toward a heavily populated area, but she has enough control over its direction to divert it to a nearby forest that is the home to no human beings but to many birds and less complex forms of life. Unquestionably, she ought to have the plane crash in the forest rather than in the city. Why so? Not because of the physical fact that she has a closer genetic affinity to those who live in the city. Not because the taxonomy employed by biologists places her in the same group as those who live in the city. Not because those who live in the city are alleged by philosophers to have a special property that all other living things lack: intrinsic value. As I see it, she should divert the plane from the city to the forest because she ought to bring about as little harm as possible. She must choose between harming birds and harming human beings, and according to my way of thinking, when normal human lives are cut short, the harm done is great in comparison with the harm done when the lives of normal birds are cut short. There are things those people would have had that would have been very good for them to have, in comparison with the things that would have been good for those birds. The concept expressed by "good for" is what the pilot needs to use to justify her diversion. She does not also need the concept of absolute goodness.[7]

7. The sort of case I discuss in this paragraph does sometimes occur, but suppose we consider one that is more far-fetched: A pilot must choose between crashing into the house of an elderly man (who presumably has only a few more years to live) and a forest filled with thousands of chimpanzees, monkeys, and other primates. Is the smallness of the amount of future good that this person has (because of his advanced age) a factor that ought to figure in the pilot's decision? I think so. Might his good be outweighed by the good that can be done by saving the many primates from death? I think it might. If the number of primates saved is sufficiently large and the length of life of the human being sufficiently small, then the plane should be made to crash into his house rather than the forest. But my principal

The ethical principle that we should choose the least harmful of our options, when all other things are equal, is uncontroversial. If animals are likely to die as a result of what we do, we should at least see to it that the number of deaths is minimized. Similarly, if we foresee that human beings will die as a result of our actions (for example, when we decide to build new highways and thereby increase the number of road accidents), we should do what we can to minimize the number of deaths (by making these roads as safe as is feasible). And when there are trade-offs to be made between human lives and the lives of other living things, we again need to minimize the amount of harm we do. One of the factors we must take into account is how bad it is for a human being to die in comparison with how bad it is for members of other species to die.

If you continue to believe, despite what I have said, that these cross-species comparisons are somehow illegitimate, your resistance to my arguments may arise from a substantive theory you tacitly hold about what it is that constitutes the good of various kinds of creatures. Surely you would reject the suggestion that the way to assess how good a life a kind of creature has (in comparison with other kinds) is to see how fast it can move through space in an hour's time. By this bizarre standard (one that will nonetheless be illuminating, for our purposes), very fast animals have better lives than slow animals. Moving through space quickly is what is good for all animals, and some animals have this benefit to a higher degree than others. We all know that this is an utterly implausible theory of what is good for a creature. But someone who entertained this idea would still be thinking meaningful thoughts. His theory would be false but not nonsense.

---

thesis regarding this dilemma is that absolute goodness should play no role in the pilot's decision.

Hedonists have a less crazy way of comparing what is good for members of diverse species. They will say that the animals that feel the most pleasure—as measured by intensity, duration, purity, and perhaps other parameters—have the best lives. If hedonism is construed as a theory about what is good *for* someone, it will say that what is good for a human being and what is good for a member of a different species can be meaningfully compared. It may be difficult to know the answer to the question "Do human beings experience more pleasure than elephants?" But that would nonetheless be a meaningful question, and the answer to it, perhaps unknowable, would provide an answer to the equally meaningful question "Is what is good for an elephant (pleasure) as good for it as what is good for a human being (pleasure)?"

Here is a different thesis about what is good for any living thing: being in good physical health. What will this theory say about the good of human beings in comparison with the good of the members of other species? Suppose George is a human being in perfect health and Spot is a dog in perfect health. George has a great advantage and Spot has a great advantage, but is one of these advantages larger than the other? Perhaps the answer is no. When we say that George is in perfect health, we use a standard of excellent physical condition that is appropriate for human beings. (He does not have to be good at sniffing his food to be healthy.) The standard we use when we pronounce Spot to be in perfect health is different: it is tailor-made for the life of a dog. Even so, I doubt that we would be failing to utter a meaningful sentence were we to say, "Human beings can be healthier than dogs." That sentence asserts that a human being who is in perfect health is healthier than a dog who is in perfect health. Someone might believe that. He might hold that the physical condition that accounts for human longevity is healthier than the physical condition that accounts for the smaller longevity of dogs. What makes for longevity, on this theory, is a constituent of health, and the longevity of the members of different species can easily be compared. Accordingly, the perfect health of a human being would be a healthier condition than the perfect health of a dog, and if what is good for creatures is constituted by physical health, healthy human beings would possess something that is better for them than what dogs possess when they attain what is good for them.

You might admit that it is *meaningful* to compare what is good for a human being to what is good for a dog, with respect to how great these benefits are, but that all such theories are *false*. Your idea would be that a true theory of what is good for someone must take the following form: to determine what is good for an individual, we must take note of the biological kind to which he or she or it belongs. If that individual is a human being, we use a standard of what is good for human beings that is appropriate for that species. If that individual is a dog, we use a standard appropriate for dogs, and so on. We say that some human beings do better than others with respect to the standard of what is good for human beings; some dogs do better than other dogs with respect to a canine standard; and so on. But we reject as false all comparisons across species.

That would be an arbitrary and dogmatic approach to our subject. There is no reason to rule out in advance the possibility that cross-species comparisons between the well-being of members of different species might be not only meaningful but also true. Whether they are true depends on the answers we give to many substantive questions: What is good for human beings? What is good for dogs? For pigs? For bats? And so on. When we have answered these questions, and only then, we will be in a position to know whether the benefits that constitute the good of human beings are even better for them than are the benefits that constitute the good of the members of other species.

greater goods)

argument

(commit to goodness simpliciter)

My own view is that there is a richness in human life at its best that is not equaled in the lives of other animals at their best. We can compare our mental lives with what our scientific theories and best commonsense conjectures tell us about the mental lives of the members of other species. Many animals, like us, are cognizers; many of them have something at least faintly akin to some of the emotions and sensations we feel (anger, fear, pleasure, pain). The correct standard, I believe, for judging whether our lives can be better than others is the degree to which we and they flourish as cognizing and feeling creatures. It is not implausible to suppose that our mental powers and the depth of our emotional lives outstrip the intelligence and feeling of other living things, and for that reason the things that are good for us are greater goods than are the things that are good for other kinds of creatures. That is why the pilot in my example is justified in diverting her plane so that it crashes in the forest and not the city.

Needless to say, not everyone believes that human life has this kind of superiority. Some hold the reverse view. Keats envied the happy lot of the nightingale who sings of summer in "full-throated ease," "pouring forth [its] soul...in such an ecstasy," knowing nothing of "the weariness, the fever, and the fret" of human life, a life in which "but to think is to be full of sorrow and leaden-eyed despairs," a life in which we are "born to death," as the "hungry generations tread [us] down."[8] Would Keats say that the pilot should therefore divert her plane to the heavily populated city in order to spare the nightingales in the forest? That is a horrible thought, and that shows, I think, that something is amiss in his pessimism. His mistake does not lie in his assumption that it is *meaningful* to speak comparatively of the lot of

8. "Ode to a Nightingale."

[handwritten annotations: "Commitment", "goodness, period?", "to", "It is okay to kill wasps-", "Kant"]

human beings and that of other creatures. He is right about that—after all, we understand his comparisons and are moved by them. If he is mistaken, that is because he underestimates the possibility that human beings, in favorable circumstances, can live in a way that is very good for them and also because he overestimates the quality of the lives of nightingales. (For further discussion of the value of humans and other animals, see appendixes A and B.)

[handwritten annotations: "w.l", "max", "H.L", "max", "(possibly not the only comparison)"]

Chapter 26

Euthanasia

I would like to call attention, as I did when I referred to Kant's opposition to suicide (chapter 21), to one of the practical consequences of our discussion. The intrinsic value of human life was cited in a 1990 decision of the U.S. Supreme Court (*Cruzan v. Director, Missouri Department of Health*) as one legitimate basis on which a state can forbid medical personnel from withdrawing life-sustaining support from a patient who has fallen into a persistent vegetative state. According to Justices Rehnquist and Scalia, even when it is contrary to the interests of those who are in this condition to continue to live, a state can legitimately prevent others from letting them die or killing them, because human lives have intrinsic value. As Ronald Dworkin reports their opinions, they held that "it is *intrinsically* a bad thing when anyone dies deliberately and prematurely." The lives of human beings "have intrinsic value. even if it is not in their *own* interests to continue living."[1]

The concept of intrinsic value being employed here is what I have been calling absolute goodness. As Dworkin says, "Something is intrinsically valuable...if its value is *independent* of what people happen to enjoy or want or need or what is good for them."[2] He describes it as a "commonplace" notion, one that "has a central place in our shared scheme of values and opinion.... Much of what we think about knowledge, experience, art, and nature, for example, presupposes that in different ways these are valuable in themselves." But Dworkin does not himself "recommend or defend any of these widespread convictions about art and nature" and allows that they may be "inconsistent superstitions."[3] His goal is rather to point out that the category of intrinsic value (or absolute goodness, as I have been calling it) is part of a widely used conceptual framework. Many people, he notes, put great art, the preservation of a species, or knowledge into this category. Rehnquist and Scalia hold that a state may legally use this category and prevent the termination of life on the grounds that it is good (period) for life to be sustained, even when this is good for no one. If they are asked, "What reason is there to keep Nancy Cruzan alive, even if doing so is not good for her, and her continued existence is costly to others, psychologically and financially?" they can reply, "Because it is good." Here the concept of absolute goodness is used to justify a medical policy that is not even alleged to be good for anyone.

The conviction of some people that human life is intrinsically valuable is sustained by their further assumption that other living things have less value or none at all. It is not life per se that is thought

1. *Life's Dominion*, p. 12 (author's emphasis).
2. Ibid., p. 71 (author's emphasis).
3. Ibid., p. 81.

by many to be valuable (otherwise it would be wrong to cut down a tree), but human life—or human life most of all. I have been arguing that there is something to this idea: many of the things that are good for human beings are good for us to a higher degree than are the things that are good for other creatures. That is not an easy idea to understand or even to express. (I had to struggle, in the previous chapter, to formulate it.) It is far simpler to entertain the thought that human life is intrinsically valuable. When God created light, he saw that it was good—but Genesis does not say that it was good *for* someone. Similarly, some hold that when we create human life, we create something that is good, whether it is good for anyone or not. Thinking along these lines can easily lead to the conclusion that suicide, assisted suicide, and euthanasia are wrong. To assess the cogency of the reasoning of the U.S. Supreme Court regarding the permissibility of euthanasia, we must decide whether absolute goodness is a reason-giving property. Our topic is not merely of academic interest.

Chapter 27

The Extinction of Humankind

One further practical implication of these reflections should be mentioned. At some time in the future, the human species will come to an end. The laws that govern the matter of our universe make this inevitable, but it is an event that may occur far sooner than need be.

This is a catastrophe that even we or our children may see looming for those who are alive several generations later. What reason would there be, in those circumstances, to take preventive action? Do earlier generations have reason to thwart a doomsday that will occur not to themselves, nor to any children or grandchildren they have, but to still more distant generations?

I earlier upheld the intelligibility of regrets about a couple's not having children and about the extinction of a species (chapters 22 and 23). About a childless couple, it is not nonsense to have the thought: "That is a shame, because the lives of any children they had would have been very good for them." Similarly, I claimed, we might regret that a species has become extinct, because in that case the world "contains within it less of what is good for its creatures." My principal claim there was simply that these thoughts are *intelligible*, not that they are true. But now I add that *these* further claims are not only intelligible but also true: when some species become extinct, there is little to regret, because what is good for some creatures is good for them only to a small degree, but should the human species become extinct millions of years before the nature of matter kills it off, that would be a catastrophe that makes all previous catastrophes pale in comparison.[1]

Who would be affected by that catastrophe? To begin with, those who are members of the last generation of human beings would be made worse off, if their lives would continue to be worth living, because those good lives would be cut short. But in addition, if doomsday is postponed by millions of years, then as a result a

---

1. For a contrasting view, see David Benatar, *Better Never to Have Been: The Harm of Coming into Existence* (Oxford: Clarendon, 2006). He argues that "it would be better if humans (and other species) became extinct. All other things being equal, my arguments also suggest that it would be better if this occurred sooner rather than later" (p. 194). The crucial premise of his arguments is that coming into existence is always a harm.

great many other human beings—those who belong to any of thousands of generations—will be alive, and if their lives are good for them, they will be the beneficiaries of the battle waged by an earlier generation against the premature extinction of humankind. As I have argued, the things that are good for human beings are very great goods for those human beings, in comparison with the benefits that other living things possess. We should want others to have those goods, and the strength of our desire should be commensurate with the magnitude of those goods. We should not care just about the generation to which we belong.[2]

But if we ask, "Which other human generations should be the objects of our concern?" any finite number that we specify in our answer (the next five generations, the next five hundred) would be arbitrary. It would be a form of stinginess, a failure of generosity, not to want good human lives to go on and on, in the only way in which this can happen. Of course, those who join together to prevent the extinction of the human race that would have occurred in a few hundred years (had they not acted) have no *personal* connection to those who later come into existence as a result of their actions. They do not know whom they are benefiting. That is because when they act, there are not already beneficiaries of their actions. But there will be. Admittedly, those future beneficiaries will realize that, had doomsday not been postponed by the measures taken by an earlier generation, they (the beneficiaries) would not have been harmed. But "do no harm" should not be the only maxim that regulates our treatment of our contemporaries or the future condition of the

2. A difficult question that I am leaving aside has to do with the relative strength of the reason we have to help future generations of human beings come into existence in comparison with the importance of helping people who are already alive. What if we must choose between these alternatives? Does the fact that people already exist give greater urgency to the need to help them? I think it does, but I do not explore that issue here.

world. We should also do what is or will be good for others, simply because it is or will be good for them.[3]

3. My views bring me into disagreement with Jeff McMahan, who holds, in *The Ethics of Killing*, that "the goods in a person's possible life provide little or no reason to cause him to exist" (p. 300). He also holds that "the expectation that a person's life would be worth *not* living *does* provide a moral reason *not* to cause that person to exist" (ibid.). The resulting asymmetry, he notes, "is notoriously difficult to defend" (ibid.). In a later essay on this question, he concedes that there is a moral reason to create lives worth living. See "Asymmetries in the Morality of Causing People to Exist," in Melinda A. Roberts and David T. Wasserman, eds., *Harming Future Persons: Ethics, Genetics, and the Non-Identity Problem* (Dordrecht, Netherlands: Springer Verlag, 2009), pp. 49–68.

Chapter 28

The Case against Absolute Goodness Reviewed

It is time to review the arguments we have been examining, and to take stock. If some things should be valued because they are, quite simply, good, we should be able to say with some confidence what they are. But every nomination of an item for this category has encountered difficulties. The problem is not that whenever some people call something good, others say that it is bad (or that it is intermediate in value) and that such a dispute cannot be rationally resolved. We have not, in other words, been asking, "How can we know which things to classify as good rather than bad"? The problem, rather, is whether this classificatory scheme of the absolutely good and the absolutely bad is necessary or useful. I have suggested that it might even impede good practical thinking. Once it is granted that we cannot dispense with the concepts of what is good for someone and what is bad for someone, it is doubtful that we need absolute goodness and badness as well. Thus far, we have found that these concepts shed no light. When we think we ought to undertake some action, hold some belief, or feel some emotion, we can give a fully adequate explanation of why we should do so without using the concepts of absolute goodness or badness. That way of using these concepts can only distort our thinking.

Can pleasures be evaluated? Yes, some of them are good *for* those who feel them, and *that* is why they are to be welcomed. Are some pains bad *for* us? Yes, some of them are bad *for* those who feel them, and *that* is why they should be shunned. But are pleasures *also* to be assessed as good (period) and pains as bad (period)? There is no need to. Someone who never counts pleasure as absolutely good or pain as absolutely bad will never go wrong. How can the goodness of pleasure be a reason to welcome it, if it can always be ignored? Ditto for pain. That is the problem of double value.

Should mathematical knowledge, or any other branch of knowledge, be pursued because it is good? If it is instrumentally or noninstrumentally good *for* someone to acquire expertise in some field, that is a reason for him to do so. But should discoveries in a field of study be sought and knowledge of the field disseminated not because doing so is good for anyone, but simply because that field of research should flourish? Those who impart knowledge for that reason are open to criticism: people are not mere instruments to be used for the creation of value. That is the ethical objection to absolute goodness: it depersonalizes our relationships.

Is there a reason to create or preserve things of beauty, regardless of whether anyone observes them? Moore believed so, and he assumed that the reason must be that beauty is good and therefore ought to exist. But even if we accept the disputable thesis that the world is a better place when it contains things of beauty regardless of whether they are observed, we have no reason to infer that this is because whatever is beautiful is also good. The world that contains beauty is perhaps a better world, but if so, that is because it contains beauty; that is all the explanation that would be needed for its superiority. We do not have to posit the existence of goodness to explain why some states of affairs are better than others.

A human being who is unable to or has no opportunity to delight in the observation of beautiful things is certainly missing something that should not be missed. Moore rightly affirms the value of our enjoyment of beauty. But are we to value beauty because in doing so we add to the sum of good things in the universe? It is more plausible to say that we should spend a pleasant day in the museum for our own sake, not because we thereby make the world a place that contains a greater amount of good. For the same reason, when we strive to preserve works of art for future generations, the best account of why we should do so is that this will be good for everyone who will enjoy them. The preservation of cultural treasures is not to be defended on the grounds that it prevents the number of absolutely valuable things in existence from diminishing, but because fine work can, in the right conditions, be beneficial: appreciating such treasures constitutes an enrichment of our lives.

Moore is also right to affirm the value of the enjoyment of affectionate human relationships. But no ethics of friendship can dispense with the concept of what is good for someone. A good friend is willing to make some sacrifices in his own well-being for that of a friend. There are benefits as well in being a good friend—and not only instrumental benefits. When you enjoy the company of a friend, that is noninstrumentally good for you; being cut off from the fellowship of others is, by itself, bad for you. We do not spend time with friends because doing so is, quite simply, good, but because it is good *for* us and our friends.

Kant uses the concept of absolute goodness when he says that a good will is unconditionally good. He does not mean that having a good will is beneficial; it is good without necessarily being good for anyone because its value shines forth even when it does not achieve the results for which it strives. But if what someone of good will tries to achieve is good *for* another, that psychological orientation calls for praise because what he aims at—something beneficial—is something he ought to aim at. We need not use the concept of absolute goodness to acknowledge the point that virtuous actions can deserve praise even when they do not succeed. Moral philosophers who want to convince us that we need to think in terms of absolute goodness need first to show us that something other than the virtues is absolutely good, if they want to reach the conclusion that the virtues are good.

When a couple decides not to have children, there is no child for whom their decision is bad. If we think that they would have been good parents, we might be tempted to be critical of their decision and to express this by saying that the world would have contained more good (period) in it, had they had a child. But a criticism of them need not employ the concept of absolute goodness. Instead, we can say that they decided badly because any child of theirs would have had great advantages.

We are rightly concerned about how many kinds of creatures have become extinct in recent times, but it is implausible to suppose that our concern must be based on the premise that when the universe contains a greater variety of species, there is more goodness in it. If the diversity of living forms were not good for anyone, its diminution would not be regrettable.

When some people have a lower degree of well-being than others through no fault of their own, is something amiss, even if that inequality brings no harms in its train? If the answer is yes, that is not because equality of well-being has a further feature—namely, the property of being absolutely good. Luck egalitarians can say that there is this reason to regret a state of affairs in which one person is worse off than another through sheer misfortune: a state of affairs in which they are equally well off would be better. Why better? Because justice consists in equal well-being—not because one state of affairs has more goodness than the other.

Are persons, in comparison with other living things, peculiarly or uniquely valuable? They can ask themselves what they should do and how they should feel; no other creatures can do that. But the idea that our species is in this way not merely different from but superior to others need not rest on the premise that there is such a thing as absolute goodness or value, and that we alone have it. We must be mindful of what is good *for* other living things, and we must harm them only if the harm is small enough in comparison with the benefits we would achieve. Positing the existence of absolute goodness does not help us think about what our relations should be with other creatures or with each other.

Putting these thoughts together, my conclusion is that we have good grounds for doubting that absolute goodness is a reason-giving property. If I am right about that, we can go further and may well wonder whether there is any basis for supposing that such goodness is *any* kind of property. We should keep in mind the obvious point that sentences need not ascribe properties to have sense. "Here is the book" was my example in chapter 1: it does not ascribe hereness to the book (there is no such property), but relates the book to a location supplied by the context. So if I say, "Here is your book" and "here is your cup of coffee," I am not saying of the book and the cup of coffee that they have some property in common: their hereness. Instead, I am relating these two items to something else: to your vicinity. Similarly, if someone says that pleasure, beauty, knowledge, virtue, and friendship are all good things, we need not take that to mean that they have some property in common (as all green things have greenness in common): namely, their goodness. He might be merely asserting that these various sorts of things bear a certain kind of relationship to other sorts of things: people have reason to value pleasure, beauty, and the like. If he insists, however, that this is not how his statement is to be construed but affirms that pleasure, beauty, and the like share in the property of goodness (even though this is not a reason-giving property), the proper response to him will be that there is no reason to believe that there is such a property.

We have seen (chapters 16 and 17) that evaluative comparisons between states of affairs—one of them being called better than the other—need not be based on a prior judgment that one more fully exemplifies the property of goodness than the other. Admittedly, there are comparisons that do have this structure: when one object is greener than another, that is because both have the property of being green, and one of them more fully shares in that property than the other. Similarly, the more beautiful of two beautiful songs has, to a higher degree, the property of being beautiful. But not all relations are grounded in properties in this way. When one box is larger than another, that is not because both have the property of largeness, one more so than the other. A large box is not made such by its sharing in the property of largeness; it is large-for-a-box, not large (period). To call a box large is to advert to a *relation* it has to some standard for the size of boxes; it is not to advert to the *property* of being large. (There is no such property.) Similarly, when we say that a certain state of affairs—someone's dying quickly and painlessly, for example—is a good thing, we can be taken to mean that it is better than some other salient state of affairs (in this case, his dying slowly and painfully).[1] It would be odd to suppose that something else is being said here: that dying quickly and painlessly has the property of being a good thing and that because it possesses that feature, it is a better state of affairs than other ways of dying. It is *only* by comparison with other ways of dying that it can be judged a good thing. Sentences that speak of some event or state of affairs as good (period) are not thereby devoid of meaning, but (to repeat) sentences need not ascribe properties to have sense. When "good" means "better than," it invokes a relation, not a property.

I earlier suggested (chapter 5) that positing the existence of absolute goodness stands to ethical theory as positing the existence of phlogiston stands to physics. The point of that comparison is that we must engage in ethical reflection, not merely in semantic analysis, to reach a sound conclusion about whether some things have the property of being, quite simply, good and whether their possession of that property is a reason to value them. The arguments I have given so far have that character: they appeal to our understanding of what counts as a good reason for acting in certain ways and having certain kinds of feelings. But I have not yet addressed the question whether speaking of absolute goodness is also *semantically* problematic, as some philosophers have argued. If they are right, my analogy between absolute goodness and phlogiston is not apt. We must now return to this piece of unfinished business.

---

1. I borrow this example from Dean Pettit, "The Semantics of 'Good.' "

Chapter 29

The Problem
of Intelligibility Revisited

Recall that according to Geach, Foot, and Thomson, it is unintelligible to say that pleasure is, quite simply, good (chapter 5). Like me, they hold that there is no useful role for absolute goodness to play in our thinking, but their way of reaching this conclusion is not the one I have taken. They think that if someone says that pleasure is good, we cannot understand him, because he has unwittingly violated a rule governing the use of "good." As a result of this mistake, what he says is neither true nor false but meaningless. Admittedly, the sentence "Pleasure is good" seems, on the surface, to be saying something. But speakers who are otherwise competent users of a language can take themselves to be saying something meaningful when, in fact, they are not. We have become accustomed to hearing this sentence and others like it ("knowledge is good," "virtue is good"). They occur frequently in philosophical texts. Perhaps our familiarity with them keeps us from asking ourselves whether we understand what they are saying. Perhaps we do not understand the Bible when it says, in Genesis, "God saw the light, that it was good." Just as we are baffled by what could be meant by someone who says that smoking is just plain bad (not bad for anyone), so we might ask, "How can light be just plain good?"

I think there is something to what these philosophers are saying. As I noted (chapter 8), if someone were to say, "smoking is bad," meaning by this not that smoking is bad for certain people, but that it is, quite simply, bad, we would be puzzled. Our immediate reaction would be not to agree with him nor to disagree with him, but to express bafflement. The statement "George is good" would produce the same reaction, if the speaker insists that he does not mean that George is a good person, good at chess, or good to talk to, but that George is just plain good. (Let's assume that he also denies that he means that George, being a human being, and therefore capable of reflective freedom, has intrinsic value and must be treated accordingly.) Since these sentences seem to lack meaning, it is tempting to think that Geach and those who follow him must be right. The sentence frame "X is good," we might suppose, is a producer of unintelligibility. Once we see how puzzling "George is good" and "smoking is bad" are, we should realize that "pleasure is good" is no more meaningful than they. We cannot intelligibly say of anything "it is good" unless we are speaking elliptically and the context supplies or we stand ready to add further words ("it is good for you" and the like).

How might friends of absolute goodness reply? Their best strategy, I think, is to propose that "smoking is bad" and "George is good" are false, not meaningless. They have a list of things that are good and a list of things that are bad. They are prepared to argue, case by case, that each of those items belongs on their list. But smoking is not on the list of things that are, quite simply, bad, nor is George on the list of things that are, quite simply, good. So if anyone were to make either of those claims, he would be wrong. Friends of absolute goodness who adopt this strategy are free to agree with us that we would be baffled by anyone who said that smoking is bad or that George is good. They can say that what baffles us is how anyone can sincerely believe and assert these statements. It should be obvious to everyone that the objection to be made to smoking is not that it is bad *simpliciter* but that it is bad for so many people. How can someone be so confused as to think that there is an additional criticism to be made of smoking, beyond its instrumental disadvantages—namely, that it is bad? It should be obvious, in other words, that "smoking is bad" is false. We would not understand *the person* who denies what is obvious by saying that smoking is not only bad for people but also bad (period). But it would be a mistake to infer that that we would not understand *the sentence* he utters. We see that it is false, and so we do understand it.

These friends of absolute goodness can continue their defense by asking us to state the linguistic rule that is allegedly violated by statements of the form "X is good." Suppose we reply that the rule is: "Do not claim of anything that it is good *simpliciter*." We would have to justify our claim that the violation of this rule produces unintelligible statements, but what would our justification be? We would have to appeal to examples: "George is good," "smoking is bad," and the like. These, we would say, are meaningless sentences, and so, too, are "pleasure is good" and "pain is bad." But if that is the justification we propose, we cannot expect the friends of absolute goodness to accept it. They claim that all of these sentences are meaningful; some of them are true, and others false, and so they must be meaningful.

Thomson proposes this generalization about what we may intelligibly say using the term "good": It is intelligible to say that A is good in a respect but unintelligible to say of A that it is good, but not good in any respect.[1] One way to speak of something as good in a respect is to say that it belongs to a kind (it is a chair, an apple, and so on) and that it is a good member of that kind (a good chair, a good apple, and so on). But there are many other ways to call something good in a certain respect. To give some of her examples: "A is good at doing crossword puzzles." "A is good for England." "A is good to look at." "A is good with children." But if one says, quite simply, "That melon is good—not a good melon, but a good thing,"

1. *Normativity*, p. 6.

one would be producing nonsense.[2] Similarly, she thinks, to speak as Moore did of pleasure and other items as good *simpliciter* violates the rule that whatever is good is good in some respect.

But friends of absolute goodness will ask why we should suppose that *all* goodness is goodness in some respect. Much of it certainly is—but all? A melon is not good *simpliciter*, but pleasure is. So say the friends of absolute goodness. Thomson would be begging the question against them were she to reply that "pleasure is good" is unintelligible because it violates the rule that all talk about what is good must assert that something is good in some respect.

Just as such statements as "smoking is bad" are perplexing—should we say that they are meaningless, or rather that they are false?—so, too, doubts can be raised about how to understand certain statements of the form "A is a good member of kind K." Suppose we are taking a walk in the woods and our companion points to the ground and asks, "Is this a good twig?" Or suppose he points to the sky and asks, "Is that a good cloud?" Twigs and clouds are perfectly good examples of kinds of things. Even so, we have no idea what is meant by these questions until further information is provided. Is our companion asking whether that twig is good for kindling? Or good for some other purpose he has in mind? Does his question about the cloud have meteorological import—is he asking whether it is likely to bring rain? Or is he planning on making a sketch of the clouds and asking whether that one will make a good subject? If he denies any such interest and insists on being told whether this twig and that cloud are good, should we say that his question lacks sense? Or that since no standard for the evaluation of these things has been supplied, and because such statements as "this is a good twig" and "this is a bad twig" presuppose the existence of

2. Ibid., p. 17.

some such standard, they are false?[3] In either case, we would not infer that because "this is a good cloud" is problematic, any statement of the form "A is a good member of kind K" is also problematic. The difficulty of understanding "this is a good twig" does not arise from the sentence form of which it is an example. Analogously, the friends of absolute goodness may claim that the difficulty of understanding someone who says that smoking is bad does not indicate that the sentence form of which it is an example is one that always produces nonsense. They claim that pain is, quite simply, bad. That should not keep them from agreeing that we would be puzzled by other statements of the form "A is bad."

3. Ziff, *Semantic Analysis*, p. 210, considers a number of similar cases: "That is a good dewdrop; that is a good pebble; that is a good chill." Thomson, citing Ziff, proposes that some kinds are not what she calls "goodness-fixing kinds." Toasters are; pebbles are not. See *Normativity*, pp. 22–24.

Chapter 30

Attributive and Predicative Uses of "Good"

Geach and Thomson believe that Moore makes a terrible mistake about the word "good." In their words, he failed to see that it is an "attributive adjective" rather than a "predicative adjective." What they mean is this: Moore says near the beginning of *Principia Ethica* that when someone speaks of good conduct, a good book, or any good thing, he is using a complex notion that must be taken apart.[1] To understand what good conduct is—surely one of the principal tasks of ethical theory—we must separately look at those two things: goodness and conduct. Goodness is the property that all good things—a good book, a good act, a good man—have in common. It follows from Moore's way of thinking about goodness that even the mundane judgment that something is (for example) a good toaster can be analyzed as containing two independent subclaims: first, it is good; second, it is a toaster. But as Geach saw, that is a mistake. To call something a good toaster is to evaluate it *as* a toaster. It is to compare it favorably with other toasters. To evaluate it in this way is not to attribute to it first the property of being good and then also, as a separate matter, the property of being a toaster.

Geach makes the further point that there are other sorts of adjectives that do combine with nouns in this aggregative way. His example is "That is a red book."[2] Here two independent points are being made about the subject of the sentence: it is red, and it is a book. It is not as a book that it is being described, when it is called red. Suppose the object in question has had all of its pages removed and is being used as a stage prop. (This is not a supposition Geach asks us to make, but it brings out his point.) Is it still a book? No matter: it remains true that it is red. Regardless of whether it is a red book, it is a red stage prop. Adjectives that combine with nouns in this decomposable way Geach calls predicative, whereas adjectives that combine with nouns as "good" does he calls attributive. The mistake Moore makes, he says, is to assume that "good" is a predicative adjective, like red. It is instead an attributive adjective, like "big." And be believes that once Moore's mistake has been exposed, his

1. See sections 1 through 4, esp. pp. 54–55.
2. "Good and Evil," p. 64.

ethical theory collapses. Moore insists that our actions must bring about as much goodness as possible, but Geach thinks there is no such thing as goodness. "There is no such thing as being just good or bad, there is only being a good or bad so-and-so."

Let's agree, at least for the sake of argument, that Moore does make the mistake of which Geach accuses him. It is, at any rate, a mistake to hold that being a good book consists in having two separate properties—being good and being a book. Similarly, being a large flea does not consist in having two separate properties—being large and being a flea. When we call a book good or a flea large, we are using "good" and "large" attributively. But Geach may nonetheless be mistaken in his further thesis that because Moore made this error, his entire moral philosophy is discredited. What is important for Moore and for friends of absolute goodness in general is that "good" is *sometimes* used in meaningful sentences as a predicative adjective. Some things are just plain good, they claim. They can agree that the word "good" is not always used in that way; it also functions as an attributive adjective. But they can reasonably ask: why can "good" not have two legitimate uses? When something is called a good toaster, the speaker is not attributing to the toaster the property of being good, but, say the friends of absolute goodness, when someone calls pleasure good, what else could he be doing but attributing to pleasure the property of being good? Why suppose that such a speaker is not making sense? Geach can impugn the meaningfulness of the statement "pleasure is good" only by assuming that because "good" operates as an attributive adjective in some sentences, it cannot operate predicatively elsewhere. But he offers no argument for that assumption. Friends of absolute goodness say that such sentences as "pleasure is good" seem meaningful to them—in fact, they think that some of these sentences are obviously true. Geach tells them that without realizing it they are speaking unintelligibly, and his argument is that *other* statements using "good"—not the ones that friends of absolute goodness most care about—make an attributive use of that adjective.

That Geach's argument is flawed in this way is, I think, undeniable. One of the merits of Thomson's discussion of this issue is that she recognizes as much. She says: "It is certainly not impossible for an adjective to have two uses, only one of which is attributive."[3] She then explains this possibility by means of an example suggested to her by Matthew Hanser.[4] The adjective that illustrates her point is "famous." Used in one way, "famous" is an attributive adjective, like "good" and like "large." Suppose A is a famous novelist who also happens to be a tennis player. We cannot infer that he is a famous tennis player, for to say that someone is a famous K is to say *only* that it is *as* a K that he is famous. We are not attributing two independent properties to someone when we say that he is a famous poet; rather, when we say this, we are ascribing to him a single property: fame as a poet.

But as Hanser notes, we also say of someone that he is just famous (period) without meaning to assert that there is something that he is famous *for*.[5] He might simply be well known because his name and face have been broadcast widely. When we say that someone is famous in this way, we are not using "famous" as an attributive adjective.[6] Someone would be missing the point we are

---

3. *Normativity*, p. 13.

4. Ibid., p. 14.

5. Of course, to be famous is always to be famous among a certain audience: those to whom the individual's name or reputation has spread. One way of being famous (to a certain group) is to be known for something; another way of being famous (to a certain group) is to be known (period).

6. We read "he is a famous native of Boston" to be attributing to the subject two independent properties: having been born in Boston and being famous. That is because we assume that being born in Boston is not the sort of thing that brings fame. If we say of the same subject, "he is also an American citizen," then it follows that he is a famous American citizen, for being an American citizen is also not something that brings fame. Such sentences ("he is a famous native of Boston," "he is a famous American citizen") are most naturally understood to be silent on the question whether the subject is famous for anything.

making, if we told him that A is famous, and he insisted that A cannot simply be famous, but must be famous for something or other. Our response to such an objection would be this: one way to be famous is to be famous for something; when that happens, one is not only well known but also known for some further feature one has. But another way to be famous is simply to be well known, without being known for any feature that one has.

Friends of absolute goodness will claim that since some adjectives evidently have both an attributive and a predicative use, nothing stands in the way of our accepting the thesis that "good" also exhibits the same duality. They say that in addition to such properties as being a good tennis player, being good to one's children, or being good for people, there is the property—possessed perhaps by pleasure, or knowledge, or virtue—of being just plain good. Certainly the fact that the former properties exist hardly shows that the latter property does not. Perhaps Geach assumes that if there is such a thing as being just plain good, then being a good tennis player would be decomposable into being good and being a tennis player. But that assumption is unwarranted: it is like saying that if someone can be just plain famous (and not famous for anything), then being a famous poet would be decomposable into being famous and a poet.

Thomson sees that she must say something to show that "good" is not like "famous" in having both an attributive and a nonattributive use. Here is how she tries to establish that the two words are not alike in this respect: "What assures us that 'famous' does have this second use is that we know what the property of being (simply) famous *is*—it is the property of being (simply) well known. What is the property that Ross claims is ascribed to knowledge, or pleasure, by a philosopher who says 'That is good' of it?"[7]

---

7. *Normativity*, p. 14 (author's emphasis).

That question is intended to have rhetorical force: Thomson means to say that we do *not* know what that property is, and she thinks we lack that knowledge because it is not there to be known. But that is a different complaint from the one she makes when she says that talk of what is good but not good in any respect is *unintelligible*.[8] If the objection to positing absolute goodness is that we do not know what it is, then its friends may reply that we need to think more imaginatively or clearly about it. The problem may reflect our limited understanding and nothing more. To dismiss that suggestion, Thomson needs to show that we already can see, by consulting the way the word "good" is used, that there is nothing for us to inquire into, when we propose to inquire into absolute goodness, because no sense can be made of such talk. We *cannot* know what is good but not good in any respect, because there is no such property, and we can see that there is no such property by reflecting on the conditions that must obtain if our talk about good is to be intelligible. The inscrutability of what is simply good—the difficulty we have in understanding it—would then be explained by the unintelligibility of ascribing mere goodness to anything.

I am doubtful that successful arguments against the friends of absolute goodness can be found, if, like those of Geach and Thomson, they bypass the question I have been posing in this investigation: what work can be done with the concept of absolute goodness in moral philosophy? I have not demanded that the friends of absolute goodness tell us what that property is. They can easily reply to that question by giving examples of the things they take to be good: pleasure, knowledge, and so on. Goodness, they may say, is a primitive concept: it cannot be analyzed further into better under-

---

8. "Unintelligible" is her term; ibid., p. 17.

stood concepts. (They might add that beauty, too, resists such an analysis, but we learn to recognize it, and it gives us reason to respond appropriately to things that possess it.) We can best understand goodness, they will suggest, by becoming aware of the important role it plays in justifying what we do and how we feel.

That idea can be made more concrete. Recall the argument rehearsed on behalf of the friends of absolute goodness in chapter 3. Think about such simple and innocent pleasures as the sensations one feels as one sits in a nice, warm bath or the pleasure of eating a delicious peach for which one has developed an appetite. Do we not seek and welcome such pleasures because we look upon them favorably? Do we not look upon them favorably because we think a reason can be given in favor of pursuing them? Can we not subject them to some sort of evaluation, on the basis of which we pursue and welcome them? And having agreed that they should be favorably evaluated, would it be mistaken to express our evaluation of them by saying that these experiences are, quite simply, *good*? How else are we to convey our positive evaluation of these pleasures, if not by calling them good? Why suppose that anything else needs to be said of them, as an explanation of why they are to be valued, beyond affirming them to be good?

Those questions seem reasonable to me. The answer I have given is that it is more illuminating to evaluate these sensations by saying, not that they are good, but that they are good *for* us. Why is that more illuminating? To answer that question, we have investigated a wide range of human experiences and moral phenomena, asking ourselves in each case: do we understand it better by thinking about it with the help of the concept of absolute goodness? I suspect that there is no shorter way to answer the question with which we began: are there things we should value because they are, quite simply, good?

APPENDIX A

Killing Persons

It is tempting to think that when one person plans to kill another, there is always at least this much to be said against his doing so: the one he proposes to kill is a *person*. What makes someone a person—rationality, self-consciousness, a certain kind of freedom—are not just any old features, like height or hair color; they are *valuable* properties and are, for that reason, to be given their due in our deliberations. Acknowledging their value in our actions consists in observing various rules that constrain the way we treat persons.

But suppose an attacker is culpably threatening to kill me, without provocation. His attack is imminent, and killing him is my only means of defense. In this case, it is permissible for me to take his life. Yet he is still rational, self-conscious, and free. If it was true before he plotted against me that he had value because he had these properties, then it remains true that he has value when I take his life. His having value, evidently, is something I can discount or entirely set aside in my deliberations in such a situation.

Of course, I have value, too (if he does). But my justification for killing him cannot *simply* be that I have value. After all, he, too, has value, and that does not give him any justification for intending to take my life.

Should we say, then, that *part* of my justification for killing him is that I have value? I do not see any reason for thinking so. It is sufficient to say that I am permitted to defend myself against wrongful attempts on my life and may kill my attacker if doing so is my only means of defense. In fact, it muddies our understanding of the situation if I advert to my value as a human being, because doing so simply invites the response that he has value as well, presumably no less value than I do. The fundamental feature of the situation is the asymmetry in our relationship: he has full responsibility for putting us into this life-or-death struggle, and I bear none; he is culpable for attacking me, and I have done nothing to merit that attack; he has made himself liable to being killed, and I have not.[1] There is no gap in my explanation of why I may

---

1. See Phillip Montague, "Self-Defense and Choosing among Lives," *Philosophical Studies* 40 (1981), pp. 207–219; Michael Otsuka, "Killing the Innocent in Self-Defense," *Philosophy and Public Affairs* 23 (1994), pp. 79–94; Jeff McMahan, "Self-Defense and the Problem of the Innocent Attacker," *Ethics* 104 (1994), pp. 252–290; and David Rodin, *War and Self-Defense* (Oxford: Clarendon, 2003), pp. 50, 56, 70, 79, 89. I am grateful to Jeff McMahan for these references.

defend myself if I fail to mention that I have value. Talk of the value of personhood does no work in this situation.

Why is it such a serious wrong on his part to attack me? Why is killing a human being such a serious business? The best explanation, I believe, will include the fact that to kill someone is to make it impossible for him ever again to do anything that is good for himself or others; it also makes it impossible for anything that is good for him ever to happen to him. The continuation of a life is a precondition for all the future advantages that come to him and from him; no benefits come to or from one who no longer exists; a life cannot go well in any respect when it is over. Those same points help explain why it is wrong to kill, for the sake of mere commercial gain, a gorilla, an elephant, or a dolphin. The goods that members of these species can enjoy are considerable, and so it is also a serious business to kill them (although not as serious as killing human beings). It is a far graver matter to kill these psychologically and socially complex creatures than it is to take the life of those far simpler animals who have sensory and signaling systems and can feel pain but, unlike primates, form no attachments, engage in no conflict resolution, undertake no parental activities, and undergo no cognitive or social development.

Let us return to a person's right to defend his life, even to the point of killing his attacker. Suppose the person attacked is near the end of his days, and he realizes that this is so. He has said his good-byes, settled his affairs, and is merely waiting for the end. As he sits quietly in his room, a young man enters and, mistaking the old man for someone else against whom he has a grievance, threatens to kill him. The old man may have to kill his attacker to save his life, and he is morally permitted to do so. But it does not follow that he would be justified were he to invoke his right of self-defense. In fact, we can easily think of the situation in a way that makes the old man wrong to kill his attacker in self-defense. If he kills the young man, he wins for himself only a few more days of life—days that would be spent idly waiting for death. But he takes from the young man a life that is likely to contain a great deal of what is good for him. It is certainly permissible for the old man to refrain from killing in self-defense; if he does refrain, forgiving his attacker for his grave offense, he merits admiration. If he is justified in showing such restraint, the explanation has nothing to do with the value of rational freedom and everything to do with the comparison just noted between the small gains he would win for himself by killing in defense and the large loss he would impose on his attacker.

Notice, incidentally, that the right to defend oneself can be invoked to justify killing not only one attacker but also several. If two intruders set upon me and will kill me unless I kill them, it is permissible for me to do so. My relationship to each of them is asymmetrical in the way described three paragraphs ago: each has made himself liable to being killed by me, but I have not made myself liable to being killed by them, individually or collectively. Nonetheless, the numbers count. It is not as defensible for me to kill two attackers to save my life as it is to kill one. If you have any doubt about that, consider what you would say in the following case: suppose thousands of people joined together to take your life (*just* your life—no one else's), and your only means of self-defense required setting off a bomb that will kill them all. Can you be justified in bringing about such massive destruction simply to save your own life? I doubt it. And if my doubt is justified, then we should say that with each increase in the number of lives you must take to defend yourself, the justification for killing in self-defense diminishes in strength. As the number who must be killed grows, it becomes more tempting to say that killing others merely to save oneself is unjustified. You should not do something extraordinarily harmful to others—extraordinarily bad *for* them—to save your life, because the good you do for yourself by saving your life eventually becomes too small to justify causing so great a harm. The asymmetry that exists between your innocence and their culpability can do only so much justificatory work; at some point, the importance of not doing what is bad to other people tips the scales in favor of allowing yourself to be killed. (If their culpability is diminished, that, too, tips the scales.) Here, once again, we apparently have no need to invoke something called "the value of persons" to think our way through the example. That would be a third factor to consider, in addition to the two we have recognized: the amount of good and bad for people that is done by killing and the moral asymmetry between culpable attackers and innocent victims. There seems to be no work for such a third factor to do.

I turn now to one further case of killing, but in this example the right to defend one's life against attack is not at issue. It is a case in which established social norms do not allow killing, even if it would be highly beneficial for the killer and only slightly harmful to the person killed. A son visits his old and ailing father in the hospital. His father has not lost his personhood: he is fully rational, cogent, and self-aware. The father knows, as do his doctors and family, that he has at best a few hours to live. Most likely, he will die in his sleep that night. He has been a terrible father to his son: he has regularly bullied and mocked him and never shown him the least affection or kindness. The son has not fared badly in his life, but his father's hostility continues to disturb him, and he is hoping for some words of kindness from him, or an apology, in this last encounter. But instead, his father once again bitterly curses his son. The son leaves his father's room in anger and sorrow, but later that night, he returns and disables the medical equipment that would have kept his father alive a few hours more. He deliberately kills his father in anger, but it is not blind anger. He thinks, not unreasonably, that this act of vengeance will be cathartic and therapeutic. He will henceforth think of himself as his father's killer, not merely his victim. His hatred for his father will not fester for the rest of his days; his mind will be emptied of that poison. Let's assume that he is right about that. He succeeds in ridding himself of a burden that would have weighed him down for the rest of his days. He benefits enormously from this murder. The father has lost a few hours of life, dying, as he sleeps, late at night rather than at dawn.

Was it morally wrong for the son to kill his father? Did he act wrongly but excusably? Or perhaps not wrongly? I will set those questions aside. Rather, what I would like to suggest is that regardless of whether what the son did was morally wrong, he did not commit as *great* a moral wrong as do other murderers. There are, in other words, murders that are far greater offenses than this one—if his act was wrong at all. We are not forced to choose between two characterizations: either his act was not morally wrong at all or it was equal in wrongness to every other wrongful killing.[2]

That is a modest proposal, and if it is right, then the fact that the father is a *person* does not have the significance we might have supposed it has. Recall that the father's rationality is in no way impeded or diminished. If this is a property that has great value whenever it is instantiated, then the father's personhood has that same full value. But when the son kills his father, that is only slightly wrong—if it is wrong at all. The value of personhood, if there is such a thing, is the same in the father as it is in any other rational being. Its value does not vary in degree from one person to another. Since the value of the father's personhood does not make killing him seriously wrong, the value of *anyone's* personhood does not explain why killing that person would be seriously wrong.

2. For an excellent and sympathetic treatment of the thesis that the wrongful killing of one person is always as wrongful as the wrongful killing of another, see McMahan, *The Ethics of Killing*, pp. 232–265. My view accords with that of Kasper Lippert-Rasmussen, "Why Killing Some People Is More Seriously Wrong Than Killing Others," *Ethics* 117 (2007), pp. 716–738.

APPENDIX B

J. David Velleman on the Value Inhering in Persons

Why is it important to care about what is good for someone?

That question might occur in an ordinary conversation between two speakers who have a particular person in mind. A knows that B has been devoting himself to the care of C but wonders whether C is really worth all that attention, so A asks B, "Why should you care so much about what is good for C?"

But that question can also be understood in a different way: it might be meant as a general challenge to our normal assumption that the category of what is good for someone should play an important role in our practical reasoning and our attitudes. We usually take it for granted that in certain situations we should care about what is good for people, or at least for certain people. But stepping back from this engagement with the needs and interests of others (as well as our own needs and interests), we can ask: why should we?

Here is one possible answer to that question: what is good for persons is important because (and only because) persons have *value*. The idea is that evaluative statements of one sort (those that advert to the beneficial and the harmful) have practical significance only when and only because evaluative statements of a different order (those that advert to absolute value or goodness) are true. What is good or bad for us human beings is important only because our humanity or personhood is important.

That is what David Velleman claims. He says, "What's good for a person is not a categorical value, any more than what's good for a purpose." He continues: "What's good for a purpose is worth caring about only out of concern for the purpose, and hence only insofar as the purpose is worth caring about. Similarly, what's good for a person is worth caring about only out of concern for the person, and hence only insofar as he is worth caring about. A person's good has only hypothetical or conditional value, which depends on the value of the person himself." In the same vein: "Things that [are] good for you would not actually merit concern unless you merited concern.... What's good for you wouldn't matter if you didn't matter."[1]

Suppose I am genuinely in doubt about whether I have a reason to care about what is good for any human beings (myself and everyone else). Someone seeking to assuage my doubts tells me that persons, because of their rational freedom, have the property of being valuable. Even if I accept that point, do I now have a better understanding of why I should care about what is good for human beings? Perhaps my recognition of their absolute value should merely lead me to congratulate them inwardly for having that property, to pat them on the back, or to build a temple in their honor, but nothing further. Why should I do what is good for them or avoid what is bad for them, out of recognition of their rationality and the value of that property? After all, I can acknowledge that someone is a great athlete but deny that this gives me any reason to look to his welfare. Similarly, even if I become convinced that I am, quite simply, valuable, how does that answer my question about whether what is good for me is something that I should be concerned about?

It might nonetheless be said that Velleman has raised a deep question that deserves an answer and that I have said nothing in this study to address it. His thought might be put in the following terms: some things are such that their good should be a matter of indifference to me. I have no reason, for example, to care about

---

1. "A Right of Self-Termination?" *Ethics* 109 (1999), pp. 606–628. The passage cited is on p. 611. See, too, Stephen Darwall, *Welfare and Rational Care* (Princeton, NJ: Princeton University Press, 2002), p. 8.

what is good for the weeds in my garden or for the paramecia in the local pond.[2] These living things have no "moral standing." Human beings do, however. That difference requires some explanation, and Velleman supplies one: we have value (because of our rationality), whereas the weeds and the paramecia have none. Sentient animals, it might be added, also have *some* moral standing, because their consciousness can be pleasant or painful. We can thus divide the world into these three categories: things that have no value of their own, others that have a lower degree of value (sentient animals), and ourselves, who alone have full value. By appealing to this trichotomy, we can sort the world into the things whose good should directly concern us (animals and humans) and those whose good should not (everything else). So we now have an answer to the question "Why should we care so much about what is good for human beings?" We can reply: because they fall into the category of things that have full value. There must be *some* explanation, after all, of why we should treat human beings and weeds so differently.

I agree with that last statement, but I propose a different explanation. Human beings and weeds should be treated differently, I suggest, because the things that are good for humans are of a sort that grounds a concern that they should have them, whereas the things that are good for weeds are of a different sort—so different that they cannot ground a concern on our part that weeds have them. Differential treatment is justified, in other words, not because humans are valuable and weeds are not, but because the advantages we can have are so different in kind from those of weeds and so much more worthy of support than are those of weeds; similarly, the harms we can suffer are so much more horrible than are the disadvantages that can accrue to weeds.

Our advantages are larger than those of weeds, but I do not mean that the *only* difference between the things that are good for human beings and those that are good for weeds (or any other sorts of plant) is a difference in quantity. We can enjoy discussing wonderful novels with friends; they can have strong root systems. Obviously, it is not the case that these are the same kind of good, differing only in degree. Our cognitive and affective enjoyments are both a much greater advantage than and a different kind of advantage from any of those available to plants.

It might be asked, "if we could do what is good for a sufficiently large number of plants, would that give us a reason so great in strength (because of the numbers involved) that it outweighs the reason we have to provide a very small number of human beings with such rich human advantages as friendship and other affective

2. Weeds—plants that are in the wrong place—can become objects of fascination and delight when those sorts of plants are in the right place, and in certain circumstances we might even take measures to ensure that they do not perish. But if we did so, we would be acting not for *their* good, as an objective that is worthy of our consideration on its own, but because they enhance the pleasure *we* take in nature. For an appreciative guide, see Richard Mabey, *Weeds: How Vagabond Plants Gatecrashed Civilization and Changed the Way We Think about Nature* (London: Profile, 2011).

enjoyments"? The answer is no, because there is a categorical difference between the kinds of goods under consideration. One of these kinds is such as to give us, in appropriate circumstances, a strong reason to provide assistance; the other is of a sort that does not give us *any* such reason. We must not infer from the fact that some things are good for weeds and the further fact that these are small goods (in comparison with those available to us) that we have some small reason to give them what help we can. To repeat: the kind of good they can have is not of a sort that gives us *any* reason to benefit them. The smallness of that good, relative to the human good, should not mislead us into thinking of it as the basis of a small reason, so that when you consider the good of two weeds, you have more reason to help them than you have to help only one of them.

To grasp the point I am making, it is helpful to keep in mind that we can express our concern for what is good for human beings without having any particular human beings in mind as the objects of our concern. Suppose I have lived through a stage of life in which I learned what it was like to be downtrodden, lonely, impoverished, and depressed. Having recovered from all that, and having become extraordinarily wealthy, I establish a foundation that will lower the chances that others will live through what I experienced. I am concerned with what is good for and what is bad for people, but there is no one about whom I make the judgment: "He has value, and that is why I am concerned about what is good for him." Rather, I don't want *anyone* to go through what I went through. If members of other species were capable of experiencing such things, I would want to make it possible for them as well to avoid such ills. It is the nature of the bad things that happened to me that serves as my grounds for establishing my foundation. Of course, as a matter of fact, it is only human beings who can experience those bad things; plants and other animals cannot. But I do not have to presuppose that human beings somehow *deserve* to have what is good for them and to avoid what is bad for them, whereas weeds do not.

So, I reject Velleman's thesis that "things that [are] good for you would not actually merit concern unless you merited concern." Do I have any answer, then, to the question I asked at the beginning of this appendix: "Why is it important to care about what is good for someone?" I believe an answer is already implicit in what I have said. If the "someone" about whom this question is asked is a weed, then the question rests on a false supposition, because it is not important to care about what is good for such things. As I have said, that is because those goods are not of a sort that we have any reason to provide. But if the question is refined, so that it is taken to mean "why is it important to care about the sorts of things that are good for or bad for human beings?" a proper response is that we must keep in mind what those goods are. It is because the kinds of goods that human beings can have are so rich,[3] so worth having—as any plausible list of them makes plain—that it is important for us to care about their having those advantages.

---

3. Recall the point made earlier (chapter 25 note 5) about how I understand the notion of a rich experience.

APPENDIX B: J. DAVID VELLEMAN

Speaking broadly and crudely, then, we can put living things into one of three categories: some of them don't "matter" (to use Velleman's term), some matter somewhat, and others matter a great deal. Plants do not matter at all (and perhaps animals that lack sensory awareness fall into this category as well).[4] Animals that are conscious of their world and feel pleasure and pain matter somewhat.[5] Persons matter a great deal. To classify some individual as mattering or not mattering is to indicate whether it should matter *to us*, in that what is good for it can, in the right circumstances, give us a reason to provide it with assistance. That an act we could perform would rescue a plant from harm or destruction (but would assist no person or animal) is by itself no reason to undertake it. By contrast, we do have some reason to alleviate the suffering of conscious nonhuman animals, should circumstances be favorable to our doing so. And when we can rescue a person from misfortune, we have, in the right circumstances, a very strong reason to do so. But we need not say, as Velleman does, that "what's good for you wouldn't matter if you didn't matter." That statement is meant to suggest that we can assess an individual's true value only by setting aside all thought of the sorts of benefits that it or she or he can have. His meaning is that we must consider whether it has some valuable property— something that is good absolutely, regardless of whether it is advantageous—and only then will we know whether we have reason to come to its assistance by helping it achieve some advantage. I have tried to show, against this, that it is precisely by looking to the different sorts of advantages available to plants, animals, and persons that we can speak of some of them as mattering more than others, and some as not mattering at all.

Return now to the question I asked in the first sentence of this appendix: "Why is it important to care about what is good for someone?" That might be taken to mean: why should we think with the category "good for" (when this means: what is advantageous or beneficial to someone)? I reply: try doing without it in your practical reasoning, and you will see that your evaluative repertoire and therefore your ability to think will become severely limited. That is the only kind of answer this question admits of.

"But whose advantage should we care about?" That is a different sort of question, requiring a different sort of answer. Our circumstances differ, and it would be madness to suppose that whomever you should care about is also someone whose good I should care about. (I do not need to care about your dog, for example, but you do.) But nearly every human being in nearly every imaginable circumstance ought to care about at least some human beings. Why is that? Part of the answer is that normal

4. As I pointed out in chapter 25 note 3, some animals (bees, for example) may be plantlike in that they lack phenomenal awareness, even though they process sensory information.
5. See chapter 25 note 7 for my willingness to countenance the possibility that the prevention of animal suffering and death, if sufficiently widespread, could justify the failure to save a person's life. In this appendix, I have put weeds and all other plants into a lower moral category, in that we can ignore how many of them we fail to assist.

adult human beings have, through a process of education and acculturation, acquired the skills that equip them to be effective, at least in some limited ways, in benefiting other human beings. But that is only part of the answer. There is much else to say. Some people we should benefit because we love them, because we are their friends or their neighbors, or because they have benefited us. We have duties to humankind in general (not to harm for no reason and to help when we can) and many special obligations. What we do not need to posit, however, to determine whose advantage we should care about, is the value of persons.

APPENDIX C

Robert Merrihew Adams on the Highest Good

In *Finite and Infinite Goods,*[1] Robert Merrihew Adams proposes what he calls a "framework for ethics" that places a transcendent and infinite goodness—God—at the center of ethical thought. "God is the supreme Good, and the goodness of other things consists in a sort of resemblance to God."[2] God has the property of goodness—indeed, God *is* that property (although God is also a person). Many other things, Adams believes, also have that property, although they have it in a derivative way, by being faint images of God. They, like God, are noninstrumentally valuable or excellent. (Adams uses "good," "excellent," and "valuable" interchangeably.) He is emphatic that the property of goodness is not the property of being good *for* someone.[3] In fact, he proposes that being good for someone is best understood as the enjoyment of something that is excellent, valuable, or good.[4] So, these two

---

1. Goodness (rather than goodness *for* someone) also plays a central role in his theory of virtue, as the subtitle of his book on that subject indicates: *A Theory of Virtue: Excellence in Being for the Good* (Oxford: Clarendon, 2006).

2. *Finite and Infinite Goodness*, p. 7.

3. Ibid., p. 13.

4. Ibid., p. 93.

properties—being good and being good for someone—are not, to his mind, independent of each other. Excellence is primary; being good for someone is definitionally dependent upon it.

What sorts of things, aside from God, are absolutely good, excellent, and valuable? Adams speaks of "the type of goodness exemplified by the beauty of a sunset, a painting, or a mathematical proof, or by the greatness of a novel, the nobility of an unselfish deed, or the quality of an athletic or a philosophical performance. It is the goodness of that which is worthy of love or admiration, honor or worship...."[5]

Let us take one of the items on this list: the greatness of a novel. Geach, Foot, and Thomson do not mean to call into question whether we can speak meaningfully of good novels. (I take a great novel to be one that is superlatively good.) In their resistance to talking about what is, quite simply, good, they take it for granted that we can speak intelligibly of what is a good member of a kind. Nor have I sought to cast doubt on such assertions. It is a further question, of course, whether a good novel resembles God or whether its being a good novel depends on that resemblance. But in any case, there is nothing controversial—nothing to which a skeptic about absolute goodness would object—in Adams's assumption that there are good novels.

The same point applies to the other examples Adams gives. A sunset can be called good. After all, if it is beautiful, we can call it a good sunset. So, too, for paintings and proofs: to the extent that they are beautiful, they are, for that reason, good—that is, good paintings and good proofs. Their goodness is not absolute, but relative: they are not good *simpliciter*, but good as paintings and as proofs. Similarly, if someone has acted nobly and unselfishly, he is, at least to that extent, a good person. If someone excels in a tennis match or in a philosophical performance, he is, at least to that extent, a good athlete or a good philosopher. All of Adams's examples can be understood as cases in which the goodness spoken of is goodness of a kind.

Adams *is* saying something controversial, of course. Great novels, he thinks, are images of God. So, too, are beautiful sunsets, unselfish deeds, excellent athletic performances, and so on. He is not merely making the mild assertion that there is such a property as being a good novel, such a property as being a good athlete, such a property as being a good person, and so on. The goodness of each of these, he believes, has this much in common with the goodness of every other: they are ways of resembling God.

Adams does not make the mistaken assumption that Geach and Thomson attribute to Moore: the assumption according to which being a good member of a kind consists in two independent properties: first, being absolutely good; second, belonging to that kind. He does not suppose that the goodness of a good novel is the very same kind of goodness that a good athlete has and that this is the goodness that we must strive to produce in all our actions. He writes that "neither Plato (as I read him) nor I maintain it is the presence of something qualitatively identical in all good things that constitutes their goodness. In our theories things are good by virtue of a relation to some one supreme Good, but the goodness is not something qualitatively identical in all of them."[6]

He does say, "God is the supreme Good,"[7] and so we may ask: Is God good *simpliciter*? Or is God a good member of a kind, for example, a good person? Or good at various things—knowing, loving, creating, and so on? If Adams were to answer, "God is good in all these ways," his statement would not conflict with anything that I have said in this book, for I have not claimed that nothing can be good *simpliciter*— not even God. Rather, I have started from *secular* assumptions, and within that framework, I have looked for something that has the property of being absolutely good. I have not asked whether God exists and, if so, whether God has the property of being good *simpliciter*. Adams and I would disagree only if he holds that we can see, from within a secular framework, that there is such a thing as absolute goodness.

There are statements in *Finite and Infinite Goods* that might be understood as affirmations that some things, other than God, are good *simpliciter*. Adams says: "Personhood is excellent."[8] Does that mean that the existence of a person is good (period)? "Fine friendships are excellent."[9] Does that mean that a good friendship is, in addition to being a good friendship, good *simpliciter*? If Adams holds that God is good *simpliciter* (in addition to being a good person and good at many activities) and that other things are good to the extent that they are images of God, what stands in the way of his holding that some things—knowledge, moral virtues, intellectual virtues, athletic skills, for example—are just plain good and that we should admire and seek these things precisely because they are good *simpliciter*? Nothing in his book is incompatible with that idea.

Consider, once again, one of the items on Adams's list of excellent things: a beautiful painting. Does that painting have the properties of both being beautiful and being good *simpliciter*? Because it is a beautiful painting, does it have the property of being, quite simply, good, and does it resemble God with respect to its being good *simpliciter*? Should we go to the museum to see it for two reasons: because it is beautiful (and resembles God in that way) and also because it is good *simpliciter* (and resembles God in this further way)?

Nothing within a secular framework supports the idea that a beautiful painting is just plain good. We would ordinarily say that a painting is a good painting because it is beautiful—not that it is just plain good because it is beautiful. If that ordinary way of speaking is all that Adams asks his readers to take for granted, he is not a friend of absolute goodness of the sort that I have been challenging in this book. But

6. Ibid., p. 39.
7. Ibid., p. 7.
8. Ibid., p. 119.
9. Ibid.

if he is asking us to think of a beautiful painting as something that is not only a good painting but also good *simpliciter*, and if he holds that we should contemplate and admire it because it is, quite simply, a good thing, then he is adopting the position that I have been questioning here.[10]

There is something that Adams and I definitely disagree about: he proposes that we take being good for a person to consist in that person's enjoyment of what is excellent[11] whereas I have argued, in *What Is Good and Why*, that we should identify being good for someone or something with the flourishing of that individual. His theory is more restricted in scope than mine, in that the concept of flourishing is applicable to all or nearly all living things, whereas only human beings and some animals (but no plants) are capable of enjoyment. According to my theory, the property of being good for a human being should be understood by being analyzed into two parts: first, we must understand what it is for something to be good for someone or something; second, we must apply that understanding to the circumstances and nature of human beings. By contrast, Adams does not examine the general notion of something being good for someone. In not doing so, he assumes that a proper understanding of what is good for a human being need not draw on a more general theory of what it is for a living being to flourish.

When Adams says that what is good for a person is a life characterized by "enjoyment of the excellent,"[12] I take him to have in mind the sorts of examples he commonly uses when he talks about the excellent: beautiful sunsets and paintings, good novels, the deeds of a good person, the excellence of a tennis match, and so on. So understood, his thesis is that for something to be good for a person consists in a combination of two elements: being good of a kind, and being enjoyed by that individual. Were he to say that certain things—for example, knowledge and virtue—are good *simpliciter*, that we should value them because they are good *simpliciter*, and that what is good for someone is the enjoyment of these absolute goods, he would be a friend of absolute goodness of the sort I have opposed.

Friends of absolute goodness might say (with Adams) that when something is good of a kind and is enjoyed, that enjoyment is good for that individual, and then they might claim, in addition, that all things that are good of a kind should be valued, even when they are not enjoyed, because they are absolutely good. Good novels, according to this theory, are to be read and valued, regardless of whether one enjoys them, because they have absolute value. They are not only good as novels but also are, quite simply, good things. These friends of absolute goodness will admit that it is not good *for* you to read a good novel that you do not enjoy, but they think that there is even in this case a reason to devote oneself to good novels: they are not only good

---

10. These remarks apply as well to Raz's proposal that (for example) a good lecture is not only good of its kind but in addition a valuable thing. See chapter 1 note 1.

11. *Finite and Infinite Goodness*, pp. 93–101.

12. Ibid., p. 93.

as novels but also good *simpliciter.* They might (unlike Moore and Ross) embed this theory in a theological framework and hold that good novels, being absolutely good, resemble God, who is absolute Goodness, and that we should therefore be devoted to them regardless of whether we enjoy them.

That theory—whether it accords with Adams's intentions or not—would border on absurdity. No one could plausibly think that someone should eat a good cucumber regardless of whether he enjoys doing so, simply because, being a good cucumber, it is also absolutely good. If someone dislikes the taste of cucumbers but has a robust appetite for a wide variety of other nourishing and tasty foods, there is no reason for him to try to alter his sensory condition. Good cucumbers are not, by virtue of being good things of a kind, also good *simpliciter,* and there is no reason to try to cultivate a taste for a certain variety of cucumbers—namely, the good ones—merely because they are good things of a kind. To generalize: the mere fact that something is good of a kind is, as yet, no reason for everyone to value or pursue it. It follows that the mere fact that a certain book belongs to some kind or other (let's say that it is a novel) and is a good thing of that kind is, as yet, no reason for everyone to want to read it or to regret not reading it. One can similarly grant that a certain video game is a good thing of its kind and nonetheless wonder whether people who play it are wasting their time. Again, I can grant that the pretzel you are offering me is a good pretzel but deny that this gives me sufficient reason to accept your offer. I may have no reason to play video games, even the good ones, nor to eat pretzels, even the good ones. That something is a good member of some kind or other does not yet speak in favor of valuing it; what we need to see, before we ought to value it, is the reason why good things of *that* particular kind should be valued. (A familiar example: that someone is a good burglar is no reason to appreciate him.)

The point I just made about good novels leaves room for the plausible thought that the greatest novels should be read and treasured by everyone. What lies behind that thought is not the assumption (which would be silly) that these marvelous novels should be read by all simply because they are good things of a kind. Nor would it be illuminating merely to point out that they are, after all, novels (not mere cucumbers) and that by being very good members of *this* kind, they ought to be enjoyed by all. What must be added is the point that these works have an effect on a receptive mind of the sort that every human being would benefit from experiencing. If someone cannot be receptive to these works, he is the worse off for it. By contrast, if someone happens not to like the way even the best cucumbers taste, he is not the worse off for that, provided that there are plenty of other kinds of equally good food for him to enjoy. The difference between the importance of being exposed to good cucumbers and good novels can be explained only by referring to the immense difference in the benefits of experiencing good members of these two kinds.

That leads me to suspect that something is amiss in Adams's thesis that what is good for someone is constituted by that person's enjoyment of what is excellent.

Suppose we take him to mean that whenever something is a good thing of some kind or other, then enjoying that thing is good for whomever enjoys it. If a certain video game is a good one, for example, and you enjoy it, then it must be good (noninstrumentally good, at any rate) for you to enjoy it. That must be wrong, for if it were true, we could entirely bypass questions that arise about the noninstrumental goodness or badness of this type of recreation. (Another sort of objection is this: a book might fall into no recognized and established kind of written work and still be such that everyone ought, for his own good, to read and enjoy it. It is not necessary that something be good of a kind, if it is to be instrumentally or noninstrumentally beneficial.)

Perhaps then we should take Adams to mean that what is good for someone is constituted by that person's enjoyment of what is good *simpliciter*. His idea, more fully spelled out, would be this: some things (beautiful sunsets, moral deeds, athletic excellence) are good *simpliciter*, and that is already a sufficient reason to value them, regardless of whether they give us pleasure. But suppose they also give us pleasure or we enjoy valuing them; in that case, there is yet another reason for us to have a favorable attitude toward them (namely, their pleasantness), and furthermore our enjoyment of them is noninstrumentally good for us.

On this reading, the framework for ethics Adams proposes includes a thesis that conflicts with the skeptical conclusion I have arrived at in this book: he assumes, but I deny, that the absolute goodness of things (beautiful sunsets and the like) gives us reason to value them. I doubt that Adams can drop this premise while leaving his framework substantially intact. He cannot embrace the idea that doing what is good for someone and doing what one enjoys are the only kinds of practical reasons we have. That would not allow him to achieve the larger theological goals at which he aims. For his purposes, he needs the assumption that the goodness (*simpliciter*) of things already constitutes a reason to value them.

Here is a further problem for Adams's theory: It would be circular were he to define what is good for a person as that individual's enjoyment of an excellent thing of a kind and then define such excellence in terms of what is good for that person. That is a difficulty for him, I think, because at least in some cases it seems that a thing's being an excellent member of its kind is constituted by its being either instrumentally or noninstrumentally advantageous (or both).

Consider, once again, a cucumber. What would make it without restriction or reservation a good cucumber is its being good *for* nearly all people to eat, and it will meet that standard if it tastes good to them and provides them with nourishment. It would in that case be both noninstrumentally beneficial for them, since they would enjoy its taste, and also instrumentally good, assuming that it promotes their health. But if a certain kind of cucumber were tasty and nutritious and therefore good for only half of the population, whereas the other half had taste buds and dietary needs that made those sorts of cucumbers bad for them, we would say that such cucumbers are good cucumbers *for* these people but bad cucumbers *for* those. There would be no answer to the question "Are they good cucumbers *simpliciter?*"

Suppose there were that sort of diversity in our reaction to sunsets. Something in the visual system of some people might make certain sunsets look brilliant to them, whereas for others those sunsets would seem dull. A particular sunset would then be noninstrumentally beneficial for some people to look at but not good for others. It could not be called, quite simply, either a good sunset or a bad sunset; we would have to speak relationally, calling one kind of sunset a good sunset for these people but not a good sunset for those. To say, "That is a good sunset for you" would mean that it is good for you to value it—to look at it with pleasure and appreciate its beauty.

Adams holds that we can explain something's being good for you in terms of your enjoyment of what is excellent—for example, your enjoyment of a beautiful and therefore good sunset. But if human beings reacted differently to sunsets, he would have to say that what makes it good for certain people to look at certain sunsets is that in doing so they enjoy what is good for them to look at. And that would be no explanation at all.

As it happens, almost all human beings react in the same way to sunsets. Some strike everyone as dull; others strike everyone as brilliant and beautiful. We have no need, in these circumstances, to say, "That is a good sunset for you." That is because what is a good sunset for one person to look at is a good sunset for anyone else to look at. So we can save breath and say, quite simply: that is an excellent sunset. But what we mean is that it would be good for anyone to look with appreciation at that sunset.

To generalize: if what it is for something to be excellent consists in its being a good thing of a kind, and its being a good thing of a kind consists in its being good for everyone to value, then the concept of what is good for someone cannot be explained in the way that Adams proposes. We go in a circle and shed no light, if we say that to be good for someone consists in the enjoyment of what it is good for someone to value.

APPENDIX D

Thomas Hurka on the Structure of Goods

In *Virtue, Vice, and Value*,[1] Thomas Hurka proposes what he calls a "recursive account" of the moral virtues and vices. He begins with a list of noninstrumental goods: pleasure, knowledge, and achievement;[2] and a corresponding list of "evils" (as he calls them—he uses "evil" where I use "bad"): pain, false belief, and failure in the pursuit of achievement.[3] Then he proposes that loving these good things (wanting them, pursuing them, taking pleasure in them) is itself a further good thing, that hating these bad things (wanting and pursuing their nonoccurrence and being pained by their occurrence) is still another good thing, that loving these bad things is yet another bad thing, and that hating these good things is also a bad thing. It seems clear that for Hurka, goodness—absolute goodness, as I have been calling it—plays a central role in moral philosophy. He notes that "consequentialist theories take goodness to be explanatorily prior to rightness,"[4] and the aim of his book is to give "a consequentialist account of the intrinsic values of virtue and vice."[5]

Moral virtues and vices, according to his theory, consist in such attitudes as those mentioned in the preceding paragraph: to be virtuous is to love good things and to hate bad things, whereas to be a bad person is to love bad things and hate good things. Benevolence, for example, consists in wanting, pursuing, or taking pleasure in other people's good—in their pleasure, knowledge, and achievement. Compassion consists in wanting and pursuing the nonoccurrence of bad things in other people and in being pained by their occurrence. Jealousy is the hatred of another person's having something good. And so on. So viewed, the virtues are noninstrumentally good and the vices noninstrumentally bad. Compassion often prompts actions that alleviate the suffering of others, and so it has instrumental value, but even when it has no consequences, it is, Hurka holds, by itself a good thing. It is a good thing because of a fundamental and substantive ethical truth: hating bad things is a good thing. It is a second-order good thing in that it consists in a complex psychological orientation toward first-order bad things.

---

1. Oxford: Oxford University Press, 2001.
2. Ibid., p. 12.
3. Ibid., p. 15.
4. Ibid., p. 3.
5. Ibid., p. 4.

It is crucial for the success of Hurka's theory that when he speaks of good and bad, he does not mean what is good *for* someone or bad *for* someone. He is not claiming that being compassionate is good for the compassionate person or even that being compassionate is good for the people who are the objects of that attitude. If he were, his theory would be easy to reject. After all, when I read in the newspaper about the sufferings of people who are thousands of miles away and I hate that bad thing—I am pained by it and wish they had not suffered so—it would be utterly implausible to suppose that my attitude by itself does them any good, and it would be perhaps only slightly less implausible to suppose that my commiseration is good for me. But Hurka is not saying anything of the sort. He means that the attitude I take toward the distant suffering of others is itself a good thing, just as pleasure, knowledge, and achievement are by themselves good things.[6]

That might make it seem as though Hurka is what I have been calling a "friend of absolute goodness." But that would be a misinterpretation, because he does not commit himself to the thesis that we should value certain things *because* they are good *simpliciter*. He does not propose any reasons to reject that thesis—that is where he and I differ—but neither does he propose any reasons to accept it. He deliberately maintains a position of neutrality between competing theories of what goodness is.

Hurka notes that some philosophers—he singles out Franz Brentano—"analyze goodness in terms of the correctness or the appropriateness of certain emotions."[7]

6. Hurka is less guarded in his more recent book, *The Best Things In Life: A Guide to What Really Matters* (New York: Oxford University Press, 2011). Here he speaks freely of what is good *for* individuals and what *benefits* them. (See pp. 2, 4, 27, 37, 66, 163, and 177 for occurrences of "good for," "better for," and "best for" and pp. 16 and 58 for occurrences of "benefit.") Speaking of a gleeful torturer, for example, he says not only that his enjoyment of the pain of others makes the world a worse place but also that it makes the torturer's life worse: "the torturer's life is... worse. It's less good *for him* to thrill at others' pain than not to, even if the thrilling gives him joy" (p. 66, emphasis added). This book is intended for a broad audience, and it would not be fair to expect of it the rigor and precision of a purely academic work. Were we to read it without making that allowance, Hurka would be saying that someone who rightly feels compassion for the suffering of another person not only makes the world a better place but also makes his life more desirable for him; his compassion, in other words, would be not only fitting but also good for him, a benefit to him. Hurka also writes in this more recent work in a manner that suggests that if something is good (period), we should want it for that reason. He says, for example, "an ideal person will... want scientific knowledge both because he thinks it's good and from natural curiosity" (p. 126). Absolute goodness, in other words, is spoken of as though it is a reason-giving property. For further discussion, see my review in *Notre Dame Philosophical Reviews* (January 2011).

7. *Virtue, Vice, and Value*, p. 4. He also makes a distinction between philosophers like Brentano, who "analyze goodness in terms of the correctness or appropriateness of certain emotions," and others—he puts Henry Sidgwick and Shelly Kagan in this category—who "analyze goodness in terms of reasons or oughts, so the good is what people have reason or ought to desire or pursue" (ibid., p. 4). Scanlon (whom Hurka does not refer to) is a member of the latter group.

(I briefly alluded to this line of thinking in chapter 2.) For them, to say that pleasure is good is not, as Moore supposes, to advert to a property that pleasure has—a property that can be appealed to as a justification for pursuing pleasure. Rather, to say that pleasure is good, according to this approach, is to say something about you, me, and pleasure, that is, about the attitudes you and I should have toward it. It is to say that we should be in favor of states of affairs that involve pleasure. Talk about the goodness of pleasure is in this way eliminable—reducible, that is, to talk that does not allude to goodness. According to this "fitting-attitude" approach, it is not the case that we should be in favor of pleasure because it is good. Its being good consists in the fact that we should favor it, and so it cannot be used as a justification for favoring it. Why, it might be asked, should we have a favorable attitude toward pleasure, according to Brentano and other like-minded theorists? That question, they must say, does not admit of an answer. There is nothing that explains why pleasure should be loved. Its lovability is a basic normative truth. It is not lovable because it is good; rather, to affirm that it is good is simply to say that when we love it, our attitude is correct.

As I have said, Hurka seeks a theory of the virtues that remains neutral between Moore and other friends of absolute goodness, on the one hand, and Brentano and other fitting-attitude theorists, on the other. Accordingly, when he lists pleasure, knowledge, and achievement as good things and holds that the moral virtues are second-order good things, we are not to take this as an affirmation or a denial of Moore's conception of goodness as a reason-giving property. He intends the thesis that pleasure and various other things are good to be acceptable to philosophers who hold that to call pleasure good is to assert that we ought to have some sort of favorable attitude toward it.

It nonetheless remains true that for Hurka it is *absolute* goodness—not goodness for someone—that plays an important role in moral philosophy. To live our lives as we should, we must know what the good things are, for it is an axiom of his ethics that some things are intrinsically good. To know which qualities are virtues and which are vices, we must identify these good things (and corresponding bad things), because virtue is loving the good and hating what is bad. But Hurka does not insist that this nonrelational sort of goodness is a ground-level *explanatory* concept, because he is open to the suggestion, which he neither accepts nor rejects, that goodness can be reduced to other concepts.

I have been assuming throughout this study that there is something appealing about the idea, which we find in Moore, that if we are going to think in terms of something's being good *simpliciter* at all, then something's having that property is a point in its favor. If courage is a good thing, for example, that certainly looks like a reason to be courageous, just as the beauty of a painting, a building, or a landscape looks like a reason to contemplate and appreciate these things. It is because that simple idea has some initial intuitive force that I have taken the trouble to examine it closely. By contrast, it initially sounds paradoxical and counterintuitive to say that when we call something like courage or friendship a good thing, we are not actually evaluating that thing by adverting to the very quality (its goodness) that recommends it, but are merely claiming that a favorable attitude toward it is appropriate, without giving any justification for such an attitude. After all, as I observed in chapter 2, it seems natural to make a distinction between the claim that pain is bad and the claim that everyone should have an unfavorable attitude toward pain wherever it exists. The second of these two statements calls on us to be compassionate people. The first is naturally understood as a statement of the reason we should be compassionate: because pain, wherever it is, is a bad thing.

So I expect that there are some readers of *Virtue, Vice, and Value* who cling to this intuitively appealing distinction and therefore reject a fitting-attitude approach to absolute goodness. They already come to his work as friends of absolute goodness, and they will be able to combine that commitment to goodness as a reason-giving property with everything its author says. Thus far, then, my quarrel is with these readers, not with Hurka himself, who does not say that goodness is a reason-giving property.

Nonetheless, there is a fundamental disagreement between us. He defends an ethical theory whose foundational premises are statements of this form: "_____ is good (period)." He fills in this blank by proposing, by way of example, that pleasure, knowledge, and achievement are good, but for his purposes, it does not matter whether *these* are the good things. He could have said, instead, that friendship, beauty, and autonomy are good. He could have said that desire-satisfaction is good. What is crucial in his theory is that ethics rests on an assumption about what is good *simpliciter*; what is morally right to do depends on a prior identification of the things that are good (period). Now, if Moore's way of thinking about goodness is correct, ethical theory gives us an answer to the question "*Why* should we value the things that this theory tells us to value?" The answer is because they have the property of goodness. On the other hand, if we reject Moore's way of thinking and accept Brentano's instead, then ethical theory gives *no* answer to the question "*Why* ought we to value the things this theory tells us to value?" Rather, what lies at the foundation of the theory is simply the axiom that certain things (for example, pleasure, knowledge, and achievement) are to be loved, appreciated, respected, or valued in some other way.

But what if it seems to us that there *is* after all a reason to value the things that an ethical theory tells us to value (although it ignores that reason)? The theory, we are supposing, tells us to value pleasure, knowledge, and achievement. By making this an axiom, it proposes that there is no reason to value these things. That will be a deep flaw in the theory—if our impression proves to be correct and there is, after all, a reason to pursue the things the theory tells us to pursue.

My own view is that there are many pleasures (not all) that we should experience because it is good *for* us to experience them and that we should value them for this reason. We benefit, in other words, by enjoying them. Similarly, there are many forms of knowledge (not all) that are noninstrumentally beneficial, and *that* is why we should acquire them; many kinds of achievement (not all) that are both noninstrumentally advantageous to the person who achieves them and instrumentally beneficial to others; and so on. Nearly all of our attitudes (and all of the worthwhile ones) are ones that are to be adopted and sustained for some reason or other. What makes certain attitudes worthwhile is precisely that there is some reason for having them. Often (perhaps always) adopting and sustaining them is good for someone (either the person who has them or others). And perhaps there are other sorts of reasons that ground our attitudes, aside from the advantages of having those attitudes. But in any case, we ought to be suspicious of the suggestion that ethical theory rests on the axiom that certain things (whether they be pleasure, knowledge, or desire-satisfaction, and so on) are simply to be valued regardless of whether they are good for anyone, regardless of whether valuing them is good for anyone, and for no reason at all. As I see it, Hurka's refusal to employ the category of what is good for someone makes his evaluative framework incomplete at the most basic level.

So whether Hurka's theory is combined with Moore's conception of goodness or with Brentano's, it will face a serious difficulty. On the one hand, it will say, following Moore, that *these* items (and here we give a list) are to be valued for one reason and one reason only: because they are good (period). We have seen the obstacles that lie along that route. On the other hand, it will say, following Brentano, that *these* items (which we list) ought to be loved, appreciated, admired (or valued in some other way) for no reason at all. The problem for this second approach is that typically we have favorable attitudes toward things because they have some attractive attribute that makes those attitudes appropriate, and often their attraction lies in the benefits they bring.[8]

To make this objection more concrete, consider an example. A factory owner, let us suppose, knows that the noise levels to which his workers are exposed will lead to considerable hearing loss over time, and yet he refuses to protect them

8. Recall (from the previous note) that Hurka mentions a third approach to goodness—that of Sidgwick and Kagan—according to which "the good is what people have reason or ought to desire or pursue" (ibid., p. 4). But this sort of theory does not simply assert, as a foundational premise, that certain things are good, without saying what it is about them that makes them so. If calling something good is not offering a reason to value it, but merely saying that there is a reason (not yet specified) to value it, then the process of reason-giving does not terminate with goodness but with something else. A theory of this sort might even give a more fundamental role to the concept of being good for someone than it does to the concept of being good. It might hold, for example, that a character trait counts as a human excellence only if possessing and expressing it is good for someone or other. Such a theory of the virtues would be quite different from the one that Hurka develops in his book. This leads me to think that his ethical theory must choose between Moore's and Brentano's approaches—must say either that goodness is the reason to value things or that the basic items of value simply should be valued, but not for any reason.

from injury because that would cut into his profits. What he does is wrong, of course. Why so? We need to hear well partly because doing so is a means to further ends, but that is not the only kind of objection to be made. When one's hearing is severely impaired, one cannot listen to the quieter sounds of nature, enjoy the subtleties of soft music, appreciate the special timbre of the voices of people we love, or notice the pleasing hum of a fan. We can agree that those changes are losses. The word "bad" should figure in our evaluation of them. But is the basic objection to them that they are bad *simpliciter*? Or they are bad *for* those who incur them? Hurka's theory adopts the first of these options. It says: what the factory owner does is wrong because it leads to things that are bad (period): the loss of the pleasures to be had by listening to nature, music, friends, and so on. Now, are we to avoid these losses *because* they are bad things? So Moore would say, but if the arguments of this book are on the right track, his answer is suspect. Should we instead adopt Brentano's suggestion and say that what the factory owner does is wrong because we ought to hate what he brings about (or have some other unfavorable attitude toward it)? Obviously, that answer leaves something out; explanation does not come to an end here. What he does is wrong because it leads to what is bad *for* his workers. *That* is why we ought to hate what he brings about. But Hurka's theory of why certain actions are morally wrong bottoms out in absolute goodness and badness.

He takes it for granted, in *Virtue, Vice, and Value*, that what we should say about pain is not that it is bad *for* many people (and other animals) who experience it, but that it is just plain bad. In an essay that appeared some fourteen years prior to the publication of that book, he argues that philosophers who, following Geach, find talk of absolute goodness to be unintelligible are mistaken.[9] To say that something is absolutely good, he suggests, is simply to say that everyone ought to desire it and pursue it. Since it is intelligible to speak of what people ought to do, he concludes that it is also intelligible to talk about what is good *simpliciter*. On this reading, if everyone has a reason to want you not to smoke, then your smoking is bad. That does not mean that smoking is bad *for you*. Rather, it is just plain bad. But as I have assumed throughout this essay, the obvious point to be made about smoking is that it is bad for you, and the claim that it is bad *simpliciter* is puzzling. We can assign a meaning to that statement and thus make it say something true. But that is not a satisfactory way to respond to Geach's question about what Moore and other friends of absolute goodness can mean when they speak in terms of good *simpliciter*. These friends of absolute goodness mean to say that the goodness of something is a reason for valuing it. Hurka's essay, by contrast, proposes that when we call something absolutely good, we should mean that everyone ought to have a certain kind of favorable attitude toward it. (Thus Hurka follows Brentano in this essay.) But it is not a satisfactory

---

9. "'Good' and 'Good For,'" *Mind* 96 (1987), pp. 71–73.

response to Geach's objection to Moore and his followers to say that when goodness and badness are interpreted in a different way—one that Moore did not intend—we can understand these concepts.

In that same essay, Hurka also argues that moral philosophers should stop talking in terms of what is good for people or bad for people.[10] "I think 'good for' is fundamentally confused, and should be banished from moral philosophy.... It can...be given too many senses, none of which is best expressed by 'good for.' "[11] One sense of "good for," he suggests, is perspectival: to be good for S, in that sense, is to be good from the point of view of S.[12] Now, "something is good from a person's point of view if she (and perhaps only she) ought morally to desire and pursue it."[13] Accordingly, for Hurka, the statement that my smoking is bad for me can be construed as an imprecise way to formulate the idea that I ought morally to have various unfavorable attitudes toward my smoking—that I ought to be repelled by it, that I must commit myself to becoming or remaining a nonsmoker, and so on. Saying that my smoking is bad (period), he further suggests, should be taken to mean that it is bad from *everyone's* point of view: everyone ought to be opposed to my smoking. By contrast, what I have taken for granted here is that if I should have an unfavorable attitude toward my own smoking or toward anyone's smoking, that attitude is grounded in facts about smoking that are independent of anyone's point of view: what smoking does to smokers is bad for them.

10. His aversion to ethical theories that emphasize what is good for people, their well-being, welfare, or interests, is also evident in one of his other major works, *Perfectionism* (New York: Oxford University Press, 1993). The "perfectionist ideal" he defends "should never be expressed in terms of well-being. It gives an account of the good human life, or what is good in a human being, but not of what is 'good for' a human in the sense tied to well-being" (pp. 17–18). He notes here that "well-being is often characterized subjectively, in terms of actual or hypothetical desires" (p. 17). The view I defend in *What Is Good and Why* is that when well-being (what is good *for* someone) is not so characterized, it has a fundamental role to play in practical thinking.

11. " 'Good' and 'Good for,'" p. 72.

12. Ibid, p. 73.

13. Ibid., p. 71.

APPENDIX E

Jeff McMahan on Impersonal Value

Suppose a human fetus has cerebral deficits that will severely limit the cognitive functioning of the child and adult it will become but that we can intervene and correct those deficits, so that it is likely to live the life of a normal human being. If the expense of doing so is reasonable, should we proceed with this intervention, and if so, why? One good reason for doing so appeals to the good of the parents and others who are responsible for the care of the child. Caring for a severely incapacitated child may be stressful and expensive for them and for the larger community. A different kind of good reason is based on the good of the fetus: it is reasonable to suppose that it is in that individual's own interests to live a normal life. According to Jeff McMahan, there is a third kind of reason as well. He says that "it is impersonally better if a fetus with cerebral deficits has those deficits corrected."[1] I do not agree that there is this third kind of reason to correct the fetus's deficit. What considerations does McMahan offer to suppose that there is?

He says that we have a reason "to ensure that, if a human being is going to come into existence, it should be one with normal cognitive capacities rather than a different one that is severely retarded. While it is preferable that an individual with normal cognitive capacities should exist, it is not better *for that individual* to exist than not to exist."[2] I take his meaning to be that when we bring into existence a normal fetus, we are not making that individual better off than he was before he came into existence or than he would have been had he not come into existence. To make a comparison between how well or badly off someone is at one time and at another time, he must be in existence at both times, and this presupposition would fail, were we to say that in bringing a normal child into existence, we are doing something that makes him better off than he was before. From this, McMahan infers that there is a different kind of reason from the one that is adverted to when we speak of what is good or bad for someone. There is impersonal goodness or value—goodness that is not good for anyone. When we bring a normal child rather than a cognitively deficient child into existence, "the world is a better place overall."[3] He means that a couple brings some

---

1. *The Ethics of Killing*, p. 329.
2. Ibid., p. 329 (author's emphasis).
3. Ibid.

degree of impersonal value into existence when they have a child who has severe cognitive deficits but that they bring about a higher amount of impersonal value when they have a normal child. They have in that way made the world a better place, even though they cannot be said to have done something that made their child better off than he was before.

His idea, then, is that just as impersonal value is increased when couples bring normal rather than subnormal children into existence, so, too, impersonal value is increased when they intervene in the development of a human fetus who has cerebral deficits. They not only do something that is good for that fetus, and good for all the caregivers of the child who the fetus will become, but also they make the world a better place by making it a world that contains a normal rather than a subnormal human being.[4]

I conjecture that McMahan finds this way of thinking attractive because he has already accepted, independently of his reflections on these questions about normal and subnormal children, a theory of value of the sort I have been questioning in this book. He writes: "Many things that have personal value have impersonal value as well. The two types of value often coincide. It is, for example, good for me if my life contains pleasure; but it is also good in itself for there to be pleasure in the world."[5] I agree with McMahan to this extent: if we are already convinced that when we do what is good for someone, we are often at the same time bringing about something that is good *simpliciter*, then there is no reason to make an exception to this general rule when we reflect on what reasons we might have for correcting the cognitive defects of a fetus or for taking measures to ensure that whatever children we have are normal rather than subnormal.

But if we have not already convinced ourselves that pleasure and other items have this double value—being both good (period) and good for individuals—then we can easily resist McMahan's proposal that we should posit this duality in the cases he considers. What should a couple have in mind, as they decide whether to take steps so that, should their sexual activities result in pregnancy, the fetus will have normal cognitive capacities rather than defects? It would be a mistake to say that they cannot have in mind what would be good for any child they have, because as of yet there is no such child. Someone who devotes himself to ensuring that future generations do not smoke cigarettes can base his work on the premise that just as it is bad for people already in existence to smoke, it will be bad for anyone who exists in the future to smoke. He is not failing to recognize the full case that can be made for his

---

4. McMahan's views about this matter are motivated by his thesis that a fetus's interests are weak because of the poverty of its current psychological state. That leads him to hold that even though there is a reason of significant strength to provide cognitive enhancement to a fetus, it cannot be significantly better *for* the fetus to be so enhanced. He invokes impersonal value to explain why enhancement is very important, even though it is not very good for the fetus.

5. *The Ethics of Killing*, p. 332.

endeavors if he does not believe that the world contains something bad, but bad for no one, when people smoke.[6] Similarly, in taking care not to produce children with serious cognitive defects, we must base our precautions on general assumptions (which will hold true in the future no less than they hold true now) about what is good for individuals, but we need not in addition attend to something called "impersonal value."

In a sense, many of the world's most admirable benefactors approach their tasks impersonally. They want to do something, for example, to help the world's poor, but there may be no specific individuals they have in mind as beneficiaries of their efforts. As Harry Frankfurt notes: "Someone who is devoted to helping the sick or the poor for their own sakes may be quite indifferent to the particularity of those whom he seeks to help. What qualifies people to be beneficiaries of his charitable concern is not that he loves them. His generosity is not a response to their identities as individuals; it is not aroused by their personal characteristics. It is induced merely by the fact that he regards them as members of a relevant class. For someone who is eager to help the sick or the poor, any sick or poor person will do."[7] They can be said to have an impersonal orientation to the individuals whose good they serve, but it is nonetheless what is good *for* others that they aim at—not good *simpliciter*. We cannot infer that there is something called absolute goodness or impersonal value from the impersonality of their orientation. Should they concern themselves not only with the current state of the world but also with the condition it will be in after the present generation is replaced by others, a full account of why they are to be admired for doing so need not advert to impersonal value.

6. This case lacks the moral complexity of the ones considered by Parfit under the heading of the "Non-Identity Problem": cases in which our actions have beneficial or harmful consequences for individuals who would not have come into existence had we not undertaken those actions. See *Reasons and Persons*, p. 359, and more generally chapter 16 (pp. 351–379). A typical example of a non-identity problem is one in which one has a choice between causing a happier person to exist and causing a different, less happy person to exist. My strategy for understanding these choices is to say that the first option (causing the happier person to exist) is good for its beneficiary by more than the second option (causing the less happy person to exist) is good for its beneficiary. We are still talking about benefits and beneficiaries and need not posit a different kind of value—absolute goodness. Adopting this strategy is compatible with upholding the view that harming an already existing person is a more serious matter than doing something that brings about that same kind of harm for someone who would not have existed in the absence of one's action.

7. Harry G. Frankfurt, *The Reasons of Love* (Princeton, NJ: Princeton University Press, 2004), p. 43.

APPENDIX F

Other Authors and Uses

Many philosophical authors and ordinary speakers use the word "good" (and other words that have the same meaning) in a way that does not commit them to the thesis that goodness is a reason-giving property. Here are some examples:

1. Plato

In the *Meno*, Socrates asks his interlocutor whether virtue is good. Meno agrees not only that virtue is good but also that it is by the possession of virtue that someone is good, and that if someone is good, he is beneficial (*ôphelimon*), because all good things (*agatha*) are beneficial (*ôphelima*, 87e2). The conversation continues with an enumeration of various things that are commonly considered beneficial: health, strength, beauty, and wealth (87e). It is agreed that sometimes these things are harmful rather than beneficial and that it is only when they are used rightly that they are good.

Something similar occurs in Plato's *Gorgias*. Socrates leads Polus to agree that everything we do is undertaken for the sake of what is good. Accordingly, even when we put someone to death, or banish him and take his property, we do so because we assume that it will be better for us (*ameinon...hêmin*) to do these things than not to (468b6). That is, if we undertake these acts, we do so because they are beneficial (*ôphelima*), and if we refrain, that is because they are harmful (*blabera*, 468c4).

Why do Plato's speakers move back and forth so readily between their words for "good" and "advantageous"? We might reply: "Because they conceive of goodness and advantage as two different properties, and they believe that whenever something has one of them, it must also have the other. Health, for example, is both good and beneficial. That is because nothing can be good without being beneficial, or beneficial without being good."

The problem with this reply is that it creates without solving a further puzzle: why is Plato assuming that these two different properties necessarily coincide? Since they are different properties, what guarantees that whenever something has one property, it also has the other?

I therefore favor a reply that creates no such mystery. We can say that sometimes Plato uses *agathon*, his word for "good," elliptically. He says that health is good, but in doing so, he is speaking in an abbreviated way. His meaning, more fully expressed, is that health is good for the healthy person. Another way to say that health is good for the healthy person is to say: health is beneficial or advantageous for him. So understood, the thesis that all that is good is beneficial is trivial: it merely reflects the way these words are used. When Plato uses *agathon* in this way, he is not speaking of it in the same way that Moore talks about absolute goodness.

Perhaps in other passages Plato does posit the kind of goodness that stands at the center of Moore's thinking. To return to a possibility I mentioned earlier (chapter 2): perhaps he conceives of the form of the good in the *Republic* not as the two-place property something has when it is good for someone—not as advantageousness—but as the property something has when it is good, regardless of whether it is also advantageous. That is one possible reading, but it is open to question, and the issue cannot be adequately addressed here. The question "Is Plato talking about what Moore later talked about?" is really many questions. In some passages, it is an easy question, and the best answer, I believe, is no. It is more difficult to say whether it is always the best answer.

2. Aristotle

The *Nicomachean Ethics* begins: "every craft and every inquiry, and likewise every action and decision, seems to aim at some good" (1094a1–2). Does Aristotle's term *agathon* here refer to the property that Moore later spoke of as absolute goodness? We have just seen that sometimes Plato moves back and forth between *agathon* and other terms that mean "beneficial" and "advantageous"—terms we use interchangeably with "good *for* someone." If Plato frequently speaks in this way, we should ask whether the same can be said of Aristotle, and whether the opening line of the *Ethics* is an instance of such usage. Might Aristotle have conveyed the same thought, had he said: "every craft and every inquiry, and likewise every action and decision, seems to aim at some advantage"?

The *Politics* opens with a sentence that also picks out the *agathon* as the focal point of human activity: "we see that every city is a certain kind of community and that every community is established for the sake of some kind of good" (1252a1–2). He soon illustrates his point in the next chapter by asserting that a slave-owning household is established for the advantage (*sumpheron*) of both master and slave (1252a34). The general point is that all communities aim at what is good *for* their members. They do not seek to increase the amount of goodness *simpliciter* that exists in the world, but have instead a less impersonal goal: mutual advantage.

We should keep in mind that Aristotle presents the *Nicomachean Ethics* as a contribution to the study of politics. It is unlikely, therefore, that its opening line is referring to a different property, when it speaks of *agathon*, from the property posited by the *Politics* as the aim of all communities. If the *Politics* proposes that advantageousness is the organizing goal of communities, then the *Ethics* posits the same property as the goal of all human striving. That advantageousness is what all communities seek is unequivocally affirmed in the *Ethics* itself: "The political community seems to have come together from the beginning and to abide for the sake of advantage [*sumpher-ontos*]. For it is at this that the lawgivers aim, and justice, they say, is the common advantage. So the other communities aim at some portion of what is advanta-geous... but the political community does not aim at the present advantage [*sumpher-ontos*], but at the whole of life..." (1160a11–23). Accordingly, we can take the opening line of the *Ethics* to be asserting that every craft, inquiry, action, and decision aim at something that is assumed to be advantageous for someone. Each aims not at the impersonal goodness that Moore takes to be the fundamental ground for all action and desire, but at something more familiar to common sense: some advantage.

Aristotle does make a distinction (as I noted in chapter 2) between something's being good (or bad) without qualification and its being qualifiedly good (or bad). A full discussion of that distinction would not be appropriate here, but here is what I think he has in mind: His ethical theory, in its search for generalization, takes many of the things that we seek to be good, and other things that we avoid to be bad. Honor and reputation, for example, are things that people justifiably want to have in their lives because they genuinely are good things. The problem is that although they are good "in the abstract" (as we might put it), they should not be sought or welcomed by certain people in certain situations. Similarly, ethical theory counts pain as a bad thing without qualification. But Aristotle holds that the remedy for a disease may be painful, and in these circumstances, undergoing what is painful may be good for someone (1152b32–33).

When ethical theory categorizes honor as good and pain as bad, it is speaking "without qualification." That is, it is speaking in a general way about the sorts of things that constitute a good or a bad human life—a life that is good *for* or bad *for* the person who is living it. But when we make choices in concrete situations, we must not always seek the things that ethical theory declares to be good or avoid the things that ethical theory declares to be bad. We should choose what is good for us then and there and shun what is bad for us then and there. People should "pray that the things that are good without qualification are also good for them, and should choose the things that are good for them" (1129b3–6). Aristotle's counsel, then, is not that we should aim at the sort of thing that Moore called absolute goodness. Goodness-for-someone is what all collective effort and individual decision-making aim at.

3. John Rawls

According to John Rawls, "the two main concepts of ethics are those of the right and the good."[1] Is he saying that one of the two main concepts of ethics is goodness *simpliciter*? Or that it is the concept of advantageousness? He does not directly address this question, but starting with the opening page of *A Theory of Justice*, it is the latter that is constantly on his mind. Such words as "advantage," "benefit," and "interest" permeate his theory. Justice "does

1. *A Theory of Justice*, revised ed. (Cambridge, MA: Belknap, 1999), p. 21.

not allow that the sacrifices imposed on a few are outweighed by the larger sum of *advantages* enjoyed by many."[2] "Although a society is a cooperative venture for mutual *advantage*, it is typically marked by a conflict as well as an identity of *interests*.... Persons are not indifferent as to how the greater *benefits* produced by their collaboration are distributed...."[3] So the theory of the good that he advances in chapter 7 of this work—what he sometimes calls "goodness as rationality"—is a theory about what is good *for* individuals.[4]

In *Political Liberalism*,[5] it is recast as a theory about what is good for the citizens of a modern democratic state; it is, in other words, not advanced as a framework in competition with traditional "comprehensive" theories about what constitutes a benefit, but as the theory of advantageousness that must guide citizens in their public interactions. But in any case it remains a theory about what is good *for* those citizens.

Whenever we see the word "good" in Rawls's writings, we can take this as an elliptical formulation. He means: what is good for someone. What is good *simpliciter*, but good for no one, plays no role in his thinking. His moral and political philosophy thus illustrates one way in which it is possible to think systematically and deeply about these subjects without taking goodness (period) to be a reason.

4. John Broome

In *Weighing Goods*,[6] John Broome uses "good" in a way that escapes my critique of absolute goodness, because he does not claim, with Moore and others, that the goodness of a state of affairs constitutes a reason for promoting it. He does not (as I believe Plato, Aristotle, and Rawls do) speak of "good" as shorthand for "advantageous to someone." The word plays a rather different role in his thinking. I have no objection to his usage. He shows us a way of speaking of goodness without taking it to be a reason-giving property.

Broome explains his use of the term "good" by making a distinction between two approaches to decision making: teleological and nonteleological. The former is extremely common and occurs most often when there are competing factors that must be weighed against each other. Suppose, to take an example he uses frequently, one must decide whether to break a promise. One reason not to do so might be that breaking a promise is intrinsically wrong. On the other hand, suppose that breaking

2. Ibid., p. 3 (my emphasis).
3. Ibid., p. 4 (my emphasis).
4. Geach's "Good and Evil" and chapter 6 of Paul Ziff's *Semantic Analysis* are cited with approval by Rawls in his presentation of goodness as rationality (*A Theory of Justice*, notes to pp. 351, 353, 355, and 356). There is a resemblance between Ziff's thesis that "good" means "answering to some interest" and Rawls's thesis that "something's being good is its having the properties that it is rational to want in things of its kind" (p. 356).
5. New York: Columbia University Press, 1996.
6. Oxford: Basil Blackwell, 1991.

my promise would enable me to prevent five other promises from being broken. How ought I to decide?

"The answer of teleology," Broome says, "is that each consideration contributes to the goodness or badness of the alternative acts. All the considerations together determine how good or bad the acts are. And which act is right is determined by the goodness of the alternatives.... The nonteleological answer, on the other hand, is that ethical considerations do not always work in this particular way. They may determine what ought to be done, not through determining the goodness of acts, but in some other way."[7]

To take a teleological approach to a particular decision, in other words, is to be open to the possibility of drawing a conclusion by weighing the strength of various considerations; the various factors, whatever they are, whose strength is assessed are called "goods" to indicate that they are to be put into the balance. A nonteleologist about that decision denies this: he holds that balancing the strength of this or that aspect of the situation is not the right way to decide it. Now, a teleologist can remain a teleologist and hold that if an act requires that (for example) one break a promise, that consideration *always* has greater weight than any other and that therefore one must not undertake that act. Furthermore, a teleologist can remain a teleologist and hold that sometimes the considerations for and against two actions under consideration are incomparable: it matters very much which he performs, but he believes that neither is better than the other and they are not equally good either. A teleologist is open to making this decision by weighing, but he believes that the nature of his alternatives prevents him from doing so on a rational basis.

So on Broome's theory, as I interpret it, for something to be a good is simply for it to be one factor that a teleological decision maker ought to take into account in his practical thinking. (It is not the reason it should be taken into account.) Nonteleological decision makers do not weigh competing factors, but come to their practical conclusions in some other way. It seems reasonable to suppose that no one is a completely nonteleological decision maker. We all think that in certain circumstances the right way to decide what to do is to weigh competing considerations or at least to sort out various considerations to see whether it is possible to weigh them.

The important point, for my purposes, is that Broome is not thinking of the goodness of an act as a property that constitutes a reason for deciding in its favor. Suppose I believe that I should never break a promise because in my opinion the wrongness of doing so is so weighty a consideration that no other fact could overcome its strength. What moves me, then, is the moral wrongness of breaking a promise: that is my *sole* reason for not breaking it. The badness of breaking the promise is not a second reason against it. It is not as though I first notice that breaking a promise has the property of being bad (and infinitely so) and then infer that it is wrong. To repeat: it is simply the wrongness of breaking the promise that grounds

7. Ibid., p. 6.

my decision. That I also think of the promise as bad (and not only wrong) simply reflects the fact that I approach my decision by asking how much the wrongness of the promise counts against it. I decide that it counts so much that nothing could justify breaking it. The infinite badness of the promise is accounted for by the great strength of the reason that is provided by its wrongness: that reason is so strong that nothing can overcome it.

In effect, then, on Broome's theory, goodness and badness pass the buck. They do not play a reason-giving role.

BIBLIOGRAPHY

Adams, Robert Merrihew. *Finite and Infinite Goods: A Framework for Ethics.* New York: Oxford University Press, 1999.

———. *A Theory of Virtue: Excellence in Being for the Good.* Oxford: Clarendon, 2006.

Allen-Hermanson, Sean. "Insects and the Problem of Simple Minds: Are Bees Natural Zombies?" *Journal of Philosophy* 105 (2008), pp. 389–415.

Anderson, Elizabeth, *Value in Ethics and Economics.* Cambridge, MA: Harvard University Press, 1993.

———. "What Is the Point of Equality?" *Ethics* 109 (1999), pp. 287–337.

Annas, Julia. *An Introduction to Plato's Republic.* Oxford: Oxford University Press, 1981.

Arneson, Richard. "Luck Egalitarianism: An Interpretation and Defense," *Philosophical Topics* 32 (2004), pp. 1–20.

Audi, Robert. *Moral Knowledge and Ethical Character.* New York: Oxford University Press, 1997.

———. *The Good in the Right: A Theory of Intuition and Intrinsic Value.* Princeton, NJ: Princeton University Press, 2004.

Benatar, David. *Better Never to Have Been: The Harm of Coming into Existence.* Oxford: Clarendon, 2006.

Bentham, Jeremy. *An Introduction to the Principles of Morals and Legislation.* Edited by J. H. Burns and H. L. A. Hart. London: Athlone, 1970.

Brentano, Franz, *The Origin of Our Knowledge of Right and Wrong*, English ed. edited by Roderick Chisholm and translated by Roderick Chisholm and Elizabeth Schneewind. London: Routledge & Kegan Paul, 1969.

Brewer, Talbot. *The Retrieval of Ethics.* Oxford: Oxford University Press, 2009.

Broome, John. *Weighing Goods.* Oxford: Basil Blackwell, 1991.

———. "Goodness Is Reducible to Betterness: The Evil of Death Is the Value of Life." In *Ethics out of Economics.* Cambridge: Cambridge University Press, 1999, pp. 162–174.

Budd, Malcolm. *Values of Art.* London: Penguin, 1995.

Butchvarov, Panayot. *Skepticism in Ethics.* Bloomington: Indiana University Press, 1989.

Carroll, Noël. *Beyond Aesthetics: Philosophical Essays.* Cambridge: Cambridge University Press, 2001.

———. "Art and Alienation." In *Art in Three Dimensions.* Oxford: Oxford University Press, 2010, pp. 143–162.

Chisholm, Roderick M. "Defining Intrinsic Value," *Analysis* 41 (1981), pp. 99–100.

Cohen, G. A. "On the Currency of Egalitarian Justice," *Ethics* 99 (1989), pp. 906–944.

Cooper, John M. "The Psychology of Justice in Plato," *American Philosophical Quarterly* 14 (1977), pp. 151–157.

Crisp, Roger. "Value, Reasons, and the Structure of Justification: How to Avoid Passing the Buck," *Analysis* 65 (2005), pp. 80–85.

———. "Goodness and Reasons: Accentuating the Negative," *Mind* 117 (2008), pp. 257–265.

Dancy, Jonathan. "Should We Pass the Buck?" In Toni Ronnow-Rasmussen and Michael J. Zimmerman (eds.), *Recent Work on Intrinsic Value.* Dordrecht, Netherlands: Springer Verlag, 2005, pp. 33–44.

Danielsson, Sven, and Jonas Olson. "Brentano and the Buck Passers," *Mind* 116 (2007), pp. 511–522.

Darwall, Stephen. *Welfare and Rational Care.* Princeton, NJ: Princeton University Press, 2002.

Dworkin, Ronald. *Life's Dominion: An Argument about Abortion, Euthanasia, and Individual Freedom.* New York: Vintage, 1994.

Ewing, A. C. *The Definition of Good.* London: Macmillan, 1947.

Foot, Philippa. "Utilitarianism and the Virtues," *Mind* 94 (1985), pp. 196–209. Reprinted in *Moral Dilemmas and Other Topics in Moral Philosophy.* Oxford: Clarendon, 2002, pp. 59–77. Citations refer to the pagination of the latter.

Frankfurt, Harry G. *The Reasons of Love.* Princeton, NJ: Princeton University Press, 2004.

Geach, P. T. "Good and Evil," *Analysis* 17 (1956), pp. 33–42. Reprinted in Philippa Foot (ed.), *Theories of Ethics.* London: Oxford University Press, 1967, pp. 64–73. Citations refer to the pagination of the latter.

Grahek, Nikola. *Feeling Pain and Being in Pain,* 2nd ed. Cambridge, MA: MIT Press, 2001.

Guyer, Paul. "History of Modern Aesthetics." In Jerrold Levinson (ed.), *The Oxford Handbook of Aesthetics.* Oxford: Oxford University Press, 2003, pp. 25–60.

Hardcastle, Valerie Gray. *The Myth of Pain.* Cambridge, MA: MIT Press, 1999.

Harris, Judith Rich. *No Two Alike: Human Nature and Human Individuality*. New York: W. W. Norton, 2006.

Heathwood, Chris. "Fitting Attitudes and Welfare." In Russ Shafer-Landau (ed.), *Oxford Studies in Metaethics*, Vol. 3. New York: Oxford University Press, 2008, pp. 47–74.

Hieronymi, Pamela. "The Wrong Kind of Reason," *Journal of Philosophy* 102 (2005), pp. 437–457.

Holtug, Nils. "Who Cares about Identity?" In Melinda A. Roberts and David T. Wasserman (eds.), *Harming Future Persons: Ethics, Genetics, and the Non-Identity Problem*. Dordrecht, Netherlands: Springer Verlag, 2009, pp. 71–92.

Hurka, Thomas. " 'Good' and 'Good For,' " *Mind* 96 (1987), pp. 71–73.

———. *Perfectionism*. New York: Oxford University Press, 1993.

———. *Virtue, Vice, and Value*. Oxford: Oxford University Press, 2001.

———. *The Best Things in Life: A Guide to What Really Matters*. New York: Oxford University Press, 2011.

Kagan, Jerome. *What Is Emotion? History, Measures, and Meanings*. New Haven, CT: Yale University Press, 2007.

Kant, Immanuel. *Lectures on Ethics*. Edited by Peter Heath and J. B. Schneewind, translated by Peter Heath. Cambridge: Cambridge University Press, 1997.

———. *Groundwork for the Metaphysics of Morals*. Translated by Arnulf Zweig. Oxford: Oxford University Press, 2002.

Korsgaard, Christine M. "Two Distinctions in Goodness," *Philosophical Review* 92 (1983), pp. 169–195. Reprinted in *Creating the Kingdom of Ends*. Cambridge: Cambridge University Press, 1996, pp. 249–274. Citations refer to the pagination of the former.

Kraut, Richard. *What Is Good and Why: The Ethics of Well-Being*. Cambridge, MA: Harvard University Press, 2007.

———. "What Is Intrinsic Goodness?" *Classical Philology* 105 (2010), pp. 450–470.

———. Review of Thomas Hurka, *The Best Things in Life: A Guide to What Really Matters*. *Notre Dame Philosophical Reviews*, 2011.

Langton, Rae. "Objective and Unconditioned Value," *Philosophical Review* 116 (2007), pp. 157–185.

Lemos, Noah M. *Intrinsic Value: Concept and Warrant*. Cambridge: Cambridge University Press, 1994.

Lippert-Rasmussen, Kasper. "Why Killing Some People Is More Seriously Wrong Than Killing Others," *Ethics* 117 (2007), pp. 716–738.

Mabey, Richard. *Weeds: How Vagabond Plants Gatecrashed Civilization and Changed the Way We Think about Nature*. London: Profile, 2011.

Mao, Douglas. *Fateful Beauty: Aesthetic Environments, Juvenile Development, and Literature, 1860–1960*. Princeton, NJ: Princeton University Press, 2008.

McMahan, Jeff. "Self-Defense and the Problem of the Innocent Attacker," *Ethics* 104 (1994), pp. 252–290.

————. *The Ethics of Killing: Problems at the Margins of Life.* New York: Oxford University Press, 2002.

————. "Asymmetries in the Morality of Causing People to Exist." In Melinda A. Roberts and David T. Wasserman (eds.), *Harming Future Persons: Ethics, Genetics, and the Non-Identity Problem.* Dordrecht, Netherlands: Springer Verlag, 2009, pp. 49–68.

Montague, Phillip. "Self-Defense and Choosing among Lives," *Philosophical Studies* 40 (1981), pp. 207–219.

Moore, G. E. *Principia Ethica.* Revised ed. Cambridge: Cambridge University Press, 1993. Original ed. 1903.

Oddie, Graham. *Value, Reality, and Desire.* Oxford: Clarendon, 2005.

Otsuka, Michael. "Killing the Innocent in Self-Defense," *Philosophy and Public Affairs* 23 (1994), pp. 79–94.

Parfit, Derek. *Reasons and Persons.* Oxford: Clarendon, 1984, reprinted with further corrections 1987.

Penner, Terry. "The Forms, the Form of the Good, and the Desire for Good in Plato's *Republic,*" *Modern Schoolman* 80, no. 3 (2003), pp. 191–234.

Pettit, Dean, "The Semantics of 'Good.'" Unpublished.

Pigden, Charles R. "Geach on Good," *Philosophical Quarterly* 40 (1990), pp. 129–154.

Rabinowicz, Wlodek, and Toni Ronnow-Rasmussen. "The Strike of the Demon: On Fitting Pro-Attitudes and Value," *Ethics* 114 (2004), pp. 391–424.

Rawls, John. *Political Liberalism.* New York: Columbia University Press, 1996.

————. *A Theory of Justice,* revised ed., Cambridge, MA: Belknap, 1999.

Raz, Joseph. *The Practice of Value.* Oxford: Clarendon, 2003.

Regan, Donald H. "Why Am I My Brother's Keeper?" In R. Jay Wallace, Philip Pettit, Samuel Scheffler, and Michael Smith (eds.), *Reason and Value: Themes from the Moral Philosophy of Joseph Raz.* Oxford: Clarendon, 2004, pp. 202–230.

Rodin, David. *War and Self-Defense.* Oxford: Clarendon, 2003.

Rosati, Connie S. "Objectivism and Relational Good," *Social Philosophy and Policy* 25 (2008), pp. 314–349.

Ross, Adam. *Mr. Peanut.* New York: Alfred A. Knopf, 2010.

Ross, W. D. *The Right and the Good.* Oxford: Oxford University Press, 1930.

————. *Foundations of Ethics.* Oxford: Clarendon, 2000.

Scanlon, T. M. *What We Owe to Each Other.* Cambridge, MA: Belknap, 1998.

Scruton, Roger. *Culture Counts: Faith and Feeling in a World Besieged.* New York: Encounter, 2007.

————. *The Roger Scruton Reader.* Compiled, edited, and with an introduction by Mark Dooley. London: Continuum, 2009.

Sidgwick, Henry. *The Methods of Ethics,* 7th ed., 1907. Reissued, Chicago: University of Chicago Press, 1962.

Sinnott-Armstrong, Walter. "For Goodness' Sake," *Southern Journal of Philosophy* 41 (2003), Supplementary Volume: "The Legacy of G. E. Moore: 100 Years of Metaethics," pp. 83–91.

Stratton-Lake, Philip, and Brad Hooker. "Scanlon versus Moore on Goodness." In Terry Horgan and Mark Timmons (eds.), *Metaethics after Moore*. Oxford: Clarendon, 2006, pp. 149–168.

Sumner, L. W. *Welfare, Happiness, and Ethics*. New York: Oxford University Press, 1996.

Tannenbaum, Julie. "Categorizing Goods." In Russ Shafer-Landau (ed.), *Oxford Studies in Metaethics*, Vol. 5. New York: Oxford University Press, 2010.

Temkin. Larry S. *Inequality*. New York: Oxford University Press, 1993.

———. "Equality, Priority, and the Leveling Down Objection." In Matthew Clayton and Andrew Williams (eds.), *The Ideal of Equality*. New York: St. Martin's Press, 2000, pp. 126–161.

Thaler, Richard H., and Cass R. Sunstein. *Nudge: Improving Decisions about Health, Wealth, and Happiness*. New Haven, CT: Yale University Press, 2008.

Thomson, Judith Jarvis. "The Right and the Good," *Journal of Philosophy* 94 (1997), pp. 273–298.

———. *Goodness and Advice*. Princeton, NJ: Princeton University Press, 2001.

———. "Reply to Sinnott-Armstrong." *Southern Journal of Philosophy* 41 (2003), Supplementary Volume, "The Legacy of G. E. Moore: 100 Years of Metaethics," pp. 92–94.

———. *Normativity*. Chicago: Open Court, 2008.

Väyrynen, Pekka. "Resisting the Buck-Passing Account." In Russ Shafer-Landau (ed.), *Oxford Studies in Metaethics*, Vol. 1. New York: Oxford University Press, 2006, pp. 295–324.

Velleman, J. David. "A Right of Self-Termination?" *Ethics* 109 (1999), pp. 606–628.

White, Nicholas P. *A Companion to Plato's Republic*. Indianapolis, IN: Hackett, 1979.

Ziff, Paul. *Semantic Analysis*. Ithaca, NY: Cornell University Press, 1960.

Zimmerman, Michael J. "In Defense of the Concept of Intrinsic Value," *Canadian Journal of Philosophy* 29 (1999), pp. 389–400.

———. *The Nature of Intrinsic Value*. Lanham, MD: Rowman & Littlefield, 2001.

INDEX

INDEX

Sidgwick, Henry 48 n. 2, 64, 92, 98–99, 100,
    200 n. 7, 203 n. 8
Sinnott-Armstrong, Walter 26 n. 8
smoking (cigarettes) 29–31, 33, 34, 38–39,
    40–42, 44–45, 47, 52, 66, 68, 96–97, 143,
    151, 152, 173–177, 204, 205, 207–208
Sophocles 58
species, extinction of 136–139, 162, 163–166,
    169
Stratton-Lake Philip 63 n. 3
suicide 127–130, 161, 163,
"sum of values in the universe" (W. D. Ross)
    81, 108, 115, 124
Sumner, L. W. 78 n. 4
Sunstein, Cass R. 149 n. 4
Supreme Court 130, 161, 163

Tannenbaum, Julie 22–23 n. 3
Temkin, Larry S. 140 n. 1
Thaler, Richard H. 149 n. 4

Thomson, Judith Jarvis 25–28, 38, 54, 62–63,
    173, 175–6, 177, 180–182, 193
Trollope, Anthony 112 n. 3

valuable. *See* intrinsic value; "sum of values
    in the universe"
Väyrynen, Pekka 63 n. 3
Velleman, J. David 187–192
virtue and vice 117–121, 129, 169, 199, 201

weeds 189, 190
White, Nicholas P. 11 n. 2
Wilde, Oscar 110 n. 2
Wittgenstein, Ludwig 25, 72
Wordsworth, William 110 n. 2

Ziff, Paul 25 n. 5, 177 n. 3, 212 n. 4
Zimmerman, Michael J. 15 n. 13, 26 n. 8

CPSIA information can be obtained at www.ICGtesting.com
Printed in the USA
BVOW05*0320260116

434259BV00003B/9/P